How China Works

D0209725

China has become known as the "workshop of the world" following its huge industrial transformation throughout the twentieth century. *How China Works* examines the importance of labor issues by charting the changes in the Chinese workplace and the impact these have had on the future of China's economic and political system.

Drawing on original fieldwork and archival research, the book presents eight key case studies that look at the micropolitics of the workplace and the globalization of production, illustrating labor relations within a range of industries across all regions of China.

Unlike previous literature in the area, *How China Works* focuses its perspective from 1910 right through to the twenty-first century, providing important historical depth with particular emphasis on the transitions to socialism in the 1950s and transitions from it in the 1980s. The book approaches the subject area from a multidisciplinary angle, introducing concepts from labor history, politics, sociology and anthropology in the China field. The contributors argue that the understanding of work in China has been overly politicized and state-centered, and instead suggest a method of study that is grounded in workplace cultures and labor processes. They pay particular attention to continuities in the Chinese workplace across divides caused by the 1949 socialist revolution and the post-Mao reforms in 1978. With China's transition to capitalism and the legitimacy of Communist one-party rule in question, *How China Works* provides a timely and topical addition to the current literature that will appeal to China academics in a wide range of social science disciplines.

Jacob Eyferth is Assistant Professor of History at Simon Fraser University, Vancouver. He is the co-editor of *Rural Development in Transitional China: The New Agriculture* (London: Frank Cass, 2003) and author of articles in *The China Quarterly* and the *Journal of Peasant Studies*.

Asia's transformations
Edited by Mark Selden
Binghamton and Cornell Universities, USA

The books in this series explore the political, social, economic and cultural consequences of Asia's transformations in the twentieth and twenty-first centuries. The series emphasizes the tumultuous interplay of local, national, regional and global forces as Asia bids to become the hub of the world economy. While focusing on the contemporary, it also looks back to analyse the antecedents of Asia's contested rise.

This series comprises several strands:

Asia's Transformations aims to address the needs of students and teachers, and the titles will be published in hardback and paperback. Titles include:

Ethnicity in Asia
Edited by Colin Mackerras

The Battle for Asia
From decolonization to
globalization
Mark T. Berger

State and Society in 21st-Century
China
Edited by Peter Hays Gries and
Stanley Rosen

Japan's Quiet Transformation
Social change and civil society in
the 21st century
Jeff Kingston

Confronting the Bush Doctrine
Critical views from the Asia-Pacific
Edited by Mel Gurtov and
Peter Van Ness

China in War and Revolution,
1895–1949
Peter Zarrow

The Future of US-Korean Relations
The imbalance of power
Edited by John Feffer

Asia's Great Cities
Each volume aims to capture the heartbeat of the contemporary city from
multiple perspectives emblematic of the authors' own deep familiarity with
the distinctive faces of the city, its history, society, culture, politics and
economics, and its evolving position in national, regional and global
frameworks. While most volumes emphasize urban developments since the
Second World War, some pay close attention to the legacy of the *longue
durée* in shaping the contemporary. Thematic and comparative volumes
address such themes as urbanization, economic and financial linkages,
architecture and space, wealth and power, gendered relationships, planning and anarchy, and ethnographies in national and regional perspective.
Titles include:

Bangkok
Place, practice and representation
Marc Askew

Beijing in the Modern World
David Strand and
Madeline Yue Dong

Shanghai
Global city
Jeff Wasserstrom

Hong Kong
Global city
Stephen Chiu and Tai-Lok Lui

Representing Calcutta
Modernity, nationalism and the
colonial uncanny
Swati Chattopadhyay

Singapore
Wealth, power and the culture of
control
Carl A. Trocki

Asia.com is a series which focuses on the ways in which new information and communication technologies are influencing politics, society and culture in Asia. Titles include:

Literature and Society is a series that seeks to demonstrate the ways in which Asian Literature is influenced by the politics, society and culture in which it is produced. Titles include:

Routledge Studies in Asia's Transformations is a forum for innovative new research intended for a high-level specialist readership, and the titles will be available in hardback only. Titles include:

Critical Asian Scholarship is a series intended to showcase the most important individual contributions to scholarship in Asian Studies. Each of the volumes presents a leading Asian scholar addressing themes that are central to his or her most significant and lasting contribution to Asian studies. The series is committed to the rich variety of research and writing on Asia, and is not restricted to any particular discipline, theoretical approach or geographical expertise.

How China Works

Perspectives on the twentieth-century industrial workplace

Edited by Jacob Eyferth

Routledge
Taylor & Francis Group

LONDON AND NEW YORK

First published 2006
by Routledge
2 Park Square, Milton Park, Abingdon, Oxon OX14 4RN

Simultaneously published in the USA and Canada
by Routledge
270 Madison Ave, New York, NY 10016

*Routledge is an imprint of the Taylor & Francis Group, an informa
business*

Typeset in Sabon by Wearset Ltd, Boldon, Tyne and Wear
Printed and bound in Great Britain by TJ Digital, Padstow, Cornwall

British Library Cataloguing in Publication Data
A catalogue record for this book is available from the British Library

Library of Congress Cataloging in Publication Data
A catalog record for this book has been requested

ISBN10: 0-415-39238-1

ISBN13: 978-0-415-39238-9

Contents

Illustrations

Figures

Tables

Contributors

Calvin Chen is Luce Assistant Professor of Politics at Mount Holyoke College. His writings include "Leninism, Developmental Stages, and Transformation: Understanding Social and Institutional Change in Contemporary China," in *World Order After Leninism* (University of Washington Press, 2006). He is currently working on a book manuscript, *Economic Reform, Local Networks, and the Politics of Production in Contemporary China*.

Jacob Eyferth is Assistant Professor of History at Simon Fraser University, Vancouver. He is the co-editor of *Rural Development in Transitional China: The New Agriculture* (Frank Cass, 2003) and author of articles in *The China Quarterly* and the *Journal of Peasant Studies*.

Mark W. Frazier is Assistant Professor of Government and the Luce Assistant Professor of East Asian Political Economy at Lawrence University. He is the author of *The Chinese Industrial Workplace: State, Revolution, and Labor Management* (Cambridge University Press, 2002) and has published articles on China's pension reforms in *The China Journal* and *Studies in Comparative International Development*. He was a 2004–2005 Fulbright Research Fellow, based in Beijing and Shanghai, where he conducted social surveys and interviews on how citizens and officials have responded to pension reforms.

Amy Hanser is Assistant Professor in the Department of Anthropology and Sociology at the University of British Columbia, Vancouver. Her publications include "Youth Job Search in Urban China: The Use of Social Connections in a Changing Labor Market," in T. Gold, D. Guthrie, and D. Wank (eds) *Social Connections in China* (Cambridge University Press, 2002).

Henrietta Harrison is Professor of History at Harvard University. Her publications include *The Making of the Republican Citizen: Ceremonies and Symbols in China, 1911–1929* (Oxford University Press, 2000), *China: Inventing the Nation* (Arnold, 2001), "Newspapers and Nationalism in Rural China, 1890–1919," *Past and Present* 166 (2000), and

The Man Awakened from Dreams: One Man's Life in a North China Village 1857–1942 (Stanford University Press, 2004).

Lida Junghans is a cultural anthropologist with a PhD degree from Harvard University. Her dissertation "Workers in Transit: Chinese Railway Workers and the Journey from Plan to Market" is based on eighteen months of research in the People's Republic of China. She currently works as a consultant in the Boston area.

Pun Ngai is Assistant Professor at the Hong Kong University of Science and Technology and has published in *The China Journal*, *Positions*, and *Cultural Anthropology*. She is the author of *Made in China: Women Factory Workers in a Global Workplace* (Duke University Press, 2005). Her research interests include Chinese migrant workers, labor resistance, and gender and cultural politics.

Minghua Zhao is Assistant Director of the Greenwich Maritime Institute at the University of Greenwich. Her research interests include state enterprise reforms, labor markets and maritime studies. She has published in *Chinese Sociology and Anthropology*, *China Review*, the *Spur* and *The China Journal*. She is also co-editor of *Women of China: Economic and Social Transformation* (Macmillan, 1999).

Acknowledgments

This book began with a workshop on "Workplaces and Work Experiences in the People's Republic of China," held at Harvard University's Fairbank Center for East Asian Research on 1–2 June 2002. I thank the Fairbank Center and its director Elizabeth Perry for their generous financial and administrative support. Thanks also to Stefanie Van Pelt, Wen-hao Tien and Abigail Ladd for their hard work which greatly contributed to the success of the workshop. While preparing the workshop, I received advice and inspiration from Tony Saich, William Kirby, James L. Watson, Martin King Whyte, Vivienne Shue, and Ching-Kwan Lee. I am indebted to all the workshop participants, including Robert Cliver and Mary Gallagher; to William Kirby, Robert Weller, Gary Leupp, and Elizabeth Remick for their insightful comments; and to the audience, in particular Peter Perdue and Regina Abrami, for two days of stimulating discussions. Mark Selden saw the manuscript through to publication, read numerous versions of the introduction, and provided well-measured doses of encouragement and criticism. This book would not have been possible without his patient help. Finally, I thank Stephanie An and Mark Langham for much needed help during the last stages of copy-editing.

Introduction

Jacob Eyferth

In 1957, on the eve of the Great Leap Forward, Mao Zedong predicted the imminent disappearance of all other classes, leaving only the working class:

> How many [people] do we now have in the working class?... Right now there are twelve million industrial workers in the factories; only twelve million out of a population of 600 million. This is a bit more than one-fiftieth.... The number is so small, but it is only this, [the working class] that has a future. All other classes are transitional classes. All they do is walk, walk along. Where do they walk to? They walk to the place of the [working class]. For instance, the peasants: the peasants will in the future become mechanized and will transform into agricultural workers.... As for the bourgeoisie, everyone knows about the bourgeoisie; the bourgeoisie is right now in the midst of a transition. It, too, must be transformed into workers. The several hundred million peasants and handicraft workers have now already transformed into collectivized peasants; in the future they will be further transformed into peasants [under the state ownership system] and agricultural workers, using machinery.
>
> (Cheng and Selden 1997: 31)

Half a century later, China is well on its way of realizing one part of Mao's vision. In terms of its employment structure, China is now a "workers' country," with more people employed in industry and services than agriculture. At the same time, of course, the part of the Maoist legacy that gave workers lifetime employment, medical care, housing, and pensions has been dismantled. Before 1950, most work, including the manufacture of commodities, took place in households or in enterprises that were essentially extensions of the household; even in major cities, the vast majority of workers were self-employed or worked in family-run stores and workshops. The transition to socialism in the 1950s transformed China's working population into wage earners, though the wages of peasants – 80 percent of the population – were calculated in work points, paid largely in grain, and fully redeemed only at the end of each growing season. Full worker status and stable monetary incomes were privileges reserved for the urban population. The reform policies of the 1980s saw a massive return to self-employment, as peasant households (and, later and in smaller numbers, segments of the urban population) became independent operators. At the same time, however, urbanization and industrialization moved ever larger numbers of people out of farming and into industrial and service employment. Today, agriculture employs less than half of the total workforce: 45 percent in 2001, against 23 percent in rural enterprises and 32 percent in the urban economy (*China Statistical Yearbook* 2002: 120–122).[1]

More people now work off-farm and outside the household than on-farm and within the household; salaried employment, rather than non-wage remuneration, has become the norm even in parts of rural China. What we see here is the formation, in the span of two generations, of the world's largest industrial workforce – a social transformation that is unprecedented in its speed and scope.

China's transition from a pre-industrial to an industrial society is usually seen as consisting of three distinct phases. Modern industry, and with it a nascent working class, emerged for the first time in the treaty ports of the early twentieth century. After 1949, this nascent working class was transformed into a much larger socialist workforce, employed in collective or state-owned work units (*danwei*), supervised and protected by the socialist "father-mother" state (Lü and Perry 1997: 8). The 1980s and 1990s, finally, saw the rise of foreign investment, private enterprise, and hybrid public–private ownership; the dismantling of the *danwei* and other socialist institutions; and the gradual fragmentation and disenfranchisement of the old *danwei* workforce. In the first years of the People's Republic of China (PRC), employment in industry (now narrowly defined as manufacture in mechanized enterprises) rose from 3.4 million in 1950 to 7.9 million in 1957. At the same time rural craft industries, which in the 1950s still produced almost all rural and a large part of urban consumer goods, were starved of raw materials and denied access to markets. When Mao in his 1957 speech claimed that the "several hundred million peasants and handicraft workers" had already been transformed "into collectivized *peasants*," this was not just a sleight of hand: in the previous three years, some fifteen million rural artisans had been transferred to the Agricultural Production Cooperatives, where most of them eventually became deskilled peasants. The introduction of quasi-industrial forms of organization in agriculture thus went hand in hand with rural deindustrialization.

The Great Leap Forward briefly swelled the ranks of the industrial workforce – sixteen million were added in 1958 alone – but did not lead to any permanent expansion. To the contrary, after the failure of the Leap, the leadership decided to retrench the privileged and expensive urban sector. The urban population was reduced by some twenty million (from a peak of 120 million); non-agricultural employment was reduced by some ten million (from a peak of forty million). Once the retrenchment was complete, rural-to-urban migration was effectively banned and a strict ceiling was imposed on the size of the urban population. In the cities, the state pursued a low wage, high employment policy, coupled with generous and comprehensive welfare provision through the *danwei*; in the countryside, local grain self-sufficiency was promoted in order to prevent a repetition of the post-Leap famine. Rural collectives were allowed to invest in small industries only as long as these increased, rather than decreased, agricultural self-sufficiency; competition with state-owned enterprises (SOEs) for raw materials, capital, or markets was explicitly banned. For ten years, industrial employment remained constant at around 7 percent of the working population. It was only in the mid-1970s that industrial employment began to rise again – this time not in the urban state-owned sector but in the countryside, where rural collectives had begun to channel savings into small-scale industries, and, after the post-Mao opening of China to foreign investment, in the coastal areas, where foreign and domestic investors took advantage of China's abundant supplies of cheap labor.

The massive changes associated with the turning points of 1949 and 1978 have led observers to assume an almost total discontinuity in the Chinese workplace. Discontinuity is taken for granted in the literature on China's early industrialization – not surprisingly, since most studies focus on large mills in the treaty ports, where the rupture with the past is much sharper than, for example, in the small silk filatures of Wuxi (Bell 1999). Continuity in the workplace tends to be conceptualized as an anachronistic survival of pre-industrial habits. While the best studies of China's early factories (Hershatter 1986; Honig 1986; Perry 1993) concede that loyalties to native place, ethnic group, or guild are meaningful forms of workers' self-expression, they still tend to regard them as extraneous to the modern workplace: a "carryover of rural practices into the industrializing cities" (Perry 1993: 12). Discontinuity is a major theme also in the literature on the 1949 transition to socialist industry. According to Andrew Walder, the Communist Party "created, almost from scratch, a new tradition of labor relations," leading to "the birth of the *second* working class in Chinese history – one created in the image of a highly centralized, industrializing socialist state" (1984: 11, 3, his italics). Scholars working on post-Mao China, finally, stress the discontinuities between the older *danwei* workforce and a new proletariat that has been called into existence by global capitalism (Lee 1998; O'Leary 1998; Pun 1999; Sargeson 1999; Chan 2001).

In all these instances, scholars focus on "typical" workplaces (the treaty port mill, the state-owned industrial *danwei*, the foreign-invested factory) to illustrate the workings of larger historical forces (economic imperialism, socialist paternalism, globalized capitalism) on the Chinese workforce. In fact, none of these "typical" formations was numerically dominant: state-owned industrial *danweis* employed less than half of all industrial labor in the 1970s (Walder 1984: 37); treaty port factories in the early twentieth century and foreign-invested factories in the early twenty-first, employed and employ much smaller percentages. This focus on "representative" types results in an overly fragmented and politicized vision of the Chinese workplace, in which change appears to be abrupt and extraneous to the workplace, caused by impersonal forces such as state power or globalization. Labor processes and labor relations appear to arrive in China fully-fledged and to be implemented in a top-down fashion by capitalist or socialist managers who act in almost perfect freedom, unencumbered by worker opposition or technical constraints.

Against such perspectives, the authors of the present volume hold that any analysis of work has to start from the actual workplace. Workplaces, in China as elsewhere, use uneven and sometimes outdated technology, are staffed by typically contentious workers, and are led by managers whose knowledge of the labor process is often very limited. Perfect managerial control, as the debate on the degradation of work under capitalism demonstrates, is well-nigh impossible (Braverman 1974; Friedman 1977; Edwards 1979). Taylorism is a powerful ideology, much in vogue in reform-period China, but as a managerial practice it is self-defeating because even fully automated production immediately breaks down without active, self-motivated worker participation. Deskilling – the "attempt to build skills into machines by means of algorithms" – is rarely permanent since "other skills tend to develop around the new machines" (Sigaut 1994: 446). Even where machinery and managerial ideologies are imports from abroad, factories depend on local sources of power, water, raw materials, spare parts, knowledge, skills, and labor, which inevitably "indigenize" the labor process. Managers may wish to create a "blank," atomized workforce, but even peasant workers, specifically selected for their lack of previous exposure to industrial work, bring specific experiences and expectations to the workplace. Workplaces, in short, are embedded in social, cultural, and technological contexts. In the following sections, I will elaborate on this proposition, drawing on three distinct literatures: the labor process approach pioneered by Michael Burawoy, recent studies of the European industrial revolution, and the literature on cultures of work in the non-Western world.

The labor process

Several chapters in this volume draw inspiration from the labor process approach pioneered by Michael Burawoy. Production, Burawoy argues, has two distinct moments: the *labor process* ("the social relations into which men and women enter as they transform raw materials into useful

products") and the *factory regime* (the "political apparatuses which reproduce those relations of the labor process through the regulation of struggles") (Burawoy 1983: 587). Most studies on work in China focus on
factory regimes: on ownership, administrative structure, formal regulations, remuneration, benefits, social welfare, and social control. While all
these aspects are important, to gain a full understanding of the workplace,
we need to know more about the motivations and strategies of managers
and workers and about the micropolitics – the concrete, daily interaction
between workers, management, and machines – of the workplace.

Technology, as feminist scholars (Cowan 1983; Hafter 1995; Liu 1994)
have long argued, is not autonomous from class and gender power struggles. While much literature has tended to stress the divide between socialist
and capitalist labor, in numerous respects, a socialist machine shop or
cotton mill resembles a capitalist machine shop or cotton mill. Power-con-
centrating technologies – the assembly line, the punch clock – were used in
Chinese factories before, during, and after state socialism and have steadily
advanced in all these eras. How workers respond to such technologies
depends partly on formal factory regimes (security and duration of job
tenure, forms of remuneration, etc.) but inferences about the labor process
based on factory regimes are risky. Intuitive assumptions about capitalist
or socialist work may be misleading: as Burawoy and Lukasz (1985)
demonstrate in their comparison between technologically similar factories
in the USA and Hungary, capitalist workplaces can be slow-paced and
bureaucratic, while work under socialism can be fiercely competitive. This
inversion, they argue, is systemic: capitalist corporations, in order to better
cope with uncertain market demand, incorporate "socialist" features
(internal bureaucracies, distribution of surplus between divisions of the
corporation), which then give rise to the "typically socialist" problems of
shortages, rushing, and shoddy work. Socialist corporations, by contrast,
in order to cope with the uncertainties of supply in shortage economies,
permit the operation of internal markets, leading (in the Hungarian
example) to high productivity and extreme competition. Or, as Burawoy
and Krotov (1992) put it, "anarchy at the level of the relations of production [i.e., unplanned distribution and appropriation of goods under
capitalism] leads to planning in the relations in production" [i.e., a bureau-
cratically planned labor process], while planned distribution and appropriation under socialism leads to "anarchy in the relations in production."
Workplaces, in short, are not microcosms of their respective societies – an
assumption that underlies much industrial sociology of China (Walder
1986; Lü and Perry 1997) – but reflect these societies in complex and
contradictory ways.

Burawoy's most important contribution, however, lies in his focus on
how workers' subjectivities shape the workplace. Earlier proponents of the
labor process approach (Braverman 1974) mechanistically assumed that
interests were determined by class position. Burawoy, by contrast, argues

that interests and identities are "manufactured" in the workplace: "any work context involves an economic dimension (production of things), a political dimension (production of social relations), and an ideological dimension (production of an experience of those relations)" (1985: 39). Work is inherently about the production of social relations and social meanings – or, to paraphrase Francesca Bray (1997: 16), one of the most important functions that work performs is to "produce people." Rather than looking at the brute mechanics of coercion and resistance, we have to look at the processes that turn workers into accomplices in their own exploitation. At Allied, where Burawoy worked, the game of "making out" dominated shop floor culture: operators set themselves certain output targets and constantly evaluated themselves and their colleagues in terms of their success or failure in the game. Such games are functional for capital, but they are also part of workers' effort to bring order and significance to their experience of work.

Workplaces, of course, are not the only sites where interests are produced and mediated. Joyce (1987: 8), in a discussion of Burawoy, emphasizes extra-work situations:

> One thinks here of such matters as the legitimation and ideological neutering of ideas of private property, technology and the market, or the social production of knowledge involved in ideologies legitimating notions of management as a distinct sphere involving special claims to competence and efficiency, and so to power.... The site of such ideologies is as likely to be in the media, in education, in the family or the state as in the work situation itself.

Gender is one among several constructs that are produced through family, education, and the media and bear directly on the organization of work. In contemporary China, sub-ethnicity, local origin, and rural/urban status further fragment the ideological terrain on which interests are organized. To understand how ideological constructs shape the reality of work at the most basic level, one only needs to look at how young female migrant workers (*dagongmei*) are ideologically constructed as "girls" and "peasants" and are made to work for wages that neither urban women nor rural men would tolerate. Although increasing numbers of these migrant workers are now becoming urbanized – Shanghai, for example, now has a permanent "migrant" population of three million, one-quarter of the total population – migration is still widely seen as temporary: a life-cycle phenomenon, akin in some ways to domestic service performed in nineteenth-century Europe. Like domestic servants, migrants need to earn enough only to cover the temporary needs of a healthy young adult who is accustomed to austere conditions. Costs associated with the long-term reproduction of their labor power – healthcare, old age security, expenses for child rearing – are borne by their home communities who raise them and are legally obliged to take them back when their productivity show signs of flagging. Migrants, like domestic servants, are assumed to reap immaterial rewards from their exposure to urban civilization, and this is seen as justifying their depressed wages. Such social meanings are *produced* largely through state and media discourses, but they are constantly *reproduced* in the factories where supervisors capitalize on gender, ethnic, and status insecurities to keep their charges under control.

China's industrial revolution

Contemporary China is – and arguably has been since at least the early twentieth century – in the throes of an industrial revolution, similar in many ways to the industrial revolutions that transformed Britain, Western Europe, North America, and Japan. Industrialization, as the latest generation of scholarship on the European industrial revolution has shown, involves the gradual transformation of entire economies, rather than the arrival of a "wave of new gadgets" on the industrial scene (Coleman 1992; O'Brien and Quinault 1993; Berg 1994a; Berg 1994b; Floud and McClosky 1994; Mokyr 1999). Such transformations are gradual and cumulative, rooted in economic practices that long predate the advent of mechanized industry. They take place not just in such glamour sectors as iron and cotton but throughout the economy; indeed, they involve not only the material production of goods but also patterns of social organization at the level of the industrial region, the village community or urban neighborhood, and the household. Most specialists now agree that productivity gains in the early phase of the European industrial revolution were caused by more efficient markets, more complex divisions of labor, and a more rational distribution of capital and labor across economic sectors rather than by mechanization. Technical progress was not limited to large-scale production in mechanized factories; much growth occurred in "traditional" agriculture, crafts, and small industries. In fact, "it was and is very difficult to make clear-cut divisions between the traditional and the modern ... as there were rarely separate organizational forms, technologies, locations or even firms to be ascribed to either" (Berg 1994a: 25).

China's industrial transformation, like those of Western Europe and Japan, was a gradual, cumulative, multi-stranded process that drew its strength from many different sources. Two concepts appear particularly relevant here: the concept of the industrial district and that of an "industrious revolution" paving the way for the industrial revolution. The latter concept, originally developed by Akira Hayami (1992) with reference to Tokugawa Japan, is best known in Jan de Vries' (1993, 1994) formulation. De Vries defines the "industrious revolution" as the increased propensity of households to produce goods and services for the market, rather than for internal consumption in the household. The income earned in this way is then used to buy more products from the market, leading to an increased supply of marketed commodities and labor and an increased demand for goods. As de Vries demonstrates, such shifts in household strategies can result in far-reaching economic transformations, even in the absence of technological change. The concept applies well to East Asia, where labor-intensive manufacture, based on the effort of the rural household to make optimal use of available resources, long preceded the introduction of mechanized factories (Sugihara 2003). It is particularly useful for understanding how changes in the ideological realm, through the aggregate decisions of households, impact on the economy. In the case of China, it allows us to understand how the state's ideological and legal interventions in basic social institutions affected the economy. From the propagation of companionate marriages in the 1950 marriage law to family planning since the 1970s; from the ideological war on household-based subsistence strategies (not to mention private money making) under the collectives to the glorification of selfishness and greed in the 1990s, the Chinese state has molded the composition, internal dynamics, and economic strategies of households to an extent that is unparalleled elsewhere in the world.

The crucial variable here is the ideologically motivated mobilization and demobilization of the labor of household dependents, in particular, young women. China has always been characterized by a high degree and generally positive valuation of female participation in production (Mann 1997). Women's work was normatively defined as "inside" work, but this did not mean that it was merely reproductive. Many of China's most important industries, in particular, textiles, relied largely on female labor, and even elite women were encouraged to develop marketable skills. What changed over time was less the extent to which women produced for the market than how and where they did so (inside or outside the household) and who accumulated the surplus produced by their labor (Pomeranz 2003). Fluctuations in the female labor supply must be understood in the light of changing gender norms and state policies that encouraged the retention of female labor by the household or collective, or, to the contrary, mandated its release into the market. The long-term trend since 1500 was towards an increased marketization of female labor, in ways that are consistent with de Vries' formulation. According to Pomeranz, this trend was temporarily interrupted in the collective period, when the ban on migration and on sideline production led to a pattern of "labor withholding." Labor that otherwise would have produced commodities for the market – either in households or in factories – was now mobilized for the production of goods and services destined for consumption in the "big household" of the collective. One result of this labor-withholding strategy was an intensified reproduction of the labor force: immobilized labor was used to improve the medical and educational infrastructure, leading to longer lives, improved health, and better education, but also to growing underemployment among an increasingly healthy and educated rural workforce.

The post-Mao period, Pomeranz argues, saw the resumption of the pre-1949 pattern in which labor, in particular female labor, was mobilized for production for the market. As several commentators have pointed out, accumulation in rural China is largely driven by the appropriation of the product of women's labor (Judd 1994; Jacka 1997; Lee 1998). Although township and village enterprise (TVE) in the 1980s and 1990s were, in some sense, communal industries, the young women who perform much of the most demanding and least remunerative work in such enterprises rarely benefit from them. Until their widespread privatization in the late 1990s, most TVEs were owned or controlled by village governments and much of the income that they generated was plowed back into communities, in the form of well-paid jobs for village members or as investment in schools, roads, and other infrastructure. However, since prevailing gender norms oblige women to marry out of their natal village, they do not benefit from improvements that are paid for by their labor. What is more, the fact that young women are not permanent members of the community encourages village leaders, along with men and married women, to intensify accumulation on the back of their daughters, rather than paying higher wages or investing in better work conditions (Pomeranz 2003: 160). Traditional gender norms thus interact with the Maoist legacy of local state developmentalism and with the market in complex ways.

Rural industry, as Pomeranz points out, has been a constant of Chinese development for the past 500 years. Like Western Europe and Japan, China underwent a long period of rural "proto-industrialization" (Li 2000); what is particular about Chinese rural industry was the fact that it has remained so preponderant for such a long time. Contrary to Maoist rhetoric, which holds that traditional craft industries collapsed long before 1949 under the onslaught of cheap foreign imports, there was no general decline. In 1933, craft industries still accounted for three-quarters of China's industrial output (Liu and Yeh 1965: 66); even in 1952, handicrafts continued to account for 42 percent of industrial output in 1952 prices (weighted in favor of heavy industry) and for an amazing 68 percent in 1933 prices. If there is a rupture in the long-term development of rural industries, it was not the sudden "take-off" (Oi 1999) of the 1980s but, to the contrary, the deindustrialization and agrarianization of the countryside in the 1950s and 1960s.

Pre-1949 China – like Western Europe and Japan during the early stages of their industrial revolutions (Sabel and Zeitlin 1985; Hudson 1989; Wigen 1995; Francks 2002) – was an economy composed of regions: relatively small areas in which firms clustered together in a number of related branches, competed for a common pool of labor, and drew on a host of supporting institutions such as guilds, formalized training and apprenticeship, informal credit markets, etc. These regions were characterized by the coexistence of firms of different size and complexity, by dense interaction between city and countryside, and by networks of patronage and mutual support that allowed for concerted action as well as cut-throat competition (Fong 1936, 1937; Bell 1999). Beginning in the 1950s and culminating in the restructuring after the Great Leap Forward, China's economic planners replaced this pattern with a system in which the main dividing line was no longer between differently specialized *regions* but between internally homogenized urban-industrial and rural-agrarian *spheres*.

From 1954 to 1956, the number of officially registered rural artisans dropped from 4.7 million to 2.2 million, while millions of so-called seasonal commodity producers were organized into rural collectives and lost their access to raw materials and markets. Handloom weaving, the most important rural industry (producing one-half of Chinese cloth in 1949), was declared obsolescent and effectively banned (Chao 1977: 266–270). Much has been made of the liberating effects of collectivization for rural women, and there can be no doubt that many women experienced remunerated work in public as an improvement over household work (Hershatter 2000). However, textile work was often highly skilled, earned considerable cash income, and was a source of pride and status. Its demise left women deskilled and consigned them to an already overcrowded agricultural sector where they faced lower wages than men and other forms of gender discrimination (Pomeranz 2003: 150). Men, too, suffered despecialization and deskilling, especially in the wake of the Great Leap Forward, when rural craft producers were turned into peasants on a massive scale (Eyferth 2003).

Rural industrialization in the reform era draws simultaneously on the Maoist tradition of resource mobilization (Oi 1999; Whiting 2001) and on pre-1949 legacies. It is most successful where it replicates the earlier pattern of small-batch production of consumer goods for distant markets, flexible (and thus often exploitative) labor relations, and dense interaction between firms of different size and complexity. Wenzhou is the best-known example of this pattern (Parris 1993; Liu Yia-ling 1992) but similar structures have been described for Guangdong (Unger and Chan 1999) and Jiangsu (Fei 1986). Industrial clusters can also be found in urban settings, from Beijing's Zhejiang village (Zhang 2001) to the computer district of Zhongguancun.

Labor migration must be understood in the context of sectoral policies that erected an artificial barrier between the city and the countryside and systematically pumped rural wealth to the cities (Knight and Song 1999). Migration on a truly massive scale (now estimated at 130 million) coexists with the systematic exclusion of migrants from social and economic citizenship in the cities. The household registration (*hukou*) system, originally conceived to prevent migration, now serves to keep migrants permanently uprooted in their new place of residence, denying them access to healthcare, education, and other services that are partly funded through their own work (Solinger 1999). The central government has announced its intention to abolish key parts of the *hukou* system, but most municipalities have already issued their own blatantly discriminatory regulations in anticipation of the abolition (Wang 2004). Moreover, the exclusion of migrants rests only partly on state regulations. Increasingly, it relies on the rhetorical construction of migrants as quasi-ethnic Others, whose presence in the cities must be tolerated for economic reasons but who cannot become full urban citizens (Anagnost 2004; Yan 2003).

The unproblematic Chinese workplace

Much workplace literature focuses on the difficult experience of the first generation of industrial workers. Factories in the early industrial revolution relied heavily on the bonded labor of workhouse and prison inmates and on women, children, and impoverished Irish immigrants, because "free-born" Englishmen refused to work in the factories even when these offered higher wages. According to Sidney Pollard (1965: 245), mechanized mills required nothing less than a new type of worker: "men who were non-accumulative, non-acquisitive, accustomed to work for subsistence, not for maximization of income, had to be made obedient to the cash stimulus, and obedient in such a way as to react precisely to the stimuli provided." As E.P. Thompson has argued in one of his best-known essays (1991), work in the pre-industrial world was task-oriented and governed by the rhythms of nature. Mechanized factories replaced this "humanly comprehensible" world of work with an abstract clock-time which workers recruited from agricultural or artisanal work experienced as extremely alienating. Thompson's work has spawned dozens of studies on workers' resistance against dehumanizing factory regimes. Ritualized drinking bouts, violence against apprentices and foremen, the observance of Saint Monday, and general indiscipline are all well-documented aspects of the European world of work (Roberts 1992).

Capitalism's violent irruption into the pre-industrial world of work is a recurrent theme also in anthropological studies of the industrialization process. Ong (1987), in her work on spirit possession among Malaysian factory women, contrasts the natural rhythms of kampong life with the oppressive discipline of the factories. Seizure by ghosts, in her interpretation, is an act of resistance against dehumanizing work. Similarly, Taussig (1980) describes Bolivian tin miners as deeply rooted in a pre-capitalist world. Unable to see surplus production for what it is – the result of their exploitation – they understand it in mythical terms as the work of the devil who enriches those who sell their soul to him. In a similar vein, much of the literature on Indian industrial work describes the survival of pre-industrial mentalities and primordial loyalties to religion, caste, and place (Chakrabarty 1989). Resistance and maladjustment to industrial work are common themes also in the literature on the Russian and Eastern European transition to socialism (Siegelbaum and Suny 1988; Kotkin 1995), on

Stalinist industrialization (Kuromiya 1994), and on the transition back from socialism to capitalism (Burawoy and Krotov 1992; Lampland 1995; Mandel and Humphrey 2002).

In contrast to all this, Chinese workers appear almost infinitely adaptable and stress-resistant. Why is it that in contemporary China, twelve-hour workdays under dehumanizing conditions and situations in which workers are frequently unpaid for weeks and months do not provoke spirit possession or the religious mystification of the workplace? Why is it that we hear so little about destructive and self-destructive behavior in the Chinese workplace, about extended drinking bouts, gambling, and violence? Is it because such behavior is indeed rare (it certainly exists – see Junghans' chapter in this volume) or because prevalent discourses have conditioned us to see the Chinese workplace as unproblematic, populated by supremely productive but culturally blank workers? Why is it that in India, working-class fragmentation along ethnic and native-place lines tends to be interpreted as the expression of *identities* and *culture* – of primordial loyalties to caste and religion – while in the Chinese case, it tends to be interpreted as the expression of (however imperfectly understood) *interests*?

Culture, of course, is not entirely absent from the study of the Chinese workplace. Perry (1993, 1994, 1996), Honig (1986, 1992, 1996), Hershatter (1986), and Bell (1999) have written in great detail about the importance of native-place ties, ethnicity, and gender in pre-1949 factories, while Perry and Li (1997) and Frazier (2002) explore cultural continuities in the post-1949 workplace. Studies on contemporary work by Lee (1998), Pun (1999), and Sargeson (1999) discuss how notions of gender and ethnicity shape and are being shaped by work. However, even in these studies, culture too often remains "thin" and abstract. Jonathan Parry's observation:

> what Ram Singh Yadav from Saran actually thinks about the machine he handles in the jute mill, how he negotiates his relationship with the Chamar from Champaran on the next machine, and whether he flirts with the Telugu woman in the same shop, is left largely unexplored
> (Parry *et al.* 1999: xii)

applies all the more to China.

The relationship between culture (ideas, consciousness, discourse) and interests has been the object of intense debates among labor historians in the West. Positions range from reformulations of Marx that seek to reground working-class history in the labor process (Burawoy 1979, 1985) to language-centered theories that see interests as discursively constructed and deny the possibility of "decod[ing] political language to reach a primal and material expression of interest since it is the discursive structure of political language itself which conceives and defines interests in the first place"

(Jones 1983: 21–22; see also Sewell 1980). Despite these differences, there is broad agreement that interests never exist in a simple, unmediated form but are constructed through language and signifying practices inside and outside the workplace. Rather than assuming that interests directly reflect economic positions, we need to look at the ideological and symbolic terrain on which interests are constructed (Joyce 1987: 7; Siegelbaum and Suny 1994: 8).

Of particular interest in this regard is Richard Biernacki's attempt to overcome the dichotomy between culture and structure by locating culture directly *in* the workplace, in the "signifying practices" at the point of production. The linguistic turn, Biernacki argues, has led labor historians to see culture as a purely discursive framework. "But the notion that culture functions through 'representations' . . . establishes a culture *for* and *around* practice, not one subsiding in the execution of its techniques. It thereby leaves in place an unreconstructed, implicitly 'economic' view of manufacture" (1997: 173). A more fruitful approach, Biernacki argues, is to see culture as directly constitutive of practices in the workplace. Biernacki illustrates this proposition by comparing nineteenth-century British and German textile mills that had developed under "compellingly similar economic circumstances" but nonetheless exhibited clear differences in the cultural specifications of labor as a commodity. German employers and workers thought of the employment relation as the sale of labor as an abstract substance: employers bought, as it were, the right to dispose over workers' time and physical strength for a fixed period of time. British employers and workers, by contrast, thought of the labor contract as the appropriation of labor as embodied in tangible products: workers were imagined as semi-independent operators who rented looms from their employers and sold the cloth back to them. These differences "structured the most fundamental aspects of industrial relations, including methods of remuneration, calculation of outputs and costs, disciplinary techniques, rights to employment, articulation of grievances, mill architecture, and even the apperception of time and space" (ibid.: 176). They also structured working-class politics: since British workers understood the labor contract as the purchase of the products of their labor, their struggles focused on the right to fair returns in the sphere of exchange. By contrast, German workers saw the employers' domination over the person of the worker as the essence of exploitation, and therefore focused on issues related to their personal dignity.

Are Chinese factory regimes rooted in shared cultural understandings, and if so, what would these be? These are empirical questions, and answers will differ across regions, time periods, and sectors. Nothing is to be gained, however, by seeing factory regimes simply as manifestations of a universal, totalizing logic, be it that of global capitalism or of the modernizing state. I see this tendency particularly in Foucault-inspired studies that interpret factory architectures or the spatial positioning of workers as forms of a totalizing power that work directly on the body of the worker. There is a danger here of seeing power as so relentless and pervasive that it blots out workers' subjectivity and reduces them to cogs in a machine. Brutal coercion and mind-numbing routines do exist in Chinese factories, but as Lee (1998: 22) reminds us, despotism is a costly method of control and management tends to resort to softer, more "hegemonic" methods whenever they are available (see Chen's chapter in this volume). Even in relatively despotic firms, management supplements strict disciplinary codes with the manipulation of shared social meanings ranging from local-origin ties and gender stereotypes to abstract notions of fairness and justice, obligation to the collectivity, and modernity and progress.

Extreme discursive positions have held little interest for students of socialist China, perhaps because the socialist state monopolized public speech and prevented the formation of alternative languages of class. However, as Perry and Li (1997) have shown, the state's control was less than monolithic, and when intra-party conflict opened up spaces for dissent, rebellious workers could and did appropriate the state's language to claim their rightful positions as the "masters of the country." The reform era saw the development of two new and very different discourses on the Chinese worker: while writers in Hong Kong, Taiwan, and the West celebrated the disciplined, hyper-productive Chinese worker (see Greenhalgh's 1994 critique of this literature), media discourses in the PRC construed large groups of workers – migrants, women, state-sector workers, and ethnic minorities – as under-achievers, crippled by peasant "feudalism" or socialist mentalities. As Pun (2005) shows, Hong Kong managers in Shenzhen construe their "northern" workers (who in fact come from southern and central China) as "red and lazy," tainted by a collectivism that is both feudal and socialist in origin. The fact that these women work eleven to fourteen hours a day, six days a week, shows us how far such claims can be removed from reality without losing their effectiveness. In a similar vein, Yan Hairong (2003) analyzes how accumulation on the back of migrant labor relies on the erasure from public consciousness of the migrants' contributions to economic development. State and media discourse in the PRC characterize rural people as deficient in *suzhi* or "quality," a term that is defined, in circular fashion, as the positive personal qualities that China's rural masses lack. The people who build, enrich, and sustain China's cities and whose labor underpins the lifestyles of the urban middle classes are thus constructed as deficient, members of an undifferentiated peasantry that through its sheer mass holds China back. Such stereotypes allow employers to construe the labor relationship as a "gift of development" (Yan 2003: 505) in which the migrant worker is a recipient rather than a producer of net worth.

Against the construction of Chinese workers as unproblematic and hyper-productive (in much Western discourse) or as deficient in personal quality (in much Chinese discourse), we can hold the rhetorical strategies of Chinese workers. One legacy of state socialism that has been impossible to remove from workers' hands has been their elevation in state discourse to the status of "masters of the country." While workers always understood this was a fiction (those who insisted on taking the fiction literally paid a high price for their mistake, see Perry and Li 1997, and Sheehan 1998), they nonetheless advanced claims to better pay and work conditions on the basis of a discourse the state could not refute. As Amy Hanser shows in Chapter 6, workers under state socialism are well positioned to understand and criticize their exploitation, not only because state rhetoric has familiarized them with the needed concepts but also because of the transparent nature of exploitation under state socialism, where the appropriation of labor and its products is not obscured by the market but carried out by identifiable state agents. However, the chapters in this volume suggest that workers do not have equal access to these rhetorical resources, and that they are most likely to critique authority relations in and outside the workplace if they experience a degree of autonomy, mastery, and professionalism in their daily experience of work.

The politics of class and place

Yan (2003) sees the denigration of migrant workers as part of an emerging neoliberal project in post-Mao China, aimed at the production of market-conscious and disciplined workers. But there is surely more to it than this. Stereotypes about migrants are currently expressed in the neoliberal idiom of market consciousness and productivity, but they derive strength and plausibility from decades of state-enforced segregation that left urban people ignorant about and distrustful of the rural population. China, of course, is not unique in having segmented labor markets; nor is it the only country in which ethnic or quasi-ethnic prejudice justifies the exclusion of large segments of the population from economic chances and the appropriation of the products of their labor. However, boundaries – between city and countryside, between different industries, between workers from different social backgrounds – appear particularly deep-rooted and persistent here. If, as Elizabeth Perry (1996) has argued, workers in China are more concerned with the politics of place than with the politics of class, this is in part because in China, local origin has long served as a basis for the formation of economic ties. But it is also because the Chinese state has turned "place" – by which Perry means social and cultural status as well as geographical origin – into a substitute for class. For fifty years, place – in the sense of a lifelong, quasi-hereditary affiliation with a territorially defined unit – was the most important determinant of income and well-being. Place has assumed the force of class and has become the ground on which workers perceive and organize their interests. Strikes and protests (as opposed to undeclared acts of everyday resistance) are most common in "old" industries (Lee 2000), where *danwei* workers act out of a sense of co-ownership of their factory, earned through decades of sacrifice and hard work.

All chapters in this volume are, in one way or another, concerned with boundaries and systems of inclusion and exclusion, but the topic is particularly central for the first four. In Chapter 1, Henrietta Harrison goes back to the very beginning of the rural–urban bifurcation, which she traces to the early twentieth century, when western-educated elites first realized how far China had fallen behind. Shanxi, the focus of Harrison's chapter, is now considered an economically backward province, best known for its disaster-prone coal mines, but this has not always been so. In the 1870s, the provincial governor claimed that only 20 to 30 percent of the province's population were supported by agriculture, while the majority relied on dispersed rural industries, with entire villages specialized in coal mining or the production of paper, saltpeter, and alum for interregional trade. What early twentieth-century Shanxi lacked was "Industry" in the sense of large-scale, mechanized production. The reformist elites that came to power in the province after 1900 misrecognized Shanxi for an agrarian province, peopled by peasants who needed to be regulated and educated into recognizing the importance of "Industry." Government indifference and hostility to existing industries, combined with changes in the patterns of international trade, led to a sharp decline in rural industry. By the time the CCP came to power, the stage for the division of China into rural and urban sectors was already set.

Sector-making required a massive redistribution of resources, among them skill and knowledge. In early twentieth-century China, technical know-how often rested in the hands of guilds, lineages, and other local groups, which jealously protected their knowledge against rival groups. Beginning in the 1920s, such local monopolies of knowledge came to be seen as illegitimate, and reformist elites began to push for their eradication. Focusing on papermaking in rural Sichuan, in Chapter 2, Jacob Eyferth documents a process of skill appropriation that culminated in the 1950s and 1960s. Through a combination of bribes and threats, agents of the socialist state wrested knowledge from the hands of artisans, translated it into scientific language, and made it available to state agents in other sectors and localities. At the same time, rural papermakers, like other artisans, were redefined as peasants whose primary obligation to state and society was to grow grain.

These changes contrast sharply with the situation in urban factories, where workers were often able to defend their control over production processes or at least to barter expertise for prestige and power. Somewhat ironically for a socialist government, CCP planners in the early 1950s tried to *increase* wage inequality and to link remuneration more closely to performance. The main reason, Mark Frazier shows in Chapter 3, was that wartime inflation had led to a severely compressed wage structure, in which unskilled workers could earn as much and sometimes more than skilled ones. The attempt to increase wage differentials was thwarted by shop floor cadres and "old" workers, who opposed performance pay not only out of self-interest (it put veteran workers at a disadvantage vis-à-vis new hires with more up-to-date technical skills) but also because they regarded it as divisive and unfair. Their protests were successful: ultimately, China adopted a wage system characterized by small differentials and rewards based on seniority rather than performance. The paradox here is that seniority wage systems are usually found in economies where employers have to compete for footloose labor, which obviously was not the case in China. Ruling out Maoist egalitarianism, Frazier concludes that the explanation for the relatively egalitarian wage system must be sought in the power of working-class cohorts to shape the workplace. It is tempting to read the resulting egalitarian wage regime as an expression of workers' cultural preference for community over competition, though Frazier argues that workers were mainly motivated by opposition to formulaic and excessively rationalized systems of wage determination.

Communities, Lida Junghans reminds us in her dystopian account of Nanjing's railway yards in the early 1990s in Chapter 4, are produced as much through exclusion as inclusion. Railway work, once second in prestige only to military service, has lost its luster; in the eyes of economic reformers, the railways have become synonymous with the *dengkaoyao* (passivity, dependence, and irresponsibility) syndrome of the collectivist past. The *danwei* system spawns bureaucratic subdivisions "like a machine gone crazy with redundant productivity." *Danweis* and their subdivisions strive for autarky, trying to provide as many goods and services as possible to their employees ("we won't let other people earn our money"). Advancement in the *danwei* system depends on "blood ties" and "apron string connections," retirees are replaced through the *dingti* system of job inheritance or through internal hiring. By containing people, Junghans argues, *danweis* create "regions of inclusion and exclusion in a context of competition over scarce goods and opportunities" and this "fosters jealousy and protectionism and spoils the opportunity for the cultivation of social trust."

Danwei bashing has, of course, become a common sport in the get-rich-first, the-devil-take-the-hindmost atmosphere of 1990s' China. Junghans documents a great deal of worker unhappiness with a system that had grown dysfunctional. This does not exclude the possibility that they thought about what others described as their "*dengkaoyao*" attitudes in rather more positive terms – perhaps as resistance to overbearing managers, solidarity with co-workers, or defense of acquired rights. It is important to see that Junghans does not describe a "Maoist" workplace but one that has already undergone years of market reforms. Indeed, as Junghans points out, there is no reason to assume that markets will level the barriers that were erected under Maoism. Markets were introduced into an environment that was already slanted in favor of certain groups, and are as likely to exacerbate existing inequities as to erode them.

Like Junghans, Amy Hanser deals with a workplace in post-socialist China that retained aspects of state socialism in Chapter 5. Work at Harbin No. X Department Store (the only non-industrial workplace in our book) was characterized by a high degree of job security and worker authority on the sales floor, as well as a great deal of worker assertiveness in interactions with management and customers, expressed in open disregard for rules and in a rough equality between sales clerks and customers. This egalitarian work culture was grounded in workers' sense of professionalism and expertise. More directly than other chapters, Hanser asks how a specific workplace culture serves as a resource for workers as they negotiate their daily work demands. In doing so, she introduces two concepts that seem to me particularly useful for the study of the socialist and post-socialist workplace. First, following Bourdieu, she explains continuity in the workplace in terms of "habitus," as a set of stable dispositions that are embedded in objective structures – authority relations, wage scales, work regulations, etc. – and reproduced through daily interactions. Like other institutions, workplaces acquire stability only to the extent that individual social actors "make them their home." This concept of the workplace as a place where people feel at home echoes Andrew Gordon's (1991: 49) description of Japanese workers in the immediate post-war years, who "hardly ever viewed the workplace ... as just a place to earn a wage [but] rather saw it as a site for the creation of community and meaning in daily life." Second, Hanser introduces Burawoy's concept of "negative class consciousness" under socialism: a critique of managerial authority based on the glaring contradictions between socialist rhetoric and practice and on the transparent nature of exploitation under socialism.

As Hanser shows, a socialist habitus, characterized by egalitarianism and a critique of authority relations, can go hand in hand with professional competence and pride in one's work, and indeed with economic efficiency. The main thrust in the Chinese workplace is of course towards the introduction of strict, rule-based management, often combined with Taylorist deskilling and far-reaching control over the private life of workers. Hierarchy is pursued with a fervor that appears motivated more by belief in "modern" (in fact, nineteenth-century) management ideologies and the rejection of community – identified with Maoism and "eating from the big pot" – than with improving enterprise performance. Yet there is also the reverse: the attempt by management – voluntarily or under pressure – to build workplace communities that in significant ways recreate the *danwei*.

In an instance of the former tendency, Pun Ngai in Chapter 6 describes how corporate codes of conduct (signed by Chinese subcontractors at the insistence of image-conscious multinationals) fail to improve labor standards. Rather than rationalizing and institutionalizing workplace management in a way that benefits workers, codes of conduct serve to hide malpractices in an endless paper trail and, ultimately, to co-opt and incorporate any oppositional discourse on labor rights. Rights granted from above, Pun suggests, remain hollow as long as actual shop floor practices produce an atomized and voiceless workforce. Zhao Minghua, in her fascinating account of work in the Chinese merchant fleet (now the third largest in the world), in Chapter 8, presents another example of atomization as a management strategy. Like Pun, she is much concerned with the regeneration of labor after work – particularly difficult in the closed world of a ship. In the past eight years, staffing levels aboard Chinese vessels have been reduced by 40 percent, largely through the laying off of cooks, political commissars, doctors, and other support staff. Smaller crews, longer working hours, and drastically reduced turnaround times in port have put Chinese seamen (there are no women on these ships) under increasing strain. In the mid-1990s, management introduced much steeper shipboard hierarchies and sharper wage differentials, not because the relatively flat wage scales and hierarchies aboard Chinese ships were dysfunctional – they are popular with both officers and ratings – but in order to align Chinese labor practices with the rigidly hierarchical practices of Western fleets and to remove the stigma of Maoist egalitarianism. These changes, Zhao concludes, have turned the "floating native land" into an increasingly cold and lonely place.

Attacks on workers' sense of community can backfire, as Calvin Chen shows in his study of two TVEs in Zhejiang in Chapter 7. The enterprises in his study appear torn between two different logics: as TVEs, they represent the territorial, local-state driven, community-based model of the 1980s; as privatized firms employing large numbers of migrant workers, they rely on impersonal management and the market. When these firms in the span of fifteen years expanded from a few dozen to several thousand employees, they turned to impersonal, rule-based management, complete with detailed job descriptions, steep hierarchies, and heavy fines. The new management style was met by workers with tacit resistance, and management was forced to return to the spirit of worker-management cooperation that had marked the beginnings of the firms. Interestingly, their attempts to construct "enterprise families" owe much to the legacy of the Maoist past: trade unions, Youth Leagues, and Women's Federations were established; workers receive little gifts to boost morale and increase identification with the factory; factories organize speech contests and other competitions to mold the thought of employees. In all this, the Party functions as the junior partner of management and as the representative of the enterprise community against the particularistic interests of worker groups. At least some aspects of *danwei* socialism seem to have found a second lease on life in rural industry.

How are we to interpret these conflicting tendencies? Will deregulation, combined with global market pressures, eradicate the last vestiges of *danwei* society and create a truly unified labor market? Will China's incompletely proletarianized workers be cut off from their moorings in *danwei* and village society and transformed into a homogenous proletariat? There is evidence of this in the atomizing factory regimes described by Zhao, Chen, and Pun. Yet what we see here is not a universal "race to the bottom" but a redrawing of boundaries in which old hierarchies and barriers are being leveled while new ones are being raised. Place and community continue to play a vital role, partly because of the continued existence of *hukou* legislation, but more importantly because the notion of the workplace as a community that is imbued with moral meaning – rather than just a place in which one earns a wage – continues to appeal to workers, even when its realization is denied.

Note

1   These figures likely overestimate the size of the farming population. Rawski and Mead (1998) argue that official statistics include as many as 100 million "phantom farmers" who no longer work on the land.

References

Anagnost, Ann (2004) "The Corporeal Politics of Quality (Suzhi)," *Public Culture*, 16(2): 189–208.

Arrighi, Giovanni, Hamashita, Takeshi and Selden, Mark (eds) (2003) *The Resurgence of East Asia: 500, 150 and 50 Year Perspectives*, London: Routledge.

Bell, Lynda (1999) *One Industry, Two Chinas: Silk Filatures and Peasant-Family Production in Wuxi County, 1865–1937*, Stanford, CA: Stanford University Press.

Berg, Maxine (1994a) *The Age of Manufactures, 1700–1820: Industry, Innovation, and Work in Britain*, London and New York: Routledge.

Berg, Maxine (1994b) "Factories, Workshops, and Industrial Organisation," in Roderick Floud and Donald McCloskey (eds) *The Economic History of Britain Since 1700*, vol. 1: *1700–1860*, Cambridge: Cambridge University Press.

Biernacki, Richard (1995) *The Fabrication of Labor: Germany and Britain, 1640–1914*, Berkeley, CA: University of California Press.

Biernacki, Richard (1997) 'Work and Culture in the Reception of Class Ideologies,' in John R. Hall (ed.) *Reworking Class*, Ithaca, NY: Cornell University Press, pp. 169–192.

Braverman, Harry (1974) *Labor and Monopoly Capital: The Degradation of Work in the Twentieth Century*, New York: Monthly Review Press.

Bray, Francesca (1997) *Technology and Gender: Fabrics of Power in Late Imperial China*, Berkeley, CA: University of California Press.

Burawoy, Michael (1979) *Manufacturing Consent: Changes in the Labor Process under Monopoly Capitalism*, Chicago: University of Chicago Press.

Burawoy, Michael (1983) "Between the Labor Process and the State: The Changing Face of Factory Regimes under Advanced Capitalism," *American Sociological Review*, 48(5): 587–605.

Burawoy, Michael (1985) *The Politics of Production: Factory Regimes under Capitalism and Socialism*, London: Verso.

Burawoy, Michael and Lukasz, Janos (1985) "Mythologies of Work: A Comparison of Firms in State Socialism and Advanced Capitalism," *American Sociological Review*, 50(6): 723–737.

Burawoy, Michael and Krotov, Pavel (1992) "The Soviet Transition from Socialism to Capitalism: Worker Control and Economic Bargaining in the Wood Economy," *American Sociological Review*, 57(February): 16–38.

Chakrabarty, Dipesh (1989) *Rethinking Working-Class History: Bengal, 1890–1940*, Princeton, NJ: Princeton University Press.

Chan, Anita (2001) *China's Workers under Assault: The Exploitation of Labor in a Globalizing Economy*, Armonk, NY: M.E. Sharpe.

Chao, Kang (Zhao Gang) (1977) *The Development of Cotton Textile Production in China*, Cambridge, MA: Harvard University Press.

Cheng, Tiejun and Selden, Mark (1997) "The Construction of Spatial Hierarchies: China's *Hukou* and *Danwei* Systems," in Timothy Cheek and Tony Saich (eds) *New Perspectives on State Socialism in China*, Armonk, NY: M.E. Sharpe, pp. 23–50.

China Statistical Yearbook (2002) *Hong Kong: International Centre for the Advancement of Science & Technology*, Beijing: China Statistical Information and Consultancy Service Centre.

Coleman, D.C. (1992) *Myth, History, and the Industrial Revolution*, London and Rio Grande: Hambledon Press.

Cowan, Ruth Schwartz (1983) *More Work for Mother: The Ironies of Household Technology from the Open Hearth to the Microwave*, New York: Basic Books.

De Vries, Jan (1993) "Between Purchasing Power and the World of Goods: Understanding the Household Economy in Early Modern Europe," in John Brewer and Roy Porter (eds) *Consumption and the World of Goods*, London: Routledge.

De Vries, Jan (1994) "The Industrial Revolution and the Industrious Revolution," *The Journal of Economic History*, 54(2): 249–270.

Edwards, Richard (1979) *Contested Terrain: The Transformation of the Workplace in the Twentieth Century*, New York: Basic Books.

Entwistle, Barbara and Henderson, Gail E. (eds) (2000) *Re-Drawing Boundaries: Work, Household and Gender in China*, Berkeley, CA: University of California Press.

Eyferth, Jacob (2003) "De-Industrialization in the Chinese Countryside: Handicrafts and Development in Jiajiang (Sichuan) 1935 to 1978," *The China Quarterly*, 173: 53–74.

Fei, Xiaotong (1986) *Small Towns in China*, Beijing: New World Press.

Floud, Roderick and McCloskey, Donald (eds) (1994) *The Economic History of Britain Since 1700*, Cambridge: Cambridge University Press.

Fong, Hsien-Ding (Fang Xianting) (1936) *The Growth and Decline of Rural Industrial Enterprise in North China*, Tianjin: Chihli Press.

Fong, Hsien-Ding (Fang Xianting) (1937) *Industrial Organisation in China*, Tianjin: Industry Series of the Nankai Institute of Economy, Bulletin 10.

Francks, Penelope (2002) "Rural Industry, Growth Linkages, and Economic Development in Nineteenth-Century Japan," *Journal of Asian Studies*, 61(1): 33–56.

Frazier, Mark (2002) *The Making of the Chinese Industrial Workplace: State, Revolution and Labor Management*, Cambridge: Cambridge University Press.

Friedman, Andrew L. (1977) *Industry and Labour: Class Struggle at Work and Monopoly Capitalism*, London: Macmillan.

Gordon, Andrew (1991) *Labour and Imperial Democracy in Prewar Japan*, Berkeley, CA: University of California Press.

Greenhalgh, Susan (1994) "De-Orientalizing the Chinese Family Firm," *American Ethnologist*, 21(4): 746–775.

Hafter, Daryl M. (1995) *European Women and Preindustrial Craft*, Bloomington, IN: Indiana University Press.

Hayami, Akira (1992) "The Industrious Revolution," *Look Japan*, 38(436): 8–10.

Hershatter, Gail (1986) *The Workers of Tianjin, 1900–1949*, Stanford, CA: Stanford University Press.

Hershatter, Gail (2000) "Local Meanings of Gender and Work in Rural Shaanxi in the 1950s," in Barbara Entwistle and Gail E. Henderson (eds) *Re-Drawing Boundaries: Work, Household and Gender in China*, Berkeley, CA: University of California Press, pp. 79–96.

Honig, Emily (1986) *Sisters and Strangers: Women in the Chinese Cotton Mills, 1919–1949*, Stanford, CA: Stanford University Press.

Honig, Emily (1992) *Creating Chinese Ethnicity: Subei People in Shanghai, 1850–1980*, New Haven, CT: Yale University Press.

Honig, Emily (1996) "Regional Identity, Labor, and Ethnicity in Contemporary China," in Elizabeth Perry (ed.) *Putting Class in its Place: Worker Identities in East Asia*, Berkeley, CA: Institute of East Asian Studies, University of California.

Hudson, Pat (1989) *Regions and Industries: A Perspective on the Industrial Revolution in Britain*, Cambridge: Cambridge University Press.

Jacka, Tamara (1997) *Women's Work in Rural China: Change and Continuity in an Era of Reform*, Cambridge: Cambridge University Press.

Jones, Gareth Stedman (1983) *Languages of Class: Studies in English Working Class History, 1832–1982*, Cambridge: Cambridge University Press.

Joyce, Patrick (ed.) (1987) *The Historical Meanings of Work*, Cambridge: Cambridge University Press.

Judd, Ellen (1994) *Gender and Power in Rural North China*, Stanford, CA: Stanford University Press.

Kau, Michael Y.M. and Leung, John K. (eds) (1986) *The Writings of Mao Zedong, 1949–1976*, Armonk, New York, NY: M.E. Sharpe.

Knight, John B. and Lina Song (1999) *The Rural–Urban Divide: Economic Disparities and Interactions in China*, Oxford: Oxford University Press.

Kotkin, Stephen (1995) *Magnetic Mountain: Stalinism as a Civilization*, Berkeley, CA: University of California Press.

Kuromiya, Hiroaki (1988) *Stalin's Industrial Revolution: Politics and Workers, 1928–1932*, Cambridge: Cambridge University Press.

Lampland, Martha (1995) *The Object of Labor: Commodification in Socialist Hungary*, Chicago: University of Chicago Press.

Lee, Ching Kwan (1998) *Gender and the South China Miracle: Two Worlds of Factory Women*, Berkeley, CA: University of California Press.

Lee, Ching Kwan (2000) "Pathways of Labor Insurgency," in Elizabeth J. Perry and Mark Selden (eds) *Chinese Society: Change, Conflict and Resistance*, London and New York: Routledge.

Li, Bozhong (2000) *Jiangnan de zaoqi gongyehua* (Protoindustrialization in the Jiangnan Region), Beijing: Shehui Kexue wenxuan.

Liu, Tessie P. (1994) *The Weaver's Knot: The Contradiction of Class Struggle and Family Solidarity in Western France, 1750–1914*, Ithaca, NY: Cornell University Press.

Liu, Ta-Chung and Kung-Chia Yeh (1965) *The Economy of the Chinese Mainland: National Income and Economic Development, 1933–1959*, Princeton, NJ: Princeton University Press.

Liu, Yia-ling (1992) "Reform from Below: The Private Economy and Local Politics in the Rural Industrialization of Wenzhou," *The China Quarterly*, 130: 293–316.

Lü, Xiaobo and Perry, Elizabeth J. (eds) (1997) *Danwei: The Changing Chinese Workplace in Historical and Comparative Perspective*, Armonk, NY: M.E. Sharpe.

Mandel, Ruth and Humphrey, Caroline (eds) (2002) *Markets and Moralities: Ethnographies of Postsocialism*, Oxford: Berg.

Mann, Susan (1997) *Precious Records: Women in China's Long Eighteenth Century*, Stanford, CA: Stanford University Press.

Mokyr, Joel (1999) *The British Industrial Revolution: An Economic Perspective*, Boulder, CO: Westview.

O'Brien, Patrick K. and Quinault, Roland E. (1993) *The Industrial Revolution and British Society*, Cambridge: Cambridge University Press.

Oi, Jean (1999) *Rural China Takes Off: Institutional Foundations of Economic Reform*, Berkeley, CA: University of California Press.

O'Leary, Greg (1998) *Adjusting to Capitalism: Chinese Workers and the State*, Armonk, NY: M.E. Sharpe.

Ong, Aihwa (1987) *Spirits of Resistance and Capitalist Discipline: Factory Women in Malaysia*, Albany, NY: SUNY Press.

Parris, Kristin (1993) "Local Initiative and National Reform: The Wenzhou Model of Development," *The China Quarterly*, 134 (June): 242–263.

Parry, Jonathan P., Breman, Jan and Kapadia, Karin (eds) (1999) *The Worlds of Indian Industrial Labour*, New Delhi and London: Sage.

Perry, Elizabeth J. (1993) *Shanghai on Strike: The Politics of Chinese Labor*, Stanford, CA: Stanford University Press.

Perry, Elizabeth J. (1994) "Shanghai's Strike Wave of 1957," *The China Quarterly*, 137: 1–27.

Perry, Elizabeth J. (ed.) (1996) *Putting Class in its Place: Worker Identities in East Asia*, Berkeley, CA: Institute of East Asian Studies.

Perry, Elizabeth J. and Li Xun (1997) *Proletarian Power: Shanghai in the Cultural Revolution*, Boulder, CO: Westview Press.

Pollard, Sydney (1965) *Genesis of Modern Management: A Study of Industrial Revolution in Great Britain*, London: Arnold.

Pomeranz, Kenneth (2000) *The Great Divergence: Europe, China, and the Making of the Modern World Economy*, Princeton, NJ: Princeton University Press.

Pomeranz, Kenneth (2003) "Women's Work, Family, and Economic Development in Europe and East Asia," in Giovanni, Arrighi, Takeshi Hamashita, and Mark Selden (eds) *The Resurgence of East Asia: 500, 150 and 50-Year Perspectives*, London: Routledge, pp. 124–172.

Pun, Ngai (1999) "Becoming Dagongmei: The Politics of Identity and Difference in Reform China," *The China Journal*, 42: 1–19.

Pun, Ngai (2005) *Made in China: Women Factory Workers in a Global Workplace*. Durham, NC: Duke University Press.

Rawski, Thomas G. and Robert W. Mead (1998) "On the Trail of China's Phantom Farmers," *World Development*, 26(5): 767–781.

Roberts, J.S. (1992) "Drink and Industrial Discipline in Nineteenth-Century Germany," in L.R. Berlanstein (ed.) *The Industrial Revolution and Work in Nineteenth-Century Europe*, London: Routledge, pp. 102–124.

Rofel, Lisa (1999) *Other Modernities: Gendered Yearnings in China After Socialism*, Berkeley, CA: University of California Press.

Ruf, Gregory A. (1998) *Cadres and Kin: Making a Socialist Village in West China, 1921–1991*, Stanford, CA: Stanford University Press.

Sabel, Charles and Zeitlin, Jonathan (1985) "Historical Alternatives to Mass Production: Politics, Markets and Technology in Nineteenth-Century Industrialization," *Past and Present*, 108: 133–176.

Sargeson, Sally (1999) *Reworking China's Proletariat*, Houndsmill: Macmillan.

Sewell, William H. (1980) *Work and Revolution in France: The Language of Labor from the Old Regime to 1848*, Cambridge: Cambridge University Press.

Sheehan, Jackie (1998) *Chinese Workers: A New History*, London: Routledge.

Siegelbaum, Lewis and Suny, Ronald G. (eds) (1994) *Making Workers Soviet*, Ithaca, NY: Cornell University Press.

Sigaut, François (1994) "Technology," in Tim Ingold (ed.) *Companion Encyclopedia of Anthropology*, London: Routledge, pp. 420–459.

Solinger, Dorothy J. (1999) *Contesting Citizenship in Urban China: Peasant Migrants, the State, and the Logic of the Market*, Berkeley, CA: University of California Press.

Sugihara, Kaoru (2003) "The East Asian Path of Economic Development: A Long-term Perspective," in Giovanni Arrighi, Takeshi Hamashita, and Mark Selden (eds) *The Resurgence of East Asia: 500, 150 and 50-Year Perspectives*, London: Routledge, pp. 78–123.

Taussig, Michael T. (1980) *The Devil and Commodity Fetishism in South America*, Chapel Hill: University of North Carolina Press.

Thompson, E.P. ([1964] 1991) "Time, Work Discipline and Industrial Capitalism," in E.P. Thompson, *Customs in Common*, Harmondsworth: Penguin, pp. 352–403.

Unger, Jonathan and Chan, Anita (1999) "Inheritors of the Boom: Private Enterprise and the Role of Local Government in a Rural South China Township," *The China Journal*, 42: 45–75.

Walder, Andrew G. (1984) "The Remaking of the Chinese Working Class, 1949–1981," *Modern China*, 10(1): 3–48.

Walder, Andrew G. (1986) *Communist Neo-Traditionalism: Work and Authority in Chinese Industry*, Berkeley, CA: University of California Press.

Wang, Fei-ling (2004) "Reformed Migration Control and New Targeted People: China's Hukou System in the 2000s," *The China Quarterly*, 177: 115–132.

Wank, David L. (1999) *Commodifying Communism: Business, Trust, and Politics in a Chinese City*, Cambridge: Cambridge University Press.

Whiting, Susan H. (2001) *Power and Wealth in Rural China: the Political Economy of Institutional Change*, New York: Cambridge University Press.

Wigen, Kären (1995) *The Making of a Japanese Periphery, 1750–1920*, Berkeley, CA: University of California Press.

Wright, Tim (2004) "The Political Economy of Coal Mine Disasters in China: 'Your Rice-Bowl or Your Life,'" *The China Quarterly*, 179: 629–646.

Yan Hairong (2003) "Neoliberal Governmentality and Neohumanism: Organizing Suzhi/Value Flow through Labor Recruitment Networks," *Cultural Anthropology*, 18(4): 493–523.

Zhang, Li (2001) *Strangers in the City: Reconfigurations of Space, Power, and Social Networks within China's Floating Population*, Stanford, CA: Stanford University Press.

Zhonghua quanguo shougongye hezuo zongshe, Zhonggong zhongyang dangshi yanjiushi (ed.) (1994) *Zhongguo shougongye hezuohua he chengzhen jiti gongye de fazhan* (Collectivization of handicrafts and development of urban collective industry in China), Beijing: Zhonggong dangshi.

1 Village industries and the making of rural–urban difference in early twentieth-century Shanxi

Henrietta Harrison

Rural north China has been slow to benefit from the reforms of the 1980s and while some commentators have pointed to differential rates of government investment, there has also been a tendency to regard the population as epitomizing the characteristics of conservative peasant farmers and thus inherently unsuited to capitalism, industrial development, and hence modernity.[1] However, as Fei Xiaotong (1948: 16–23) observed, late imperial China provided an environment where manufacturing took place in the countryside close to supplies of fuel and raw materials, while cities were primarily political and administrative centers. Moreover, since 1979, rural industry has in fact been central to China's rapid economic development. This chapter uses an area of central Shanxi province to argue that the stereotypical image of rural China, which ultimately came to shape many of the features of the Chinese industrial workplace described in this book, is a construction of the early twentieth century. An examination of central Shanxi in the 1890s and 1900s shows the existence of a large proto-industrial economy, which had grown up on the basis of coal mining. From the sixteenth century onwards the mining industry expanded dramatically and local manufacturing grew with it. Moreover, Shanxi's well-known involvement in nationwide trading and banking networks provided capital to invest, so that by the end of the nineteenth century the rural population included a large, specialized, and disciplined proto-industrial workforce.

In theory, the Qing state tended to ignore manufacturing and commerce, since its Confucian ideology emphasized agriculture and administration as the core activities underpinning a properly ordered society. This vision of an agricultural countryside was easy enough to maintain since many families whose primary income came from industry or commerce did also farm some land. However, when it came to practicalities, Qing officials were well aware that the majority of Shanxi's population were engaged in commerce and industry and that the province regularly imported large quantities of grain from considerable distances (Shaanxi and Inner Mongolia).[2] Indeed, in the 1870s, the provincial governor claimed that only 20 to 30 percent of the province's population was supported by agriculture (Zhu 1958: 1.409). The reformers and modernizers, who dominated both central and provincial governments for most of the twentieth century, took over the idea of a countryside dominated by agriculture and administration, but for them this was no longer a vision of the proper order of things, but rather a description of China's backwardness. They looked not to a golden age of the past, but to a vision of modernity that found its embodiment in the city. Closely linked to this image was the belief in the necessity of large-scale urban industry as the basis for national strength and prosperity. So much for the vision; in actual fact, the early twentieth century saw the progressive destruction of Shanxi's rural industry and commerce caused by political instability, civil war, rampant inflation, world recession, and finally foreign invasion. Government policies designed to promote and protect the new urban industries exacerbated the difficulties. By the time the Chinese Communist Party came to power in 1949, the Shanxi countryside had indeed become a primarily agricultural area. Subsequent government policies were based on the urban image of modernity learnt from the modernizers of the early twentieth century, but also on the specific conditions of the late 1940s. The result was the policies described in the introduction to this volume that concentrated industrial development in urban areas and suppressed attempts to revive rural industries. It is these policies that have created the peasant stereotype that now itself damages the prospects of Shanxi's rural areas.

Proto-industrialization in late Qing Central Shanxi

This chapter concentrates on the marketing area of the town of Jinci, which is located about fifteen miles south of Taiyuan, the provincial capital of Shanxi. Jinci is famous for a spectacular temple complex dating from the sixth century. However, the razing of the nearby Qi capital in the tenth century left an ordinary market town, lying at the foot of the mountains that surround the Fen river plain. Its main feature was the spring of the Jin River, which provided a reliable source of water and enabled some twenty villages to irrigate their land and even grow paddy-field rice despite Shanxi's arid climate. Coal is said to have been mined in the mountains since the Tang dynasty (*Taiyuan shi* 1994: 259). Somewhat more reliably, a local genealogy records that the family's founding ancestor observed coal mines in the mountains in the tenth century (*Qingxu xiangzhi* 1999: 228). The mountains also produce lime, alum-bearing shales, iron ores, and china clay (*Shanxi kuangwu* 1919: 551, 556). This part of Shanxi was a major iron-producing area as early as the eleventh century and production expanded in the fourteenth century when the Ming government formally permitted commoners to enter the business (Qiao 1978: 8–16). The early years of the Qing dynasty saw the reduction of mining and its related industries since large numbers of miners were seen as a threat by the state, but coal mining boomed in the eighteenth century when government bans were lifted (*Jinzhong diqu* 1993: 173). Given the difficulty of transporting coal, it is hardly surprising that many industrial workshops were located at the foot of the mountains. The Ming dynasty gazetteer for the prefecture lists alum, silk, hemp, cotton, tin, saltpeter, iron, and lime as local products (*Taiyuan fuzhi* 1991: 59). In the late Qing, the county produced coal, two types of alum, lime, red ochre, pottery, earthenware, reeds, coarse paper, white paper, reed mats, and vegetables (Liu 1990: 375). A few miles south were villages that specialized in the production of saltpeter, which was used to make alum and gunpowder, while to the east other villages made carbonate of soda.[3]

Chiqiao village, which is adjacent to Jinci town, specialized in making coarse paper. The process used required a mixture of wheat and rice straw, abundant fresh water, coal to boil the pulp, and lime to break up the fibers, all of which were available locally. The origins of the industry are unclear, but it is clear that the villagers were heavily dependent on it by 1844 when there was a dispute over the Chiqiao villagers' right to wash pulp in the pools within the Jinci temple complex during the few days every year when the Jin river was dammed up for the irrigation channels to be cleared (Liu 1986: 784). Elderly men whom I interviewed in the early 1990s insisted that this had been the villagers' primary occupation. Liu Dapeng, who kept a diary of his life in the village from 1897 to 1942, described the situation in the 1900s by saying that more than 80 percent of the villagers made paper and fewer than 20 percent farmed (1986: 143–149). A survey conducted in the 1930s, when the industry was in steep decline, found seventy-eight families engaged in the industry, 61 percent of the village's total population. Twenty-five of these families had no land and their businesses operated throughout the year, while the rest had some land and would close down their businesses during the busiest agricultural seasons (Ying 1933: 4–5, 9). By the 1930s, many of the village's inhabitants were papermakers who had migrated from Xinyang county in Henan, presumably as a result of the progressive collapse of law and order that followed the 1911 revolution in that province. The migrants included both business owners and laborers. People who grew up in Chiqiao at this time remember that more than half of the village's population was from Henan. Papermaking provided an income, a way of life and a sense of identity that bound the community together. Indeed, almost every aspect of life revolved around the industry, even for those villagers who did not make paper themselves. Liu Dapeng commented that the sound of the grinding of the pulp did not cease all night (1986: 143–149). Papermaking was also central to the village's ritual life. There was a temple to Cai Lun, said to be the inventor of paper and subsequently its tutelary deity, and his birthday was the main annual festival. Opera was put on in front of his temple, buyers came from considerable distances, and all the families in the village, including those who were not involved in the industry, entertained visitors (Liu 1990: 32, 193, 210–211). The festivities were paid for by a tax on the pulp vats (Ying 1933: 13). Some Chiqiao villagers farmed and there were also shopkeepers, traders, alum makers, and many who made a living during the winter by bringing coal down from the mountains for sale, but papermaking was indeed Chiqiao's primary activity and the villagers identified themselves above all as papermakers.

Such specialized village economies were typical of the area (Shi 1998). The adjacent village of Zhifang, whose name literally means "paper workshop," also specialized in making paper (*Taiyuan shi* 1994: 270). Beyond Zhifang were several villages that grew paddy-field rice, which was a specialized cash crop in this part of north China, but some of these also had other specialities. Beidasi, which lay immediately to the east of Chiqiao, had for generations sent many of its men out to trade in Mongolia.[4] In fact, trade was often also a village speciality: certain villages on the central Shanxi plain were well known for the fact that the majority of their adult men worked in commerce away from home (Liu Rongting 1935). Immediately to the west, the mountain villages specialized in coal mining. Liu Dapeng commented that outsiders, whether they were wealthy men from the plains villages or powerful ones from Taiyuan city, were never able to make a profit in competition with the mountain people who had mined for generations (1986: 1388).

As Eyferth argues in the Introduction to this volume, specialized village industries of this sort were linked to regional markets for their products, in this case either on the north China plain or in the Shanxi-Shaanxi macroregion. The cheap, coarse paper produced in Chiqiao, which was used primarily in mortar (the long fibers strengthened the mortar and the lime in the paper made it more adhesive) but also for wrapping and as toilet paper, was sold not only in local villages and in Taiyuan city, but also in Shaanxi (Ying 1933: 11). Hemp paper made further down the Fen River valley was sold as far away as Beijing in the 1870s (Williamson 1870: 340–341). In the 1930s, a large general goods store in the railway terminus town of Yuci sold craft-made paper from Anhui, Shaanxi, Shandong, Hunan and Guangdong provinces, as well as machine-made paper from Finland, Switzerland, the USA, and Sweden, and a little from the north China city of Changchun (Zhou 1987). Moreover, as the sale of paper for the making of mortar implies, the trade in local products often supplied other specialized local industries, forming elaborate chains of production. So, for example, in 1917, disturbances in north Shanxi, where hemp was grown and processed into oil, caused a rise in the price of coal in central Taigu county. This was a result of the fact that this hemp oil was used to light the mines in Taiyuan county that supplied the Taigu area (*North China Herald*, 22 December 1917).

Skills that could be passed down within the community were essential to this kind of village specialization: when the great famine of the 1870s decimated the population of the mountain areas, Mingxian valley, which ran up from Chiqiao into the hills, simply lost the knowledge needed to make alum, a previously profitable industry (Liu 1986: 1139). But skills concentrations could also be reinforced as a result of catastrophes, as happened with the Henan papermakers who traveled hundreds of miles to settle in the papermaking village of Chiqiao. Villagers today remember that the Henan people brought with them a new type of finer frame for molding the sheets of paper. Thus, the village's geography and the villagers' skills reinforced each other.

Village specialization had the effect of producing a skilled and highly disciplined workforce. The production process in the papermaking village of Chiqiao was similar to that described for papermaking in Sichuan by Eyferth in Chapter 2 in this volume. As in Sichuan, certain stages of the process required considerable skill and much of the work was agonizingly hard and repetitive. In Chiqiao, the hardest, but least skilled, work was that of the men who stood up to their waists in the river for hours even in the depths of the north China winter, washing the lime that had been used to soften the straw out of the paper pulp. A local rhyme went, "In Chiqiao and Zhifang life is bitter/They take off their trousers and go down into the water."[5] In the 1930s and 1940s, when heroin was cheap and widely available, these men used to take it before they stepped into the water simply to dull the pain.[6] When the pulp had been washed, it was placed in vats and the skilled work of molding it into sheets began. The molders used a fine mesh frame which they scooped through the pulp. The work was heavy since the wet frame full of pulp needed to be lifted up and tipped over for each sheet to be formed. It was also skilled since the slightest unevenness of the hands would produce a sheet that was too thick on one side (see Figures 2.1 and 2.2 in Chapter 2). In the 1930s, molders' rates of pay were calculated on the assumption that they would produce 1,000 sheets a day, which would work out as 1.6 sheets a minute over a ten-hour working day. For this a piece worker would earn forty cents. It was a relatively good rate of pay: roughly that of a farm laborer at harvest time, and considerably more than that of the paper washers, who could earn only thirty cents for a day of almost unimaginably hard work. Finally, the paper was pasted onto the walls of houses or onto special heated drying walls to dry. This work, much of which took place within the home, was largely done by women. Often a child was employed to separate the sheets of paper and hand them up to the woman who did the pasting, and those who did even this light work remember the agony of handling the wet paper in the bitterly cold winters. A paster who worked for a full day would earn only sixteen cents. No wonder many of those families who labored for piece-work rates making paper were so poor that they bought grain in the morning for lunch and in the evening for dinner, and if they could not find paid work for the day would work simply for their food (Ying 1933: 8; Liu 1990: 450).

Part of the discipline, especially for the piece workers, was no doubt induced simply by poverty and necessity, but there was also a strong element of skill and pride. Many of the small workshops did not employ outsiders at all, but only the wife and children of the owner (Ying Kui 1933: 5–6). Patterns of work fitted strictly into this family context, with the men washing the pulp and molding the paper while the women pasted up the wet sheets to dry and prepared them for sale. Children learnt the skills from their parents. Work was a demonstration of one's position in the family, and this is particularly true of the work of molding. No paper has been made in Chiqiao since the late 1970s, and in recent years many men who spent their lives in the industry have been buried with their molding frames. When I interviewed in the village in the 1990s, the men spoke with great nostalgia of papermaking and particularly the work of molding, often standing up to illustrate to me the motions involved. Since the 1980s, the village's main industry has been the manufacture of children's clothing, which was started and originally controlled by the village branch of the Women's Federation, while many men have left to work driving vehicles in Taiyuan city. Talking about the skills involved in papermaking allowed these men to return to a world in which their place at the head of the family and the village's social order was confirmed by the skill and strength they displayed molding paper.

Similar patterns can be seen in the work of the miners, which was even harder than that of the papermakers. Mines varied from small pits dug into the mountainside and operated by two or three men for a few months, through drift mines driven horizontally into the side of the hill and using oxen to extract the coal, to a few shaft mines that used porters and pulley systems to bring the coal to the surface (Liu 1986: 1339–1341, 1449). The coal was sold at the pit head to carters and porters, who then transported it down to the plain and sold it on (ibid.: 1227; 1990: 205). Since the mountain roads were impassable in the summer and much of the coal was sold for domestic heating, the mines usually opened only in the winter (*North China Herald*, 30 January 1915). Strong young men supported their families during the winter, when there was little farm work available, by taking a wheelbarrow up into the mountains and bringing the coal down (Wang 1995). In 1935 the county government claimed that there were 1,303 miners in the county, though this quite probably referred only to the natives for whom this was a primary occupation (*Taiyuan shi* 1994: 259). Mining involved a mix between the highly skilled labor of the men who identified the seams of coal and hewed the blocks from the coal face, and the almost entirely unskilled labor of dragging those blocks to the surface. The foremen and hewers were mostly local men from the mountain villages and, during the boom years of the late 1910s, mine owners would ruthlessly poach them from one another (*Xishan meikuang* 1961: 24). The foreman, who was known as the "head of the mine" or "the inspector," would identify the seams and manage the underground operations. There are many folk tales of the strange power of these men, and the revenge they could wreak on owners who did not treat them well. One told of a mysterious beggar called Zhang Makuang who arrived at a mine and was appointed foreman because the owner had dreamed that he must employ a man with that name. For as long as Zhang stayed, the mine was hugely prosperous, but one day he saw two white goats, symbols of the mine god, and after that he refused to continue working. A few days later the mine flooded (Liu 1986: 1545). Other stories told of a foreman who flooded the mine when he was not given a high enough seat at a banquet, and another who did the same when he found out that the mine owner intended to replace him (*Xishan meikuang* 1961: 50–51; Liu 1986: 1120). The work of the hewers was unpleasant and dangerous but it too was highly skilled. Often they would contract the coal face from the mine owner and then pay a commission on the coal they mined (*Shanxi kuangwu* 1919: 29; *Xishan meikuang* 1961: 45). Both hewers and foremen might well become rich enough to own their own mines (*Xishan meikuang* 1961: 38). At the coal face two hewers would work with two porters, usually all of them having close personal connections. As the rhyme went:

> The employer is my sister's husband, the manager is my mother's brother.
> Those who aren't relatives have no contacts and don't get work.
>
> (*Xishan meikuang* 1961: 30)

But many mines also employed large numbers of migrant laborers as porters. These men were known as "wild ghosts without souls," "dead monkeys," or "dead hands" and had little or no protection against those above them (*Xishan meikuang* 1961: 31, 47). In the worst cases, they were sold as bonded labor to the mines at the beginning of the winter season, kept under lock and key, forced to work 14–16 hour days, and emerged in the spring with little more than they had before they started (*Xishan meikuang* 1961: 40–43).[7] Migrant laborers were undoubtedly exploited, but locals who spent their lives in the industry had opportunities for social mobility, even if the result of that social mobility was merely the ability to rent a small patch of land and work with a couple of local partners digging coal from the ground. However, the modernizing reforms of the twentieth century made this increasingly difficult as time went on.

Rural industries under reform and modernization

So what happened to Shanxi's proto-industrialization? The term proto-industrialization was coined by historians of Europe to suggest a stage that leads into modern industry (though in recent years it has become clear that even in Europe such links were not always direct). In a similar vein, development economists talk of a virtuous circle in which diversification into non-agricultural activity will lead to higher incomes, increased consumer demand, and thus further development. In this scenario, individual households may continue, as happened in Japan, to be engaged in some agricultural activities, while also becoming involved in industrial enterprises

(Francks 2002). The central Shanxi economy of the late nineteenth century appears to have been moving towards further industrialization and development and yet central Shanxi today is agricultural and impoverished. As we shall see, the chain of development was broken in the early twentieth century in part by government policies that favored a particular model of modernity and in part by external political events.

The modern education system that began in Shanxi in the 1900s created a new urban elite. The network of modern schools was centered on the cities, producing graduates who had spent most of their youth in the cities and expected to find jobs there on graduation. The old system, in which many men who became officials received much of their training under family tutors in their home villages and often returned there on retirement, faded. The result was a reformist elite whose own social mobility had involved moving from the countryside into the cities and who consequently tended to be ignorant of rural life (Luo 1998). Members of this elite were inclined towards the vision of modernity that equated the countryside with backwardness and tended naturally towards policies designed to implement a highly urban vision of modernity. This modernizing elite existed across the country, but was particularly influential in Shanxi since Yan Xishan, who ruled the province from 1911 to 1937, was a keen proponent of this type of modernization. Indeed, he won for Shanxi the title of "the model province" in response to his efforts to transform the province in line with his vision.[8]

But this was not just a matter of the leader's personal predilections: even before Yan Xishan came to power, industrial modernization in Shanxi had involved the founding of large factories and other heavily capitalized operations. Hu Pingzhi, who was governor in the late 1890s, founded an arsenal and a match factory, though the match factory was closed down when he left the province (*North China Herald*, 14 February 1900). He also oversaw the disastrous sale of concessions of Shanxi's coal reserves to the British-dominated Peking Syndicate. This led to vigorous protests, primarily by students motivated by nationalist feeling, but also by the landowners and miners whose property and rights were being conceded. When the concession was eventually repurchased by the Shanxi provincial government, however, these rights did not revert to their original owners but were transferred to the Baojin (literally "Protect Shanxi") Company, a government-sponsored enterprise that was to replace the Peking Syndicate and was committed to large-scale, modern-style production. Just as much as the sale of rights to foreigners, the so-called rights recovery movement turned out to involve the government taking over the mineral rights on land that was often already being mined by traditional methods and transferring those rights to a large modern company. In the wake of this, 1916 saw demonstrations and mass meetings in Taiyuan city when the Baojin Company came into conflict with a local syndicate which had tried to mine in an area included in the concession (*North China Herald*, 14 October 1916; Quan 1972).

Meanwhile, Yan Xishan hugely expanded the operations of the arsenal founded in the 1890s until by 1926 it employed 10,000 workers and included a steel mill and a machine-making operation. In the 1930s, these factories and mills grew into a vast industrial complex located outside the north gate of Taiyuan city. Private entrepreneurs followed the government's lead in establishing factories around the walls of the city, including an electric power plant, a flour mill, another match factory and a paper mill (Lu 1989; Yao n.d.). The paper mill, which produced newsprint as well as several other types of paper, was established at the city's south gate in 1931. It used machines powered by electricity to grind the pulp and mould the paper, and its total capital was 500,000 *yuan* (*Shanxi kaocha* 1936: 114). The scale of the operation is evident from a comparison with Chiqiao where the average paper workshop had a total capital of 45 *yuan* (Ying 1933: 7).

However, these huge, heavily capitalized modern industries did not necessarily compete successfully with their small rural counterparts, especially in terms of price. Some of the coarse paper made in Chiqiao was sold for toilet paper in Taiyuan city. Reports on the use of handmade and factory-made toilet paper in Beijing in the late 1920s suggest the way in which such products competed with factory-made materials. Most of Beijing's supply of toilet paper came from small handicraft workshops in Zhejiang province. When military activities cut off the usual supplies, people had to use factory-made Japanese paper which cost more than twice as much as the Zhejiang paper. However, the newspaper commented that people were happy to use the Japanese paper since the Zhejiang paper was coarse and limey and health specialists thought that it caused disease (*Beijing yishibao*, 27 April 1928, 1 May 1928). It is clear that people would in fact have continued to use the cheaper handmade paper if it had been available, but also that journalists justified the shift to factory-made paper in terms of hygiene which was an important part of the vision of modernity at the time (Rogaski 2003). In Taiyuan county, small-scale coal mines using traditional methods and little capital caused the same kind of problems for large modern enterprises. But in this case the problem was even more severe, since the modern-style coal mines could not even produce a higher quality product to justify their higher prices.

Traditional mines operated with the minimum capital investment, a practice which has certain obvious advantages in mining since any coal mine will eventually be worked to a degree where it is no longer practical and will have to be closed. This factor was particularly important given the great abundance of coal in Shanxi. Here I disagree with Quan Han-sheng (1972), who argued that modern coal mining techniques were essential to growth in late nineteenth-century China since accessible seams of coal had been used up by centuries of exploitation. At least in this part of Shanxi, coal was (and remains today) both abundant and accessible. When Baron Ferdinand von Richthofen traveled in this part of Shanxi in the

1870s to inspect its coal resources, he noted that the coal lay in horizontal seams and outcrops were exposed on the hillsides so that mining was very easy (1903: 132). The most basic mines were simply holes dug into the hillside by two or three laborers and worked for a few months until the coal ran out and the workers moved on to the next outcrop. Such operations had no capital at all unless one counted the few simple tools used by the miners (Liu 1986: 1339–1341). Most of the larger mines were drift mines running roughly horizontally into the side of the hill, though there were also a few shaft mines that used windlasses to shift the coal to the surface (Williamson 1870: 154). Of the 120 mines in Taiyuan county that were recorded in a 1918 government survey, only twenty-six were classified as large. Of these one had capital of 20,000 *yuan*, six had more than 1,000 *yuan*, and the remaining fifteen had capital of 500 *yuan* or less. Looking in more detail at two of the valleys near Jinci, we find that apart from the modern-style Jinfeng Company, the capital of most large mines was around 500 *yuan*. Smaller mines could be worth much less: Liu Dapeng took over Houwa mine in 1929 for the cost of 44.25 *yuan* plus a gift of 11.75 *yuan*. The full value of all the shares in this mine at the time was 130 *yuan* (Liu 1990: 391).

Such low capital investment was possible because of the ease of working the seams. Since the coal was overlaid by hard sandstone, which formed a solid roof, the mines could do without the expense of setting up timber pit props (Von Richthofen 1903: 132). Ventilation relied on the natural circulation of the air through narrow shafts dug up to the surface, though sometimes, especially when mines were worked in the summer months, fires might be set under the shafts to force the circulation. Tools, which were usually provided by the miners rather than the pit owner, consisted merely of a pickaxe, shovel, hammer, drill, and basket. The miners carried hemp oil lamps tied to their heads or between their teeth; the shallowness of the workings and the absence of coal gas meant that there was little risk of explosions. The largest capital investment was in the oxen used by some of the larger mines to draw the coal to the surface. With this minimal investment, mines worked efficiently. The worst problem was drainage. Sometimes the seam was worked in such a way as to allow the water to run out through the tunnels to the entrance, or the lowest parts of the seam were worked first and the water allowed to flow into the abandoned workings. Alternatively, drainage tunnels might be dug to allow the water to escape. A few mines where the quality of the coal was very high employed a night shift of porters to carry the water to the surface in leather sacks (*Xishan meikuang* 1961: 27–28; *Shanxi kuangwu* 1919: 113–114). If coal had been in short supply, the use of steam pumps would have given modern-style mines an advantage, but in fact flooded mines were simply abandoned and new ones opened. As the local proverb went, "When the water blocks you or the lamps don't shine, give the coal to later generations" (Liu 1986: 1120).

Attempts were made, mostly by outsiders, to operate mines along the large-scale mechanized lines that appealed so heavily to the vision of modernity. In the 1900s, two southerners from Zhejiang and Jiangsu provinces opened a 200-foot deep shaft mine, which took three years to dig and required 10,000 taels of capital. The coal was very hard and of exceptionally good quality, but the mine suffered from explosions and drainage problems. It was operated for twenty years but never made a profit. The level of personal commitment to such modernizing projects is suggested by the fact that it was only closed down when the owners died (Liu 1986: 1247). Another attempt at modern-style mining was made by a Cantonese man who took over an old and not particularly profitable mine in 1916 and determined to modernize it and use it to mine shale for the production of alum, which was at the time an extremely profitable business. The new owner bought rails in Tianjin and had them laid from the alum works to the pit head. He also bought wheeled carts that could be loaded up and pushed along the rails by a man. Although the system saved the ongoing cost of buying and keeping oxen, the huge investment in the rails and carts made it unlikely that the mine would ever be able to make money (ibid.: 1244).

As these examples suggest, it was difficult for modern-style mines to compete successfully with traditional ones. However, modern-style mines were helped by a number of government policies, most importantly the government's claim to all mineral rights and the resulting requirement that all mines register. Registration was a costly and troublesome process which involved filling in forms, providing maps of the area and paying a flat fee. During the 1910s, local industry boomed (probably because of the collapse of imports from Europe during World War I) and both modern and traditional mines could make a good profit; there was little effort to make small mines register. Officials commented that since many mines had little capital and were run by laborers who made barely enough to feed themselves, it was impractical to require them to register (*Shanxi kuangwu* 1919: 611). But when the world recession and the provincial financial crisis of the early 1930s caused the demand for coal to collapse, the large mines ceased to make a profit and the government began to demand that the small mines register. The cost of registration could come to 70 *yuan*, which was simply unaffordable for the impoverished laborers who ran these small mines. In Liu Dapeng's opinion, the aim was to put the small mines out of business, and the registration requirement certainly succeeded in this: that year the small mines in Taiyuan and many other counties were all forced to close (1933, 1986: 1339–1341; 1990: 474–475). In the end, the problems of unemployment and destitution that this caused were so severe that several counties petitioned the provincial government and the small mines were allowed to open again. The text of the government response, however, indicates the government's bias towards the large modern mines. It says that in future people may open small mines where there are poor roads, little coal or no coal yet discovered, but only on condition that they do not prevent the large mines from making a profit.[9]

Not only did the state favor modern-style, usually urban, industry over existing proto-industrial enterprises, but by the 1930s it had come to ignore the very existence of rural industry. Government records simply did not include small-scale rural producers, and as a result the provincial government seems to have been extraordinarily ignorant of their existence. This is well illustrated by the ten-year plan for political and economic development created by the Shanxi provincial government in the aftermath of the industrial crisis of the early 1930s. Counties were required to produce details of how they intended to implement the plan and Taiyuan county's response is indicative of even local governments' ability to overlook rural industry. The section of the text that covers economic development deals with irrigation, cotton and tobacco growing, forestry, sheep farming, mining, industry, commerce, and road building. Many of these items, which were drawn from the provincial government's plan, were far from relevant to the county, which does not in fact seem to have been suitable for cotton, tobacco, or large-scale sheep farming. The plan for mining involved forcing the small mines to amalgamate to form large units and imposing unified selling for each of the county's seven valleys. However, the most extraordinary section is that on industrial development which entirely ignores the county's existing industries and suggests that the county girls' school should provide classes to teach women to make straw hats (*Taiyuan xian* 1934). Here the county's rural industries have completely disappeared from the view of the state (Scott 1998). Perhaps more dangerous, however, was the fact that even those members of the modernizing elite who did still see rural industries had come to regard them, in the face of all the evidence, as agricultural sidelines. Ying Kui, whose detailed survey of Chiqiao papermaking was written in the 1930s, noted that 61 percent of Chiqiao people were engaged in the industry and that for many it was their only occupation, but nevertheless classified their activities as an "important sideline" (1933: 1).

This view that rural industries were merely a sideline was to have dramatic and far-reaching effects in the 1950s and 1960s, as Eyferth's chapter in this volume shows. But no Chinese government during the early twentieth century had anything like the ability to implement its ideas that the Chinese Communist Party achieved after 1949. Under Yan Xishan, ignorance, neglect, and even suppression would probably not have destroyed Taiyuan county's rural industries if it had not been for a variety of external factors. The earliest of these was the collapse of Shanxi's trade with Mongolia and Russia beginning with the rerouting of the Russian tea trade via Vladivostok, and ending with the Russian Revolution, which effectively closed the border to Shanxi merchants. By this time the powerful Shanxi banks, which had dealt with much of China's internal trade and particularly the profitable Yangzi trade, had been brought down by the fall of the Qing government.[10] Thus, Shanxi's two major sources of external revenue were destroyed and this had a huge impact on rural industry.

Rural industries were seldom funded by a single owner. Most local enterprises were divided between a number of shareholders, and received capital from a variety of sources. In the village of Zhifang, next to Chiqiao, about half the capital invested in paper making came from landowners and merchants in the nearby town of Jinci (Ying 1933: 8). Liu Dapeng records in detail the exact nature of his shareholding in the mines he owned and precisely what each share made him responsible for. Moreover, even the money he himself invested was not his own but was collected by him from other wealthier men. The great Shanxi merchants and bankers had been the ultimate source of much of this capital and when their businesses outside the province failed, sources of investment for rural industry were much reduced. At the same time, many of those who had been employed in trade and commerce became unemployed and returned to their home villages; often farming the family's fields was their only alternative source of employment. The disintegration of the economy was completed by the war years that followed, first, under Yan Xishan who entered the country's civil war in the late 1920s and then as a result of the Japanese invasion of central Shanxi in 1938. During the 1930s, first Yan Xishan and then the Japanese extracted taxes and other contributions from the economy to such an extent that most surviving businesses were destroyed. The collapse of the merchants and bankers who provided the investment and the related rise in rural unemployment made subsistence agriculture a far more important part of Shanxi's economy in 1940 than it had been in 1900.

Conclusion

When the Chinese Communist Party came to power in 1949, it brought with it the ideas that had influenced its leading members growing up in China over the past fifty years. Even though these ideas drew from the Party's Marxist heritage and its Soviet backers, which ideas were taken up and how they were used was the result of Chinese culture at that time. The idea of a rural economy dominated by peasant farmers was shared both by Marxism and by common non-Marxist approaches to modernization at the time. Moreover, it fitted easily with the earlier Confucian emphasis on agriculture as the root of the economy. As a result, this idea of the agrarian nature of the rural economy had already come to shape government policy well before 1949. Finally, which ideas made sense to the party was also related to the specific economic and social conditions of that crucial moment in the 1940s when the party came to power. The policies adopted after the revolution, which were remarkably stable in their overall direction despite the many shifts of political forces, were thus shaped both by ideological currents that preceded the revolution and by the contingent circumstances of the time when the party came to power. The idea of a conservative, agricultural, North China peasant culture set against a vision of modernity based upon large-scale urban industrial production is the product of this process.

In recent years, that idea has been bolstered by images of the process of the late twentieth-century state bringing industrialization to rural China. After the gradual decline and final collapse of the Chiqiao papermaking industry in the 1970s, the village has been the site of a household-based enterprise manufacturing children's clothes which have been sold to Tianjin for the Russian market. Profits have fluctuated depending on the state of the Russian economy. Meanwhile, many local attempts to reopen small-scale mines have been attacked by the government on the grounds that they cause pollution and have appallingly high death and injury rates for their workers. It is, however, claimed on the streets that the profits of the major state-owned mines fluctuate depending on the provincial government's level of success in closing down smaller, more informal mines. Clearly changes in central government policy have played an important role in Chiqiao's current economic success, but it would be wrong to see such rural industry simply as the benefits of modernity finally reaching the countryside. Rural industries with a skilled and specialized workforce existed in the area long before the arrival of the twentieth-century's vision of modernity and have suffered as much from that vision as they have gained.

Acknowledgments

I am grateful to Penny Francks for all her help with this chapter.

Notes

1 This image was set forth with startling clarity in the famous Chinese television series *River Elegy* (see also Wang Xiaoqiang 1991). In terms of the English language literature, it manifests itself rather in a tacit acceptance of the inevitability of more rapid development by the eastern seacoast provinces.
2 For the theory, see Rowe (2001). For Shanxi, see Cao Xinyu (1998).
3 *Qingyuan xiangzhi* (1882: 10.17a); Wesleyan Methodist Missionary Society (London). Archive. Special Series. Biographical. Box 632(3) China Papers of D. Hill 1876–1878.
4 Interview Wu Jiongsheng, Beidasi village, local historian.
5 Interview, Jinsheng, 6 September 1999.
6 Interviews, Beidasi, Summer 2002.
7 See also Liu Dapeng (1986: 1343); interview Liu Zuoqing, Jinsheng, 6 September 1999; Guo Yuanchou (1987); Wu Zhenhua (1990).
8 For a general history of Yan Xishan's rule in Shanxi, see Gillin (1967).
9 Shanxi sheng dang'anguan [Shanxi provincial archives. Taiyuan] B30/3/119 p. 6.
10 The best general accounts of Shanxi's economic history during this period are Qu and Pang (1984), Huang (1992) and Zhang (1995).

References

Beijing yishibao [Beijing Times].

Cao Xinyu (1998) "Qingdai Shanxi de liangshi fanyun luxian" [Grain transport routes in Qing dynasty Shanxi], *Zhongguo lishi dili luncong.*

Fei Xiaotong (1948) *Xiangtu chongjian* [Rebuilding the countryside], Shanghai: Guanchashe.

Francks, Penelope (2002) "Rural Industry, Growth Linkages, and Economic Development in Nineteenth-Century Japan," *Journal of Asian Studies*, 61(1): 33–56.

Gillin, Donald D. (1967) *Warlord: Yen Hsi-shan in Shansi Province 1911–1949*, Princeton, NJ: Princeton University Press.

Guo Yuanchou (1987) "Feng Yuxiang jiangjun zai Jinci" [General Feng Yuxiang in Jinci], *Taiyuan wenshi ziliao*, 6.

Huang Jianhui (1992) *Shanxi piaohao shi* [A history of the Shanxi banks], Taiyuan: Shanxi jingji chubanshe.

Jinzhong diqu zhi [Central Shanxi district gazetteer] (1993) Taiyuan: Shanxi renmin chubanshe.

Liu Dapeng (1933) *Taiyuan xian xianzhuang yipie* [A glance at present conditions in Taiyuan county], photocopy of manuscript: Shanxi Provincial Library.

Liu Dapeng (1986) *Jinci zhi* [Jinci gazetteer], ed. Mu Xiang and Lu Wenxing, Taiyuan: Shanxi renmin chubanshe.

Liu Dapeng (1990) *Tuixiangzhai riji* [Diary from the chamber to which one retires to ponder], ed. Qiao Zhiqiang, Taiyuan: Shanxi renmin chubanshe.

Liu Rongting (1935) "Shanxi Qixian Dongzuodun, Xizuodun liang cun ji Taigu xian Yangyi zhen, Pingyao xian Daobeicun jingshangzhe xiankuang diaocha zhi yanjiu" [Research on an investigation into the present conditions of businessmen in the two villages of Dongzuodun and Xizuodun in Qixian county, and Yangyi town in Taigu county, and Daobei village in Pingyao county in Shanxi], *Xin nongcun*, 22.

Lu Jun (1989) "Xibei shiye gongsi he Shanxi jindai gongye" [The Northwest Industrial Company and Shanxi's modern industry], *Shanxi wenshi ziliao*, 63.

Luo Zhitian (1998) "Qingji kejuzhi gaige de shehui yingxiang" [The social influence of the late Qing reforms to the examination system], *Zhongguo shehui kexue*, 4.

North China Herald, various editions.

Qiao Zhiqiang (1978) *Shanxi tiezhi shi* [A history of Shanxi iron working], Taiyuan: Shanxi renmin chubanshe.

Qingxu xianzhi [Qingxu county gazetteer] (1999) Taiyuan: Shanxi guji chubanshe.

Qingyuan xiangzhi [Qingyuan district gazetteer] (1882) Gengyang shuyuan.

Qu Shaomiao and Pang Yicai (1984) *Shanxi waimao zhi* [An account of Shanxi's foreign trade], Taiyuan: Shanxi sheng difangzhi bianzuan weiyuanhui bangongshi.

Quan Hansheng (1972) *Zhongguo jingjishi luncong* [Collected essays on Chinese economic history], Xianggang: Xinya yanjiusuo.

Rogaski, Ruth (2003) *Hygienic Modernity: Meanings of Health and Disease in Treaty Port China*, Berkeley, CA: University of California Press.

Rowe, William T. (2001) *Saving the World: Chen Hongmou and Elite Consciousness in Eighteenth-Century China*, Stanford, CA: Stanford University Press.

Scott, James C. (1998) *Seeing Like a State: How Certain Schemes to Improve the Human Condition Have Failed*, New Haven, CT: Yale University Press.

Shanxi kaocha baogao [Report on an investigation of Shanxi] (1936), Quanguo jingji weiyuanhui.

Shanxi kuangwu zhilue [A brief survey of Shanxi minerals] (*c.*1919).

Shanxi sheng dang'anguan [Shanxi provincial archives], Taiyuan.

Shanxi sheng zhengxie wenshi ziliao yanjiu weiyuanhui (1981) *Yan Xishan tongzhi Shanxi shishi* [A true account of Yan Xishan's rule of Shanxi], Taiyuan: Shanxi renmin chubanshe.

Shi, Jianyun (1998) "Shangpin shengchan, shehui fengong yu shengchanli jinbu – jindai Huabei nongcun shougongye de biange" [Commercial production, social division of labor and improvements in productivity: changes in handicraft industries in modern North China villages], *Zhongguo shehui jingjishi yanjiu*, 4.

Taiyuan fuzhi [Taiyuan prefecture gazetteer] (1991) 1st edn. Ming, Wanli period, Taiyuan: Shanxi renmin chubanshe.

Taiyuan shi nanjiaoqu zhi [Taiyuan city southern suburban district gazetteer] (1994) Beijing: Sanlian shudian.

Taiyuan xian xianzheng shinian jianshi jihuaan [Taiyuan county government ten-year construction plan] (*c.*1934).

Von Richthofen, Ferdinand (1903) *Baron Richthofen's Letters, 1870–1872*, Shanghai: North China Herald.

Wang, Shuren (1995) "Taiyuan xian de tuiche" [Taiyuan county wheelbarrows] *Jinyang wenshi ziliao*, 4.

Wang Xiaoqiang and Bai Nanfeng (1991) *The Poverty of Plenty*, Basingstoke: Macmillan.

Wesleyan Methodist Missionary Society (London). Archive. Special Series. Biographical. Box 632(3) China Papers of D. Hill 1876–1878.

Williamson, Alexander (1870) *Journeys in North China, Manchuria, and Eastern Mongolia; with some Account of Corea*, London: Smith, Elder.

Wu Zhenhua, Hao Shoushen (1990) "Feng Yuxiang jiefang budaiyao" [Feng Yuxiang liberated the mines where sacks were used to carry coal], *Jinyang wenshi ziliao*, 3.

Xishan meikuang shi [A history of coal mining in the Western Hills] (1961) (ed. Taiyuan Xishan kuangwuju Xishan meikuangshi bianxiezu).

Yao Daili (unpublished) "Taiyuan jiu chengshi de guoqu, xianzai he jianglai" [The past, present and future of the old city of Taiyuan].

Ying Kui (1933) "Lancun, Zhifang, Chiqiao san cun zhi caozhi diaocha" [An investigation into the paper made from straw in the three villages of Lancun, Zhifang and Chiqiao], *Xin nongcun*, Taiyuan, 3–4.

Zhang Zhengming (1995) *Jinshang xingshuai shi* [A history of the rise and fall of the Shanxi merchants], Taiyuan: Shanxi guji chubanshe.

Zhou, Pichen (1987) "Yi gongxing shun he ji zahuozhuang" [Memoir of Gongxingshun and record of a general goods store], *Shanxi wenshi ziliao*, 49.

Zhu Shoupeng (ed.) (1958) *Guangxu chao donghua lu* [Records from the Donghua Gate for the Guangxu reign], Beijing: Zhonghua shuju.

2 Socialist deskilling

The struggle over skills in a rural craft industry, 1949–1965

Jacob Eyferth

Control over production processes depends on a secure grasp of production-related skills and knowledge. As long as shop floor workers have a better understanding of how things are produced than managers, managers will find it difficult or impossible to impose their will on them. Even in the industrialized countries of Western Europe and North America, managerial control over production was imposed relatively late (in most industries not before the early twentieth century) and only against stiff worker resistance. Deskilling – the process by which management wrested control over skills from the hands of workers and fragmented complex operations into simple tasks that could be performed by unskilled labor – has been studied in much detail for the West (Braverman 1974).[1] Little work, however, has been done on deskilling under socialism. There is no reason to assume that deskilling does not take place in socialist countries. Lenin's enthusiasm for Taylorist "scientific management" is well known (Bailes 1977; Scoville 2001), and Chinese leaders shared Lenin's vision of rapid, state-led industrialization and his disdain for historically rooted institutions – the guilds, kinship groups, and networks of artisans that controlled much of the "technostructure" in pre-revolutionary industry. Socialist China, like the Soviet Union, was what James Scott has called a "high modernist" regime: aggressively anti-traditional, obsessed with order and control, and possessed of an almost religious belief in the necessity and rationality of state planning (Scott 1998; Kirby 2000). Both countries started from low levels of mechanization and pursued industrialization at breakneck speed, leading to a much sharper clash between proto-industrial, artisanal production structures and centralized industry than in Western Europe, North America, or Japan.

Nor is there any reason to assume that workers under socialism are more willing to relinquish control of their skills than their capitalist counterparts. This chapter argues that the struggle over technological control lies at the heart of the transformation of the Chinese workplace in the early PRC. Socialist managers, similar to their capitalist counterparts, tried to wrest technological control from the hands of workers; workers, in China as elsewhere, resented and resisted their deskilling and acquiesced to it only if they felt that they were given adequate compensation. The data for this chapter come from the handmade paper industry of Jiajiang County, Sichuan. The focus is on what I call "skill extraction": the effort of state officials, especially in the 1950s, to penetrate the "opaque" (Behagg 1982) workplace of the paper industry, master production skills, sift and organize the newfound knowledge, translate it into written form, and pass it on to an audience of state-appointed experts. Skill extraction was carried out with energy and ruthlessness and was, on the whole, successful – though, paradoxically, it left the labor process in the paper industry virtually unchanged.

Socialist deindustrialization

Until the 1950s, most commodities in China were produced in households and small workshops, often in the countryside (compare Harrison's chapter in this volume). Socialist industrialization entailed the separation of the economy into rural-agrarian and urban-industrial spheres and the closing down of most traditional rural industries – a process that was only partly compensated by the growth of new rural industries in the 1960s and 1970s. In this process, millions of artisans and semi-specialized sideline producers were redefined as peasants and eventually deskilled. The number of rural artisans dropped from 4.7 million in 1954 to 2.2 million in 1957; in addition, twelve million "household-based seasonal commodity producers" (a category that included skilled, specialized artisans) were made to join the agricultural collectives (Zhongguo laodong 1987: 13, 83, 86). After a brief expansion during the Great Leap Forward, employment in rural industries and handicrafts dropped to an all-time low of 0.4 million in 1963. Despite the much advertised expansion of rural small-scale industry in the 1970s, rural industrial employment remained below 1954 levels for twenty years, until 1975.[2]

The Jiajiang paper industry

Paper production in Jiajiang (in western Sichuan, 120 km south of Chengdu) dates back to the seventeenth century. The industry reached its peak after the outbreak of the Sino-Japanese war, when Jiajiang, together with a handful of other counties, supplied the paper needs of the Chinese government and the publishing industries that had sprung up in Chongqing, Kunming, and Chengdu. In 1943, an estimated 60,000 persons – one-third of the county's population – worked in the paper industry and in related trades. Paper output dropped after the war, due to inflation and resumed paper imports from abroad. When the People's Liberation Army arrived in Jiajiang in early 1950, it recognized the importance of paper as a product (like its predecessor, the CCP urgently needed paper for education and propaganda work) and as a source of income for the local population, which was close to starvation following the collapse of the paper market. One of the first actions of the new government was therefore to revive the industry by bringing relief grain into the paper districts. In 1951, paper output rose to 4,700 tons, 40 percent below the peak of the wartime boom but probably not much lower than in the pre-war period. From that year on, output declined, reaching an all-time low of 500 tons in 1977. In 1978, the industry was rescued from collapse by Li Xiannian, then vice premier in charge of economic planning. Thanks to Li's intervention and to the opening of grain and paper markets in the late 1970s, the industry revived and expanded in the 1980s and 1990s, eventually becoming the largest of its kind in China. Today, production is still manual (largely because painters and calligraphers pay high prices for handmade paper). Despite some recent setbacks, Jiajiang is still China's leading producer of handmade paper (Eyferth 2003).

The technostructure of Jiajiang papermaking before 1949

Papermaking is a complex and demanding craft with an elaborate division of labor. It consists of six basic steps:

1 the harvest, cutting, crushing, and soaking of bamboo;
2 the transformation of bamboo into "stuff" (*liaozi*) by steaming in giant wooden pots, followed by washing and fermentation;
3 pulping, traditionally in foot-operated hammer mills;
4 molding the sheets (Figure 2.1);
5 pasting the sheets on drying walls (Figure 2.2);
6 finishing and packing.

All steps, with the exception of the first, require manual dexterity; steps 2 and 3 also require a kind of knowledge that is best described as "folk chemistry." Pulpers add dyestuff for color, sizing to reduce absorption, resin to make the paper glossy, or special fibers for extra tensile strength. Steaming is similarly crucial, because the temperature and acidity of the boiling "stuff" determine fiber strength and the way the paper ages. A master papermaker knows how much lime or potash is needed to soften knotty bamboo, or how much mucilage must be added to prevent clotting in the vat. Such knowledge is tacit and context-dependent, gained from experience and not easily translated into words. Very few individuals ever master all steps of the production process, largely because of the division of labor between men (who steam, pulp, and mold) and women (who dry and finish the paper).

Papermaking skills were reproduced at different levels: in the household, the residential cluster – there are no nucleated villages in this part of China (Skinner 1964) – and the agnatic kinship group. Within residential and agnatic communities, knowledge circulated freely. Paper workshops

Figure 2.1 Molding a sheet of paper (source: Author's photograph, Jiajiang 1996).

Figure 2.2 Pasting the wet paper sheet onto a drying wall (source: Author's photograph, Jiajiang 1996).

were open structures, which made the preservation of secrets almost impossible. Kinship ideology in the paper districts saw papermaking knowledge as a collective resource, similar in some ways to lineage land in other parts of China. As one recent artifact – a stele, erected in 1993 in the heart of the paper districts – puts it, "the art of papermaking was bestowed on us by the ancestors" and "the teaching of the ancestors" must be passed on to future generations (Jiadanqiao stele 1993). For local people, this implies that lineage members must not monopolize knowledge for themselves but ought to share it with other members. Social norms, combined with the need of resource-poor household workshops to cooperate with their neighbors, ensured a constant circulation of knowledge between producers. Before collectivization, strong moral pressure was brought to bear on wealthy producers to help relatives and neighbors, and those who tried to opt out of mutual aid obligations were penalized by neighbors wielding the "weapons of the weak" – slander, sabotage, and theft (Eyferth 2000: 65–78).

Guilds, chambers of commerce, and religious associations added more layers to Jiajiang's technostructure. These institutions ensured that innovations spread quickly through the system. In the war years, papermakers adopted a whole host of innovations (the use of chloride bleach, sizing, glazing, new fibers, and new formats) that lowered production costs and made Jiajiang paper suitable for machine printing. Without government intervention, these innovations spread from enterprising papermakers who learned them from books or paper merchants to the most remote corners of the paper districts.[3] The institutions that facilitated the circulation of knowledge in the paper districts also aimed to prevent its leaking to outside competitors, but with much less success. Despite complaints from state officials about the secretiveness of Jiajiang papermakers, information flowed in and out of the system with relative ease.

Craft control and the state

Paper was a strategic resource during the Sino-Japanese war, and Sichuan, China's main industrial base after the loss of coastal China, was expected to supply most of the demand. Papermakers were "encouraged" to mass-produce newsprint and sell it to the state at mandated low prices. This they were unwilling to do, especially since buyers (including agents of state institutions) competed for their goods and were willing to pay high prices. Like the reformist elites described by Harrison, representatives of the central and provincial government, who already thought of the paper-makers as unenlightened peasants, became increasingly hostile to the industry, as the following quote shows:

Jiajiang papermakers have passed on their secrets from father to son for ten or twenty generations. Even friends and relatives who visit the workshops ... are not told any secrets. This shows the fierceness of their conservatism. Their ignorance of progress stems from the same reason. A government wanting to promote industry must smash these evil habits, otherwise it cannot succeed.

(anon. 1935: 89–90)

When the CCP arrived in Jiajiang in early 1950, it found itself in a situation similar to that of the Guomindang during the war: it needed large quantities of newsprint paper to mobilize the population for a war and for its new social policies, and most of that paper had to come from rural handicraft producers. As delegates from the paper industry were told at a 1950 conference in Chongqing, "Paper is one of the indispensable weapons [in the movement to resist America and aid Korea]. We have to mobilize the greatest enthusiasm and energy to fulfill this most historical, militant, internationalist glorious production task." Handicraft producers, who at that time produced ten times more paper than the factory sector, tried to evade this "glorious task," preferring to sell to their paper to the highest open market bidder (Sichuan Provincial Archives 1951). For several years, papermakers resisted state attempts to gain control over their output, but ultimately they failed.

The declared aim of collectivization was to overcome the "half-worker half-peasant, dispersed and backward situation" of household-based papermaking; its declared model was the centralized factory. Private workshops had usually consisted of a single paper vat and employed four to six workers, most of them household members. Collective workshops, by contrast, contained five to fifteen vats and employed up to sixty men and women, working under the supervision of a small managerial staff selected from the ranks of papermakers. Since there are no economies of scale in manual papermaking, the massing of vats in a single workshop did not increase productivity. Scale would have paid off only in combination with mechanization, but this was explicitly not on the agenda: rural workshops were told not to mechanize because this would have increased competition for scarce industrial inputs. Important as it was, paper was less important than scarce steel: apart from a few locally produced knives and rakes, traditional paper workshops contained virtually no iron or steel implements. Steel-reinforced pressure steamers, which could have reduced fuel consumption by one-half and turnover time by 90 percent, were never made available to rural producers.

Though Maoist class analysis allows for the existence of isolated craftspeople in rural market towns and villages, it does not acknowledge the existence of large, concentrated proto-industrial populations. Rural people, whatever their actual occupation, were therefore classified as peasants. Jiajiang papermakers underwent the usual sequence of rural campaigns – land reform, formation of agricultural and handicraft cooperatives, and collectivization – though the primary object of redistribution and collectivization in the Jiajiang hills was not land but industrial infrastructure: bamboo groves, soaking ponds, trip hammers, steamers, and drying walls.

Collectivization, official sources make quite clear, aimed at reducing total grain expenditure and at improving the ratio between state input (mainly grain) and collective output (paper). Jiajiang, with its large non-agricultural population, had always been grain-deficient; when grain became a state monopoly, papermakers therefore became clients of the State Grain Bureau. Since papermakers were now technically peasants, supplies to them were classified as "reverse sales" (*fan xiao*). Such sales were still relatively common in the 1950s, but there was a growing sense that peasants should be grain producers, not consumers, and that the provision of grain to rural people was anomalous and needed to be justified.[4] From 1953 on, the county administration began to carefully monitor the flow of grain and paper through the system. Between 1951 and 1958, the number of persons entitled to full industrial rations – classified as "paper-making" or "industrial population" (*zaozhi renkou, gongye renkou*) – was reduced from 21,000 to 2,500. At the same time, the status and income of the remaining recipients rose. By 1957, registered papermakers enjoyed quasi-urban status: fixed cash incomes, high and secure grain rations, special supplies of meat and sugar – and in some cases, even the ultimate badge of recognition in a workers' state: membership in the trade union.[5]

This system of entitlements collapsed in the Great Leap Forward and the ensuing famine, which wiped out one-quarter of the population of the paper districts. In the aftermath of the famine, paper production was reorganized as a rural sideline owned and managed by agricultural production teams. A brief recovery in 1962–1965 was followed by a radical retrenchment, as the government embarked on a "grain first" policy that emphasized local self-sufficiency and discouraged specialization (Yang 1996). Papermakers were forced to cut down their bamboo groves and plant maize on the steep slopes. By the mid-1970s, most papermakers had become self-sufficient peasants, living in poverty on rapidly eroding land.

Skill extraction

As Harrison argues in Chapter 1 in this volume, the early decades of the twentieth century saw a rising interest in local industrialization among western-educated officials and elites. Industry, previously discussed primarily in the context of local livelihood (*minsheng*) and social order, was increasingly seen as the means to save the nation (*yi shiye jiu guo*) – and therefore too important to be left in the hands of mere "peasants." In Sichuan, industrial reform took off only in 1935, after the Guomindang ousted Liu Wenhui's warlord regime. In the next years, dozens of technicians, engineers, and industrial reformers visited the paper districts. Though their official mission was to teach, there is no evidence that they imparted any useful knowledge to local papermakers; instead, they concentrated on mapping and cataloguing existing technologies. Why did officials and elites bent on modern industrialization study craft technologies? First, mechanized paper mills simply could not meet demands. In 1943, after the wartime relocation of several large coastal paper mills to Sichuan, mechanized production accounted for less than one-quarter of Sichuan's paper output; after the war, when the factories had been relocated, the ratio dropped to one-tenth. Even with heavy investment (which, given development priorities and resource constraints in the 1930s and 1940s, neither private industry nor the state could provide), it would take decades to replace handmade paper. Manual production, by contrast, could be expanded rapidly and at low cost.

Another reason for the reliance on traditional techniques was that industrial paper mills in China, as practically everywhere else in the world, used wood pulp made from softwood timber, even though China is one of the most heavily deforested countries in the world. Annual grasses, a category that includes bamboo, are much more plentiful than timber and grow closer to the areas where paper is needed. However, grasses are too stiff to be ground to pulp; they have to be "digested" using a combination of heat and chemicals to soften and wash out the lignin. Bamboo paper technology was developed in China in the twelfth century, but it had never been applied on an industrial scale. By the mid-1950s, some pulp mills had been converted to bamboo, but the search for low-cost, fuel-efficient ways to make paper from bamboo still continued (Du 1958; Sichuan sheng 1958). It was in this area that engineers had much to learn from handicraft producers.

Like their Guomindang predecessors, representatives of the socialist state who tried to study these technologies initially encountered hostility. It was not until land reform, which in the paper districts began in 1953, that the new state began to gain a foothold in the paper districts. Land reform, in fact, was a misnomer: since agricultural land had little value in this region of poor, acidic soils, redistribution focused on bamboo groves and paper workshops – and indeed on skills, which were expropriated and redistributed like other resources. Owners of large workshops were often highly skilled, but also likely to hire more than the two workers that were considered compatible with poor or middle peasant status. Rather than risk jail or worse, most of them chose to share their knowledge with poorer neighbors, land reform activists, and ultimately the state, thus demonstrating their loyalty to the new regime.[6]

Intimidated workshop owners were not the only ones to opt for cooperation. For generations, papermakers had thought secrecy essential for survival. In the early 1950s, it seemed as if they had entered into a new compact with the state that obliterated the need for secrecy. State agents bought their paper at guaranteed and relatively high prices; cash incomes rose, grain rations were generous and appeared secure. Those who were classified as "industrial personnel," in particular, enjoyed high living standards and high status. State cadres argued that local protectionism was a thing of the past, the outcome of an irrational system that pitted small producer against small producer and labor against capital. Under socialism, there was no need for competition; knowledge would circulate freely, to the benefit of all. These arguments carried most weight with local activists: young men and women, most of them in their late teens when they joined the revolution, often from impoverished families. When these activists rose through the ranks to become leaders of workshops, brigades, and communes, they became the main conduits for the flow of information from local papermakers to the state.

Their official counterpart was the Jiajiang Handicraft Management Bureau (HMB), established in 1950 as part of the handicraft administration (later reorganized as the Second Ministry of Light Industry). In 1950, as soon as the Jiajiang hills had become safe for official travel, the HMB convened meetings with local paper traders, agents of state trading companies, and representatives of papermaking communities. The government, HMB cadres explained in these meetings, supported papermaking; what it expected in return was a concerted effort of all parties to overcome past inefficiencies. If papermakers wanted the state to buy their paper and to supply bleach, soda, and grain, they had to provide precise information on input and output and allow outside observers in their workshops.

By 1953, the HMB had complete and accurate information on all parts of the production process. This information was carefully sifted and catalogued; techniques from different workshops, localities, and production districts were compared; best practices were identified and refined in model workshops (*shifan zaozhichang*). Jiajiang, like other paper districts, opened a model workshop in 1951 which remained operational until 1966, although lack of funds and poor management forced it to close down several times. Model workshops were explicitly ordered not to mechanize; their task was to systematize and improve existing craft technologies. Much of their work focused on shortening the production cycle and on developing ways to process new fibers such as sugar cane and straw. Industry journals published articles on how to build water-powered grinding mills and pulp beaters, increase the fuel efficiency of steamers, reduce soaking times by using caustic soda instead of potash, etc. (Du 1957; Lu 1958a, 1958b; Sichuan sheng 1958). These were cheap and practical technologies, well suited to the needs of medium-sized paper workshops.

Skill transfer

Once extracted and processed, knowledge was circulated in writing. The most common medium was the survey report (*diaocha baogao*), produced for internal use in the nationwide handicraft administration, written in standardized language and characterized by careful attention to detail. Technical reports were also published in industry journals with provincial or nationwide circulation. Such reports were accompanied by drawings that grew increasingly accurate over the years. Nobody would have been able to reconstruct production technology from the crude woodcuts published in the Republican era (Figure 2.3). Articles from the 1950s, by contrast, were accompanied by accurate floor plans and cross-sections, tables, flow charts, and step-by-step descriptions of the production process (Figure 2.4). Knowledge in the paper industry used to be tacit, residing in the hands and eyes of workers who knew how to do certain things but rarely felt the need to express their knowledge verbally. This tacit and context-specific knowledge was now translated into general formulas that worked as well in one locality as in any other. Ironically, although the aim was to break down barriers to circulation, the audience for this reformulated knowledge did not include the people who had originally supplied much of the information: even if they were literate, papermakers were unable to read it in its newly encoded form.

A second type of knowledge circulation involved the migration of young men and women from Jiajiang to other bamboo-rich regions, where they taught their skills to local people. During the Great Leap Forward, young papermakers were mobilized to migrate to the borderlands of Southwest Sichuan or the mountains along the Shaanxi–Sichuan border. Teaching the skills was relatively easy; as one participant put it, "those with clever hands learn them in a week; others take about a month." The problem was that farm boys and girls were unable to get used to the machine-like work rhythm in the paper workshops. Papermaking is strenuous and repetitive work: a good vatman or brusher works for ten to twelve hours without slacking, performing the same motions 500 to 1,000 times a day. Jiajiang people believe that their capacity for sustained work comes from the local "water and soil" (*shuitu*) and needs to be imbibed at an early age. An alternative explanation is that skills are embedded in social networks, outside of which they are difficult to reproduce.

The failure to transform the labor process in Jiajiang

Most of the technologies developed in the model workshops were cheap: a water-driven stamp mill could be built for 80 *yuan*; airtight steamer lids that raised fiber yields by 50 percent could be had for less than 20 *yuan* (Lu 1958a, 1958b). Most new implements could be built from locally available materials and be maintained at low cost. These were adapted technologies, well suited to unmechanized production in remote rural areas. However, few of them ever spread throughout the paper districts. When asked about change under the collectives, most papermakers recall only the "hanging mold," a device to reduce the strain on people's backs when they lift the paper mold. Even this was not widely adopted, as most

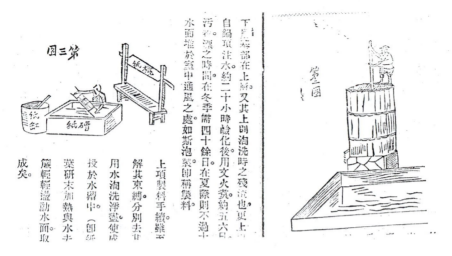

Figure 2.3 Woodcut illustration of a paper workshop, 1923 (source: Su Shiliang (1923)).

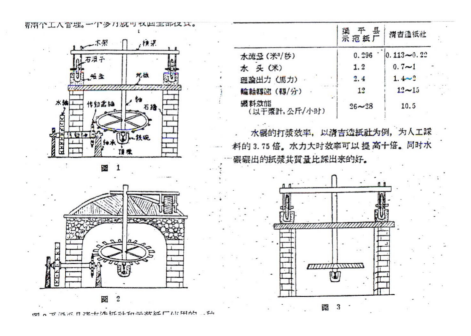

Figure 2.4 Blueprint of a paper workshop, 1958 (source: Lu Deheng (1958a: 19)).

papermakers found it inconvenient. There were a few less obvious changes: collective workshops tended to use cheaper, tougher bamboo, which required more aggressive solvents; they also used larger steamers and soaking pits. Production became bulkier and therefore slower, despite the declared aim of shortening the production cycle. Products became standardized: in contrast to the pre-1949 period, when Jiajiang workshops produced several hundred types of paper, most workshops in the late 1950s and early 1960s produced only *duifang*, a drab, coarse all-purpose paper. None of these changes altered the labor process in a significant way.

Why this failure to transform the labor process? Cynics might argue, with some justification, that officials mined Jiajiang for information and closed down the industry as soon as all useful knowledge was extracted. The provincial HMB considered the Jiajiang industry too large for its resource base: Jiajiang imported one-third of its bamboo and one-half of its grain from neighboring counties. This, in the view of state planners, was irrational: it seemed easier and cheaper to move skilled workers or disembodied skills to concentrations of raw materials than vice versa. Knowledge was not recognized as a production factor, and no thought was given to the conditions necessary for its reproduction (Sichuan Provincial Archives 1951).

However, it seems unlikely that the HMB planned to phase out the industry from the beginning, if only because it was reorganized too often to pursue any systematic plans.[7] The closure of the industry after the Great Leap Forward seems to have been the final outcome of a long tug-of-war in which county officials grew increasingly frustrated with an industry that they were unable to control. In the early 1950s, HMB officials envisaged a gradual transformation of the paper industry, described as "democratization, rationalization, and enterprisation" (*minzhuhua, helihua, qiyehua*). What they meant by this was a voluntary restructuring along rational, almost Taylorist lines: papermakers would eliminate slack time, increase job differentiation, establish clear hierarchies, and generally reorganize the labor process in ways that would boost productivity. Rationalization would then allow them to accumulate funds and invest in machinery. Mechanization, in short, would come as a final reward *after* a Taylorist restructuring of the labor process.

Both papermakers and local officials thought of mechanization in terms of status and entitlement, as a formal upgrading that would seal the promotion of the industry into the privileged state sector. This led to a curious inversion, in which the Second Ministry of Light Industry opposed mechanization as too costly, while papermakers pleaded, in a sense, for their own deskilling. However, papermakers were unenthusiastic about rationalization *without* mechanization, which from their point of view was pointless and perverse: pointless because they knew (as administrators were soon to find out) that manual papermaking had exhausted its potential for improvement and could not be made more efficient without mechanization; perverse because it denied them the prize – inclusion in the modern sector – that they expected in return for relinquishing craft control. One worker drew an analogy with the imperial examinations: "not only do we not become officials [i.e. reap the material rewards of mechanization] but we are also deprived of the *xiucai* title [i.e. lose craft control]" (*qiu guan bude, fan ba xiucai diule*) (Sichuan Provincial Archives 1956: 13).

Rationalization without mechanization proved a complete failure. The centralized "factories" (in fact, large unmechanized workshops) built between 1956 and 1958 were plagued by administrative incompetence and rivalries between cooperatives that had been forced to merge. Without mechanization, workshops were unable to sustain their enlarged bureaucratic overhead; after each merger, they gravitated back to their former size and structure. The workshops that survived consisted of around five vats employing twenty workers, closely linked by co-residence and kinship and led by a small staff of local people.

The Great Leap Forward and the demise of papermaking

The Great Leap Forward and the ensuing famine wiped out the collective structure in the Jiajiang hills. The paper districts with their dense non-agricultural population were devastated by the famine. Average population loss between the last population count before the famine and the first count after it was 4 percent in the agricultural plains of Jiajiang. In the hills, where people depended on the exchange of paper for grain, losses reached 24 percent; in the townships where papermaking was most concentrated, a staggering 40 percent (Eyferth 2003). During the famine, people began to cut down their bamboo and plant maize and sweet potatoes on the slopes. After 1961, paper production picked up again, but by that time the collective structure had crumbled and people had reverted to household production. Generous grain supplies and high paper prices between 1961 and 1965 helped to corral papermakers back into the collectives (now designated *agricultural* production teams), but many teams illegally contracted the running of the workshops out to households or small teams. By 1962, the HMB had lost control not only of the labor process but also of the flow of raw materials and finished products: an estimated 60 percent of the output slipped through the hands of the HMB and the state trading companies to be sold on the black market (Jiajiang xian n.d.: 56).

In 1961, the central government launched a series of movements to reconsolidate industry after the excesses of the Leap. One of these, called "trimming and simplifying the workforce" (*jingjian zhigong*),[8] aimed at reducing urban population and industrial employment after the massive influx of unskilled rural labor during the Great Leap Forward; in the handicraft sector, it also aimed at re-establishing state control. Although work teams were explicitly told that "trimming and simplifying is not a political campaign" and that there were to be "no struggle meetings, no forced capping, pulling of braids, or beating with sticks" (Zhongguo Shougongye 1994: 296), "trimming and simplifying" quickly morphed into an aggressive campaign that eventually merged with the urban Five-Anti and the rural Four Clean-up movements. In Jiajiang, teams that continued to make paper were accused of "eating guilty conscience grain" (*chi kuixin liang*) and "not sitting straight on their buttocks" (*pigu zuo wai* – i.e. neglecting agriculture). Documents from the campaign show the range of tactics employed by handicraft coops in their desperate effort to survive: various forms of subcontracting, underreporting of profits, excessive payment of dividends and wages, sale of state-supplied materials and finished products on the black market, etc. They also document a growing state exasperation with recalcitrant handicraft producers. Following Lenin, the CCP had always considered artisans a hybrid class: like peasants, they were part working class, part owners of means of production, and in this later quality they were prone to the "daily, hourly, spontaneous, large-scale reproduction of capitalism and the bourgeoisie" (ibid.: 27). Resistance to state-imposed controls only demonstrated that handicrafts, because of their "local and dispersed nature," were particularly prone to "splittism, localism, bureaucratism … individualist and capitalist tendencies," which in their extreme forms constituted "criminal activities aimed at a capitalist restoration" (Sichuan Provincial Archives 1963: 5–6).

Deskilling and the socialist state

CCP leaders liked to think of socialist industrialization as an entirely new beginning, a start from scratch that owed nothing to the country's tainted feudal past. However, no industrialization ever starts from scratch. Lack of funds made sure that much of the inherited industrial hardware continued to be used; Soviet blueprints, which provided much of the industrial software, were available only for the advanced sectors in the more industrialized parts of the country. Especially in the less developed sectors of the interior provinces, state planners had to rely on the skills, knowledge, and inventiveness of workers.

Despite the Maoist rhetoric of workplace democracy, socialist managers in China were as intent on increasing their control over the workplace as their more openly Taylorist colleagues in the Soviet Union and the West.[9] However, complete deskilling required mechanization – the embedding of control into machines – or, short of this, hands-on supervision, coupled with generous wages to buy workers' consent. These were costly solutions, made even more costly by the association (in official rhetoric and paper-makers' minds) of factory production with urban benefits and status, rather than with stricter discipline and increased productivity. In which sense, then, were papermakers deskilled?

Labor market theorists have long argued that skill is primarily a social construct: a claim by groups of workers to status and rewards, based on a monopoly over crucial production processes and the capacity to defend this claim against rival groups of workers and employers (Edwards 1979; Sabel 1982). Deskilling, then, has several aspects: the loss of technical competence as a consequence of mechanization, the loss of craft control over production in result of managerial supervision, and the loss of symbolic title to a trade. In the first two senses, deskilling in Jiajiang remained incomplete: though the number of skilled workers dropped, those who continued to make paper retained their skills and were able to resuscitate the industry in the 1980s. Despite product standardization and HMB control over raw materials, day-to-day management of the workshops remained in the hands of artisans.

Papermakers were deskilled, however, in the sense that they lost their exclusive title to the industry. If skill denotes a measure of control over the terms under which one sells one's labor, derived from a successfully defended monopoly over certain techniques, papermakers became thoroughly deskilled in the 1950s – even though they remained manually skilled. CCP rhetoric encouraged urban workers to think of themselves as masters of their workplace, and core industrial workers took a proprietary interest in crucial production processes – certainly enough to defend their position against competition from temporary workers, women, or other "unskilled" groups (Perry and Li 1997; Frazier 2002). Rural people, by contrast, were denied a position from which they could have launched proprietary claims over industrial techniques. For a brief moment in the early 1950s, wage workers in the paper industry were told that they, too, were workers and thus "masters of the country," but soon after, the initially permeable boundaries between rural-agrarian and the urban-industrial sectors became impermeable, and papermakers – like other rural people – found themselves on the wrong side of the fence. Rural industrial production was not ruled out: peasants could engage in "sidelines" as long as this did not interfere with their obligation to produce food grain for the state. However, the idea that rural people could be skilled specialists came to be seen as almost a contradiction in terms: rural people were peasants, and peasants could not have industrial skills.[10]

Deskilling of this type prepared the ground for China's rapid industrialization in the past twenty years. China's main competitive advantage in the global economy is its cheap and productive workforce, in particular the millions of young rural men and women who staff township and village enterprises and coastal factories. Managers and employers treat rural workers as peasants with "rough hands and rough feet" who handle precision tools as if they were about to plow a furrow (Pun 1999: 4). In reality, of course, these are often dexterous and dedicated workers, often from families that derive as much of their income from sidelines, handicrafts, or trade as from farming (Lee 1998). More generally, migrants come from a rural culture in which skill-intensive commodity production has been a normal part of life for centuries, and in which children learn complex manual skills at an early age and are expected to train and retrain themselves several times in the course of their lives. There is an obvious disjunction between the skillfulness of many rural workers (the famous "nimble fingers") and their inability to translate their skills into social status and material rewards. It is this disjunction that renders rural Chinese both productive and cheap and underpins much of China's economic growth in the last decades.

Notes

1 Braverman's thesis has been criticized on two accounts. First, Taylorism in its original form was an ideology rather than a practice. Absolute managerial control is self-defeating; even the most basic production process cannot be sustained without the active participation of informed workers. Second, Braverman saw deskilling as an inexorable process, driven by the logic of monopoly capitalism. This ignores the fact that the "attempt to build skills into machines by means of algorithms [is] constantly foiled because other skills tend to develop around the new machines" (Sigaut 1994: 445), and the ways workers' resistance can alter the course of technological development.

2 Employment in rural collective industry passed the 4.7 million mark in 1975. If we include the twelve million "household-based seasonal commodity producers" in the 1954 figure, the 1954 level was not reached until the early 1980s.

3 The 1980s saw a similar innovation spurt, once again stimulated by market demand.

4 It takes roughly one pound of hulled rice to feed the workers needed to produce one pound of paper.

5 This was in contravention to central guidelines and was soon rescinded. As artisans and peasants, Jiajiang papermakers were doubly barred from becoming union members.

6 The campaign against "bandits and local bullies" in 1950 was particularly violent in the paper districts, where thousands of unemployed papermakers joined pro-Guomindang "bandit" gangs. As one former militia man recalled, "the four biggest power holders in each village were shot." Many of the victims were wealthy papermakers.

7 The HMB was reorganized nine times between 1953 and 1978 and suspended twice. It managed the industry in conjunction with the agricultural communes, six state agencies that bought paper (often competing with each other) and five agencies that supplied papermakers with raw materials.

8 In the case of handicrafts, *jingjian shougongye duiwu*, since the term "staff and workers" (*zhigong*) was reserved for state-owned industry.

9 Even the supposedly democratic "technological innovation movement" of the 1960s was tightly controlled. Regulations stipulated that innovation work must be carried out "step by step and in a planned fashion," must increase product quality and diversity, serve agriculture, and so on.

10 Many papermakers I interviewed denied that they had any skills (*jishu*), often explicitly linking their lack of skill to the fact that they were peasants. This does not mean that they were unaware of their often very high level of expertise and dexterity but that the word for skill has connotations of formal qualification and entitlement that are associated with the urban world.

References

Anon. (1934) "Jiajiang zhizhi gongye gaikuang" [Description of the paper industry in Jiajiang], *Sichuan Yuebao*, (5)6: 155–161.

Anon. (1935) "Jiajiang zhiye diaocha" [Survey of the Jiajiang paper industry], *Sichuan Jingji Yuekan*, 3(1): 89–90.

Bailes, Kendall E. (1977) "Alexei Gastev and the Soviet Controversy over Taylorism," *Soviet Studies*, 29(3): 373–394.

Behagg, Clive (1982) "Secrecy, Ritual, and Folk Violence: The Opacity of the Workplace in the First Half of the 19th Century," in R. Storch, *Popular Culture and Custom in 19th Century England*, London: Macmillan.

Braverman, Harry (1974) *Labour and Monopoly Capital: The Degradation of Work in the Twentieth Century*, New York: Monthly Review Press.

Burawoy, Michael and Krotov, Pavel (1992) "The Soviet Transition from Socialism to Capitalism: Worker Control and Economic Bargaining in the Wood Economy," *American Sociological Review*, 57(February): 16–38.

Du Shihua (1957) "Shougong zhujiang de zhizao jiqi gaijin fangfa" [Manual production of bamboo pulp and the way to reform it], *Zaozhi Gongye*, 7: 25–29.

Edwards, Richard (1979) *Contested Terrain: The Transformation of the Workplace in the Twentieth Century*, London: Macmillan.

Eyferth, Jacob (2000) "Eating Rice from Bamboo Roots: The History of a Papermaking Community in West China, 1839–1998," PhD thesis, Leiden.

Eyferth, Jacob (2003) "De-Industrialization in the Chinese Countryside: Handicrafts and Development in Jiajiang (Sichuan), 1935 to 1978," *The China Quarterly*, 173(March): 53–73.

Frazier, Mark (2002) *The Making of the Chinese Industrial Workplace: State, Revolution and Labor Management*, Cambridge: Cambridge University Press.

Jiadanqiao stele (1993), text reproduced in Eyferth (2000) "Eating Rice from Bamboo Roots: The History of a Papermaking Community in West China, 1839–1998," PhD thesis, Leiden: 321.

Jiajiang xian erqing gongyeju (ed.) (no date) *Jiajiang zhishi* [A history of Jiajiang paper]. Jiajiang: xeroxed manuscript.

Kirby, William C. (2000) "Engineering China: Birth of the Developmental State, 1928–1937," in Yeh Wen-hsin (ed.) *Becoming Chinese: Passages to Modernity and Beyond*, Berkeley, CA: University of California Press.

Lee, Ching Kwan (1998) *Gender and the South China Miracle: Two Worlds of Factory Women*, Berkeley, CA: University of California Press.

Lu Deheng (1958a) "Bian shougongzhi shengchan zhouqi 100 tian wei 3 tian" [Reduce the production cycle in handmade paper production from 100 to 3 days], *Zaozhi Gongye*, 10: 19–20.

Lu Deheng (1958b) "Shougongzhi shengchan zhong de jishu gexin" [Technological innovation in handmade paper production], *Zaozhi Gongye*, 6: 12–13.

Perry, Elizabeth J. and Li Xun (1997) *Proletarian Power: Shanghai in the Cultural Revolution*, Boulder, CO: Westview Press.

Pun, Ngai (1999) "Becoming Dagongmei: the Politics of Identity and Difference in Reform China," *The China Journal*, 42: 1–19.

Sabel, Charles F. (1982) *Work and Politics: The Division of Labor in Industry*, Cambridge: Cambridge University Press.

Schran, Peter (1964) "Handicrafts in Communist China," *The China Quarterly*, 17: 151–173.

Scott, James (1998) *Seeing Like a State: How Certain Schemes to Improve the Human Condition Have Failed*, New Haven, CT: Yale University Press.

Scoville, James G. (2001) "The Taylorization of Vladimir Ilich Lenin," *Industrial Relations*, 40(October): 620–626.

Sichuan Provincial Archives, Gongyeting series, 19:3 (1951) *Chuanxiqu shoujie zhiye huiyi zongjie* [Summary of the first meeting of the paper industry of the West Sichuan district].

Sichuan Provincial Archives, Shouguanting series, *jianchuan* 074 (1956) *Guanyu guanche 'Zhonggong Zhongyang pizhuan Zhongyang shougongye guanliju, quanguo shougongye hezuo zongshe deng weiyuanhui dangzu guanyu dangqian shougongye hezuohua zhong jige wenti de baogao* [re: Strictly enforce the CCP Center's endorsement of the report of the party groups of the Central Handicraft Management Bureau and the All China Handicraft Cooperative on several issues in the present collectivization of handicrafts].

Sichuan Provincial Archives, Shouguanting series, *jianchuan* 074 (1963) *Guanyu zhaokai quansheng shougongye gongzuo huiyi de qingkuang baogao* [Report on the opening of the province-wide conference on handicraft work].

Sichuan sheng shougongzhi shengchan jishu jingyan jiaoliuhui (1958) "Shougongzhi shengchan zhong shiyong daiyong yuanliao he gaijin shengchan gongju de jingyan" [Experiences on the use and replacement of raw materials in handmade paper production and the improvement of production tools], *Zaozhi Gongye* 4: 14–15.

Sigaut, François (1994) "Technology," in Tim Ingold (ed.) *Companion Encyclopedia of Anthropology*, London: Routledge, pp. 420–459.

Skinner, G. William (1964–1965) "Marketing and Social Structure in Rural China," I-III, *Journal of Asian Studies* 24(1): 5–43; 24(2): 195–228; 25(1): 363–399.

Su Shiliang (1923) "Jiajiang xian zhiye de gaikuang" [The situation of the paper industry in Jiajiang], *Nongmin zazhi*, 1(1).

Veilleux, Louis (1978) *The Paper Industry in China from 1949 to the Cultural Revolution*, Toronto: University of Toronto-York University.

Walder, Andrew G. (1986) *Communist Neo-Traditionalism: Work and Authority in Chinese Industry*, Berkeley, CA: University of California Press.

Yang, Dali (1996) *Calamity and Reform in China: State, Rural Society, and Institutional Change since the Great Leap Famine*, Stanford, CA: Stanford University Press.

Zhongguo laodong gongzi tongji ziliao zoubianzu (1987) *Zhongguo laodong gongzi tongji ziliao, 1949–1985* [Statistical materials on China's labor and wages, 1949–1985], Beijing: Zhongguo tongji chubanshi.

Zhonghua quanguo shougongye hezuo zongshe (ed.) (1994) *Zhongguo Shougongye hezuohua he chengzhen jiti gongye de fazhan* [The collectivization of China's handicrafts and development of collective industry in towns and cities], vol. 2, Beijing: Dangxiao.

3 Commanding heights industrialization and wage determination in the Chinese factory, 1950–1957

Mark W. Frazier

Within any workplace, few questions are as contentious as the issue of who earns how much for which jobs. Wage levels and remunerative systems broadly reflect the supply and demand for labor, but the economics of labor markets does little to dampen the intensity of the debate over what constitutes a "proper" wage (or salary level) and a "fair day's work." These questions are fought over not by the faceless "labor market participants" of neo-classical economics but by groups and individuals who work alongside one another, within their workplaces. Whatever equilibrium emerges as a more or less acceptable outcome does not necessarily reflect the intersection of labor supply and demand curves. The level and manner of compensation thus signify a sort of compromise among different groups within the workplace over what represents a "full day's pay for a full day's work."

Just as the labor market structure outside the workplace is not always an accurate predictor of the wage bargains that eventually emerge within the firm, the power of the state and its policies should not be overly privileged in explaining the levels and forms that wages take. This point is especially important to our understanding of the role of the state in planned economies. Wage policy in planned economies predicts actual wage outcomes no more reliably than does labor supply and demand in a market economy. States possess the power to impose new wage regulations, but they often lack the ability to monitor compliance in every workplace. As state agents put regulations into practice, unintended consequences and conflicts arise that can lead to wage patterns quite unlike those envisioned in initial regulations.

This chapter explores the Chinese workplace during the transition to socialism in the 1950s. My objective is to explain how inter-group divisions among the industrial elite of China's state enterprises generated a system of seniority wages, marked by narrow wage differentials and a fundamental aversion to production-based pay. This pattern stands in marked contrast to the wage regimes found in other socialist planned economies. It also differs substantially from seniority wage systems found at various times and places in capitalist economies.

While a low-wage, low-consumption pattern is understandable in the context of the "small society" of the work unit (*danwei*), which provided extensive non-wage benefits, it does not necessarily follow that the work unit structure would produce seniority-based wages, narrow differences in pay, and an absence of output-based compensation (Walder 1986; Lü and Perry 1997; Frazier 2002). One might then turn to explanations that view the Chinese factory wage regime as a product of prevailing belief systems, based on Maoist ideology or cultural norms, which might have given rise to egalitarian or collective-based systems of compensation, or perhaps to pay based on conceptions of group status. A cultural explanation for the pattern of wage compensation that eventually emerged in the Chinese industrial workplace in the 1950s could be sharpened by specifying the process by which Maoism or other norms were brought into the factory, who transmitted the new norms, and how they compromised or enforced existing beliefs about wage compensation in the factory. If we take seriously the Chinese Communist Party's efforts in the early 1950s to transform both the structure of industry and the "thinking" of industrial workers and managers, then the wage regime that emerged ought to reflect specific structural constraints that existed at the time as well as contending preferences of those within the factory. As Jacob Eyferth argues in the Introduction to this volume, the Chinese revolution was also an industrial revolution, and this perspective helps begin to explain the particular form of labor compensation that emerged in the 1950s and took hold as a centerpiece of the Chinese industrial workplace for much of the remainder of the twentieth century.

Commanding heights industrialization

During the 1950s the Chinese state embarked upon an industrialization drive that increased the number of industrial workers from 3.4 million to 7.9 million over seven years and raised the gross value of industrial output from 19.1 billion *yuan* to 78.4 billion *yuan*.[1] Industrial and planning agencies sought to concentrate and maximize capital accumulation within a state sector that grew from 2,500 central-government administered factories in 1952 to 9,300 by 1957. At the same time, local governments consolidated nearly 165,000 private industrial enterprises down to 48,700 collective firms (Chinese Academy of Social Sciences and National Archives 1998: 1173). The newly-established PRC government would rely heavily on profits in the state industrial sector as a source of revenue. Thus it was vital to maintain careful controls on the growth of industrial wages. Historical precedent offered plenty of evidence of the hazards of wage policy in the context of national industrialization drives: the Nationalist government, admittedly in wartime conditions, had failed to control wage and price inflation in the industrial sector; meanwhile the Soviet Union's otherwise impressive industrialization push since the late 1920s, which

PRC planners clearly sought to emulate, had brought a twelve-fold increase in prices and a six-fold increase in wages between 1928 and 1940 (Eckstein 1977: 172).

For all the distinctive traits of the Chinese state of the 1950s, it did share with contemporary and earlier industrializing states the fundamental objective of creating a wage regime commensurate with the goals of rapid industrial growth. In China as elsewhere, state agencies concentrated capital investment in the "commanding heights" of the state-owned sector and sought to impose a wage regime that induced high rates of labor productivity growth while keeping a lid on the growth of wages. In this respect, the PRC's industrial policy succeeded – real wages during the First Five-Year Plan (1953–1957) advanced at only 4 percent per annum (Howe 1973: 33–34). However, the wage regime that emerged by the end of the 1950s was almost the antithesis of the productivity-, skill-, and output-based system envisioned by PRC industrial planners.

The wage-rank hierarchy that Chinese planners borrowed from the Soviet Union in the early 1950s called for skill-based pay criteria. However, as frequently noted among observers of the Chinese workplace since the 1950s, the wage ladder became a mere reflection of seniority rather than skill. Wage adjustments, or promotions up the wage ladder (toward the highest-paying grade eight for production workers), were possible only when the planning bureaucracy permitted firms to designate particular workers for higher levels of pay. Over time, a worker's position on the wage ladder reflected the year in which he or she had entered industrial employment (Walder 1986: 79; Granick 1990: 54–55; Peng 1992: 208–209).

Moreover, the wage regime in China contained surprisingly narrow wage differentials between the highest and lowest paid workers. While state guidelines mandated intra-industry wage ratios of 2.75 to 1 in the machinery sector, in actual practice, for example, the vast majority of workers were classified in wage grades that resulted in a 1.77 to 1 ratio between the highest and lowest paid production workers (Frazier 2002: 185–186). Including managerial personnel in the income differentials, the "compressed" nature of wage distribution remains striking: the highest paid factory officials earned only two to three times as much as the lowest paid production worker, a ratio far smaller than the 5 to 1 differential between managers and workers in Soviet factories (Richman 1969: 804–805) (Figure 3.1). As late as the 1980s, the wage range for industrial workers in the typical Chinese state-owned enterprise was 2.5 to 1 (Granick 1990: 54).

While top-down wage administration did lend a good deal of control and coordination to the central planners in the industrial bureaucracy, at the firm level, the process of determining a worker's initial wage level and making subsequent adjustments to it provided some room for negotiation between employee and manager. First, during the process of "wage

Figure 3.1 Soviet influences: the No. 1 Auto Factory (source: Author's photograph).

reform" in the 1950s, when current workers were classified by skill, job task, and corresponding wage level, informal bargaining was widespread. While enterprise managers had to follow state guidelines for attaching a certain income to particular job categories (the government's wage matrix varied slightly depending on local prices), the actual task of classifying individual workers based on skills proved cumbersome. Second, in subsequent wage adjustments, state officials allocated fixed sums to each enterprise that would be used for expanding the wage bill. These allocations generally represented small percentage increases, but they set off a round of further informal bargaining as managers, supervisors, and workers arranged how the expanded wage bill would be allocated.

Finally, the Chinese wage regime departed significantly from other state-led industrialization experiences by the fact that over-quota production bonuses, after their controversial implementation in the mid-1950s, were altogether abolished at the outset of the Great Leap Forward (1958) and did not make a comeback until the 1980s. While the rejection of output-based pay reflected the ideological preferences of the Great Leap Forward and later of those who gained power during the Cultural Revolution, it is significant that the aversion to linking additional pay to additional output existed within factories themselves well before it became national policy to eschew material incentive as an instrument of motivation for industrial workers.

In sum, the Chinese wage regime, with its *de facto* seniority system, narrow wage differentials, and rejection of over-quota bonus payments, diverged in important respects from the visions of industrial bureaucrats who strove to maximize output through the use of a skill-based wage structure and over-quota bonus payments. Explaining why China's industrial workplaces evolved seniority norms poses a problem if we rely solely on a labor market perspective. Firms and trade unions in market economies establish seniority practices as a means of encouraging careers within the same firm and protecting against the threat of labor turnover or, from the union's perspective, the threat of workforce reduction. Andrew Gordon (1985) persuasively explains Japan's seniority wage system (*nenko*) as the outcome of negotiations among workers, managers, and state officials during Japan's pre-war industrialization drive. Here and in other industrializing market economies, seniority-based wages arose as a solution to the extraordinarily high rates of turnover. During subsequent unionization struggles in the 1920s, workers sought to preserve the seniority system. However, this explanation cannot account for China's seniority wage pattern during the command economy, since retaining workers was easily accomplished in the absence of a labor market. Even had labor been scarce, enterprise managers in China by the mid-1950s could no longer freely adjust the wage bill.

By the same token, comparison with other command economies does not suggest viable explanations for the narrow wage differentials and absence of production bonuses in the Chinese factory. The Soviet industrialization drive of the late 1920s initially also brought "leveling" tendencies in wages, but by the early 1930s, the Soviet state had succeeded in imposing expanded wage differentials and the widespread use of production bonuses (Shearer 1996: 221; Kuromiya 1988: 283–284). One possible explanation for the divergent outcome in China is that Chinese workers had firmly established preferences for some pre-existing wage regime, informal or otherwise, and resisted the strictures of the command economy. Was it the case that seniority systems, narrow wage differences, and an aversion to output-linked pay were common in the factories of pre-socialist China? What prevailing norms and conditions existed in Chinese factories at the time that wage reform was imposed in the mid-1950s?

Compressed wage structure

Discussions of the relatively flat wage structure of the Chinese socialist workplace during the 1960s and 1970s assumed that this wage pattern reflected the prevailing Maoist aversion to income differentials, with their implicit threat of capitalist tendencies (Richman 1969: 804–805; Andors 1977: 218–221). While there is no doubt that Maoism was consistent with the compressed wage structure in industrial firms, the problem with an ideological explanation for China's narrow wage differentials is that they existed well before the heyday of Maoist ideology and even before the Chinese Communist Party took power in 1949.

The source of this pre-1949 "egalitarianism" in the wage structure no doubt reflected something of a tradition of CCP industrial management in the factories of base areas and a preference for egalitarianism in compensation levels, but previous discussions of wage policy in Maoist China have overlooked an important structural cause that acted as a backdrop to wage reform in the early 1950s: recovery from the hyperinflation that raged through the urban economies of China during the late 1940s. Hyperinflation distorted the existing wage structure in such a way that wage differentials were tightly compressed, even "inverted," meaning that less-skilled occupations and industries had higher average real wages than did jobs and sectors that used relatively higher-skilled labor. Christopher Howe, relying on secondary sources, showed some time ago how the hyperinflation of the late 1940s caused real wages in Shanghai industries to rise as much as three- and four-fold between 1936 and 1946 (1973: 22–27). In addition, wages in the textile industry rose rapidly relative to other industries, such as machinery. Within industrial sectors, wage differentials between unskilled and skilled workers in Shanghai declined to a ratio of only 1 to 1.5. In the machinery industry, the ratio of the highest to lowest paid production workers was 1 to 1.09 and in cotton spinning, 1 to 1.36 (ibid.: 17–19). Inflationary conditions caused average wages to rise and eroded wage differentials between the lowest and highest paid workers. This was the result more directly of Nationalist government policy to link wages to price indexes and to control wages by placing caps on the highest wage earners (ibid.: 26).

My examination of factory-specific and Nationalist government archives confirms that hyperinflation and the Nationalist response to it caused the distortion in the wage structure that Howe discussed (Frazier 2002: 66–91). As Communist Party officials in Shanghai and other cities set about installing the eight-grade wage system on China's industrial sector, they wrote frequently of the problem of "egalitarianism" and "inversion" in wages. As an official in the Shanghai Municipal Trade Union wrote of the inverted wage structure, "A wage system like this will neither stimulate production nor raise skill levels, and will also foster an egalitarian viewpoint among workers" (Shanghai Municipal Archives, Series C1-2-338). The objective of wage reform was to freeze or limit wage increases in the light industrial sectors and less skilled occupations and to increase wages in heavy industrial sectors and skilled occupations. Wage reform began in the early 1950s in the existing state-owned sector, in firms taken over from the Nationalist government. Wage reform continued in the mid-1950s in factories brought under state ownership with the collectivization of industry.

Archival reports from particular firms, local governments and trade unions, as well as national industrial ministries, suggest that the process of wage reform did succeed in widening the drastically narrow wage differentials, but not always in ways that the central government planners had intended. At the Jiangnan Shipyard in Shanghai, management appeared to have avoided disputes over wages by simply placing most workers in the middle rungs of the eight-grade wage scale (SMA, Series A36-2-072). At the Shenxin Number Six Mill, which had recently been brought under state ownership, factory floor supervisors complained that wage settings were held in small-group meetings, as the new Communist Party supervisors insisted they be. Such open appraisals of individual workers, the supervisors noted, allowed workers to bring up issues such as a worker's tenure, family conditions, attitude, and "work style." These criteria, the CCP enterprise committee agreed, were irrelevant to the skill-based wage settings and adjustments they were attempting to implement (Shanghai No. 31 Cotton Mill, Series 56).

More generally, enterprise managers found it impossible to follow the arcane standards of the central ministries for assessing how to place an individual worker at a given wage rank. A welder in the machinery industry, for example, might qualify for placement anywhere between grade three and grade six. That much was clear, but determining the precise grade level for each welder provoked controversy. After all, managers were being asked to take a group of welders and rank them based on the highly ambiguous criterion of skill. The wage-rank system, with its uniform standards, also presumed that the endowments of production machinery varied little from firm to firm. In actual fact, it was often impossible for enterprise managers and supervisors to follow the guidelines and criteria for particular industrial tasks that determined wage ranks (Howe 1973: 108–109). At the Guangdong Textile Mill, managers sought to avoid disputes over wages by simply not making public the skill standards for particular jobs (GMA, Series 92-478) The state's insistence on attaching a skill-based wage grade to every worker in China was especially problematic within the service sector. The managers of a Shanghai department store implemented wage reform by applying a rather questionable "skills" test on the store's clerks, who were asked to assess the quality of cigarette brands in a sort of blind taste-test – despite the fact that many were non-smokers (SMA, Series C1-2-2723).

Wage reform resulted in most workers being put on the same or proximate wage grade levels. As new workers arrived in factories, they invariably found themselves slotted for grades one and two, or the lowest rung for their particular occupation. Here, it is worth stressing that for the largest and oldest factories, the number of temporary and contract workers was quite small, sometimes amounting to only a handful, according to personnel records. Temporary and contract workers could be found more often in formerly private firms, generally of small and medium scale, that were nationalized in the mid-1950s. If one were to include temporary and contract workers and their earnings in an overall measure of wage differentials, then undoubtedly the flattened wage structure would look quite a bit steeper.[2] To the often-cited workforce divisions such as gender, skill, and native-place, we might add the political criterion of whether one had engaged in work prior to "liberation" in 1949. This cohort distinction had an important bearing on the emergence of the seniority wage system and aversion to output-based wage compensation.

Seniority wages

Factory archives and party documents from the 1950s make explicit reference to a segment of the workforce known as "old workers" (*lao gongren*), whose status derived not from their age but from the fact that they had entered the workforce prior to "liberation" and had thus suffered at the hands of capitalist and bureaucratic capitalist owners. PRC civilian and military cadres throughout the 1950s and 1960s had their pensions and other employment benefits based on the time they had first "participated in the work of the revolution" or entered "revolutionary ranks" (Lu 1993: 17). Urban workers in cities under Nationalist rule prior to 1948–1949 had a somewhat more challenging task in demonstrating that they had conducted "revolutionary work," since few could legitimately claim to have participated in underground trade unions. Nonetheless, urban workers were rewarded for their engagement in "pre-liberation" work when it came to determining their initial wage grade and their subsequent wage adjustments.

During wage reform in Chinese factories throughout the 1950s, Communist Party cadres implemented wage policy in the familiar (to them at least) idiom of the mass campaign. Trade union members, model workers, labor supervisors, and others were mobilized to exchange opinions about wages in open meetings in their workshops and production teams. While the atmosphere lacked the charge of prior campaigns directed against corruption, collaboration, and various other potentially counter-revolutionary acts, the wage meetings did open up the rather contentious issue of which colleagues deserved to be rewarded over others with higher levels of pay. While it was the task of CCP cadres to persuade workers to suppress their impulses for higher wages and to put the nation ahead of themselves and their families, the eventual announcement by management of wage grade settings brought forth a wave of complaints from workers who felt overlooked in the wage setting process. Workers appeared to be aware of the fact that it would be difficult in subsequent years to advance up the wage ladder. As textile workers in Shanghai said in the mid-1950s of their initial wage setting, "once it's set, it's yours for life" (SMA, Series C16-2-99). During the infrequent nationwide wage adjustments of the late 1950s and early 1960s, employees who possessed status as "old workers" received most of the scarce supply of incremental wage increases. As one official explained, "This was done because it was felt that someone with more seniority, who had worked in the mill before liberation, had contributed more to the nation."[3] Seniority *cum* political status as the criterion for wage adjustments meant that over time, younger employees who had attained similar, if not more advanced technical skills, still earned less than a worker who had entered factory work before 1949. It is true that some factories in China had seniority wage structures during the pre-1949 period – and indeed, some enterprises before 1949 had wage ranks based on skill. But wage reform lessened to a great degree the power of shop floor supervisors to control a worker's fate by controlling their pay levels – and of course their job security.[4]

It is important to note that government policy to tie wage adjustments to the tenure of one's factory employment became explicit after this practice was institutionalized within firms in the 1950s. During the 1959 national wage adjustments, guidelines called for promotions to be given only to those who had been employed before 1957, with special consideration to those who had "pre-liberation" work experience. The 1963 and 1971 wage adjustments made similar provisions for those who had entered the workforce in the 1950s but had yet to receive wage adjustments. By the early 1960s, many "old workers" were at or near retirement, and wage adjustments mattered little to them. But they were not without political sway to enterprise cadres, who had the retirees convey their personal histories to assembled groups of workers during wage meetings (Frazier 2002: 228). The intent was to use the bitter personal experiences of workers who had labored in the same enterprise pre-1949 as a means of stemming the demands from new workers, the beneficiaries of work unit health insurance, guaranteed employment, etc., for higher wages. The "speaking bitterness" sessions informally gave "old workers" political status at the expense of post-1949 workforce entrants.

Production bonuses

As Burawoy and others have shown in factory ethnographies, one trait shared by socialist and monopoly capitalist industrial firms is informal bargaining between workers and shop floor administrators over production quotas and related pay. In both types of firms, the threat to firm profits posed by overproduction is minimal, so factory production lines are geared to optimize output. Bonus payments for production beyond a quota can be offered as a pecuniary incentive to increase individual output. The shop floor debate centers on quota-setting and the allocation of workers to tasks that offer relatively more promising prospects of exceeding given quotas (Haraszti 1977; Burawoy 1985; Burawoy and Lukács 1985). One key contrast between socialist and monopoly capitalist firms, Burawoy argues, is that the latter enjoy union contracts that generally guarantee wages but do not ensure future employment. In socialist factories, on the other hand, employment is assured whereas wage increases are not (Burawoy and Lukács 1985: 727). Exceeding production quotas thus becomes critical to workers in the factory of a command economy. The unreliable supply of inputs further complicates matters for the industrial employee in the socialist firm (Burawoy 1985: 168). Thus, in China, as in other command economies, factory officials and party cadres attempt to mobilize the workforce through "socialist competitions" that result in high levels of individual output. These levels then become, not without some irony, the output norms or standards that workers must exceed in order to qualify for over-quota production bonuses.

The PRC industrial authorities achieved some success in introducing such production bonuses during the 1950s. By the end of the First Five-Year Plan, about 330,000 of Shanghai's 974,000 production workers were earning some form of production-related bonuses (SMA, Series A36-1-248). In the machine industry, this amounted to 70 to 80 percent of the workforce and 50 to 60 percent of textile mill workers (SMA, Series C1-2-2723). Nationwide, by 1956, the total wage bill for production workers of 184.2 million *yuan* included 77.2 million *yuan* (42 percent) in output-based pay (Chinese Academy of Social Sciences and National Archives 1998b: 573). While these and other figures reflect a substantial diffusion of production-quota systems, such incentive systems proved very difficult to administer in practice.

First, the inevitable delays in supply quickly discouraged many workers from pursuing the extra levels of pay through increased production. Given the very uneven distribution of capital equipment across Chinese industrial firms and within factories themselves, some workers clearly were advantaged over others. Workers who had access to new or renovated machines could churn out goods at rates that easily exceeded the quotas that had been set by the physical exertions of a model worker a few years prior. Reports also suggest that enterprise managers were distributing bonuses using questionable criteria – as a way to pass along income adjustments to as many personnel as possible, whether they fit the strict eligibility criteria or not (Frazier 2002: 153–154).

Perhaps most seriously from the perspective of CCP industrial and union cadres, however, such production incentive systems created an unhealthy division within the workforce. Specifically, a rivalry between older and younger workers had emerged by the mid-1950s (SMA, Series C1-2-2724; SMA, Series A36-1-136). Those who had just joined the ranks of industrial workers and had been trained in the operation of more technically sophisticated equipment found that they were earning, thanks to production bonuses, as much as those older workers who might have a higher wage grade rank and considerably longer job tenure. The recent recruits under state socialism were accused by their seniors of chasing cash over ideals – of "serving the *renminbi*" instead of "serving the people (*renmin*)" (SMA, Series A36-1-136). As one Shanghai fitter in the Jiangnan Shipyard remarked, "post-liberation" apprentices earned at least 50 *yuan* a month, leading them to less wholesome pursuits than that of enhancing productivity:

> They brainstorm over how to spend their money. They study dancing, look for girlfriends, and don't put in any time learning technical skills. But skill is something that is acquired from a life of bitter experience. There's a huge difference between the grade 3 worker of today and the grade 3 worker of the past.
>
> (SMA, Series C1-2-2257)

With the advent of the Great Leap Forward, calls for the abolition of piece-rates and over-quota bonuses arose from many quarters and received the support of many in the CCP leadership. Only a few months after Shanghai's *Jiefang Ribao* (Liberation Daily) trumpeted the news that the city's shipyard workers had abolished over-quota production bonuses, all such incentive pay systems had disappeared (SMA, Series A36-1-248). Veteran workers in Guangzhou advocated the same, proclaiming, "We want politics, not cash, to take command" (GMA, Series 92-216). Although incentive pay systems were restored in the early 1960s, when the portion of the state enterprise workforce participating in some form of output-based pay rose from 5 percent in 1960 to 20 percent in 1963, wages remained closely tied to "mass appraisals" and "political attitude" rather than formal criteria of production (Yuan 1990: 256). During the Cultural Revolution, incentive pay once again was abolished, not to be revived on a nationwide scale in state enterprises until the early 1980s.

Commanding heights industrialization and working class cohorts

The argument presented here for the origins of the socialist wage regime in Chinese factories thus relies heavily on material and political influences that shaped China's transition to a command economy. I have emphasized the importance of cohort divisions that this transition created, with an older group of pre-revolutionary workers at odds with younger workers over wage determination and production bonuses. Given that China's labor and industrial planners had so closely modeled their centrally planned economy on Soviet blueprints, it is illuminating to examine how working-class cohort divisions might have given shape to the wage regime of the Soviet Union.

As was the case in China, the Soviet Union's industrial workforce rapidly expanded during the initial phases of commanding heights industrialization. The number of industrial workers doubled, from three million to six million, during the First Five Year Plan (1928–1932) (Kuromiya

1988: 290). Here too, fault-lines quickly appeared dividing older workers with years of experience in pre-command economy factories and newer workers who had just entered industrial employment (ibid.: 89). However, whereas the Chinese Communist Party would venerate pre-revolutionary workers as the "backbone of politics" during the late 1950s and beyond, in the Soviet Union, a nearly inverse result obtained. By the onset of the First Five-Year Plan (FFYP), Communist Party leaders, including Stalin himself, branded old Soviet workers as "labor aristocrats," putting them in a condemned category with kulaks (ibid.: 87). As wage reform in the FFYP swept through the industrial sector of the Soviet Union, the policy objective was to reduce wage differentials. It took intervention by Stalin himself with a major speech on labor and wage policy in 1931 to reverse the serious wage leveling tendency (ibid.: 283–284). In short order, a drastic program of anti-egalitarian wage policy brought about expanded wage spreads and, significantly, the rise of "shock workers" and Stakhanovites, individuals who earned large portions of income through over-quota bonuses (Sil 1997: 126).

Thus, in the Soviet case, a cohort division of a rather different sort produced a substantially different outcome in wage regime. Unlike China, urban and industrial centers in the Soviet Union encountered extreme shortages of labor during the process of industrialization. This led planners and enterprise managers to shift large numbers (up to three million) of first generation workers from peasant households into factories. These new recruits lacked technical skills, but they constituted an important constituency of "shock workers" for the Stalinist leadership bent on a leap forward in industrial output. Scarcities drove managers to raise wages at a pace that doubled total wage expenditures between 1930 and 1932 and prompted the Soviet government to criminalize violations of wage policy (Kuromiya 1988: 291). In China, by contrast, the gates were opened at times in the 1950s for rural to urban labor migration but were quickly shut.

Wage regimes, in both the Soviet and Chinese cases, appear to reflect political conflict among different groups of workers that first undergo the process of rapid industrialization under a command economy. The resolution of this conflict reflects the contests over the implementation of national wage policy within the factory. Clearly labor scarcities in the Soviet Union and relative abundance in China factored into the resolution of the clash of cohorts. Moreover, the generally higher levels of capital endowments in Soviet factories produced a faster "de-skilling" of the older generation, as first-generation rural migrants obtained positions in assembly lines. In China, by contrast, where capital investment was far scarcer, the older cohort served as critical intermediaries to instruct recent workforce entrants in how to get the most from older equipment. To the extent that new machinery and sectors that used them undermined the status and pay of the older cohort in China, tensions flared and criticisms of the production-based quota system emerged. Finally, the Chinese Communist Party's heavy emphasis on face-to-face meetings to discuss mass campaigns, "thought work," and even wage standards provided an occasion for the older cohort of workers to enhance their political status as the arbiters of pre- and post-1949 working conditions and wages.

Conclusion

This chapter has stressed a set of exogenous factors – wartime inflation and rapid industrialization – as crucial to understanding the wage regime that emerged within Chinese factories by the late 1950s. However, we should be cautious about placing too much emphasis on context. While hyperinflation in the 1940s followed by rapid industrialization in the 1950s influenced the broad parameters for wage policy, these external forces did not preordain the outcome of the debate over pay that raged within the Chinese industrial workplace. As this chapter shows, that debate was fueled by an abiding opposition to the new wage regime among older workers who had come of age in factories prior to the First Five-Year Plan.

It is tempting to conclude that a deeper set of cultural preferences lay beneath debates over wages, that in resisting the wage regime of the First Five-Year Plan, Chinese workers asserted the primacy of community over competition, and the roughly equal distribution of income over differentials in it. After all, opposition to the new stratified wage regime of the 1950s was led by older workers, whose training and introduction to workplace norms had taken place among communities of migrant workers and guild members, with their emphasis on group identity and cohesion. Yet, I would argue that this explanation stresses solidarity at the expense of a more universal source of opposition among workers to formulaic, excessively rationalized, wage determination. In applying the Soviet model, the CCP planners took an elusive, subjective assessment – a worker's skill – as something that could be standardized, quantified, measured, and ultimately tied to one's pay. This opposition to the scientific application of pay reflects both values and material interests, and is difficult therefore to label as a distinctly cultural phenomenon. For older Chinese workers in the 1950s, new wage scales and technologies upon which they were based threatened to erode their pay and attach new meanings to the concept of "skill." The First Five-Year Plan and its wage regime thus challenged the older generation both in terms of their well-being and their workplace values.

In this regard, the experience of the Chinese workplace during the command economy resonates beyond the time and circumstances of the 1950s. Elsewhere in this volume, we see owners of township and village enterprises and department store directors (in Chapters by Calvin Chen and Amy Hanser in this volume) during the reform era seeking to impose rules and order on an existing workplace culture with mixed results. These rules seek to differentiate, with positive inducements and negative sanctions, groups of workers on the basis of productivity, skill, and even behavior and appearance. Like the workers of the 1950s who resisted efforts at differentiation on the basis of skill, TVE workers and department store staff engage in individual and collective behaviors that openly defy managerial initiatives to impose rules and lessen workers' autonomy in their workplace. The transition from socialism, like the transition to socialism, engages managers and workers in a struggle over the multiple meanings of work, wages, and fair compensation.

Notes

1 The employment figure refers to workers and staff in industrial enterprises (not including collectives). Output calculated is based on 1952 fixed prices (Chinese Academy of Social Sciences and National Archives 1998a: 1117, 1173).
2 I am grateful to Jacob Eyferth for contributing this observation.
3 Author's interview, Factory Director's Office and Personnel Department, Shanghai No. 31 Cotton Mill, Jan. 14, 1995.
4 This erosion of personal authority among shop floor supervisors in the early 1950s was reversed by the early 1960s when supervisors became the arbiters of Maoist ideology and controlled their workers through the politicized, patron–client reward system which Walder (1986) has documented.

References

Andors, Stephen (1977) *China's Industrial Revolution: Politics, Planning, and Management, 1949 to the Present*, New York: Pantheon Books.
Burawoy, Michael (1985) *The Politics of Production: Factory Regimes under Capitalism and Socialism*, London: Verso Press.
Burawoy, Michael and Lukács, János (1985) "Mythologies of Work: A Comparison of Firms in State Socialism and Advanced Capitalism," *American Sociological Review* 50(6): 723–738.
Chinese Academy of Social Sciences and National Archives (ed.) (1998a) *Zhonghua renmin gongheguo jingji dang'an ziliao xuanbian, 1953–1957: gongye juan* [Selected Economic Archival Materials from the People's Republic of China: industrial files], Beijing: Zhongguo wujia chubanshe.
Chinese Academy of Social Sciences and National Archives (ed.) (1998b) *Zhonghua renmin gongheguo jingji dang'an ziliao xuanbian, 1953–1957: laodong gongzi he zhigong baoxian fuli juan* [Selected Economic Archival Materials from the People's Republic of China: labor, wages, and employee insurance and welfare files], Beijing: Zhongguo wujia chubanshe.
Eckstein, Alexander (1977) *China's Economic Revolution*, New York: Cambridge University Press.
Frazier, Mark W. (2002) *The Making of the Chinese Industrial Workplace: State, Revolution, and Labor Management*, New York: Cambridge University Press.
Gordon, Andrew (1985) *The Evolution of Labor Relations in Japan: Heavy Industry, 1853–1955*, Cambridge, MA: Harvard University Press.

Granick, David (1990) *Chinese State Enterprises: A Regional Property Rights Analysis*, Chicago: University of Chicago Press.

Guangzhou Municipal Archives: Series 92–478.

Haraszti, Miklós (1977) *A Worker in a Workers' State*, trans. Michael Wright, New York: Pelican Books.

Howe, Christopher (1973) *Wage Patterns and Wage Policy in Modern China, 1919–1972*, New York: Cambridge University Press.

Kuromiya, Hiroaki (1988) *Stalin's Industrial Revolution: Politics and Workers, 1928–1932*, New York: Cambridge University Press.

Lu, Feng (1993) "The Origins and Formation of the Unit (Danwei) System," *Chinese Sociology and Anthropology*, 25(3): 1–95.

Lü, Xiaobo and Perry, Elizabeth J. (eds) (1997) *Danwei: the Changing Chinese Workplace in Historical and Comparative Perspective*, Armonk, NY: M.E. Sharpe.

Peng, Yusheng (1992) "Wage Determination in Rural and Urban China: A Comparison of Public and Private Industrial Sectors," *American Sociological Review*, 57(2): 198–214.

Richman, Barry M. (1969) *Industrial Society in Communist China*, New York: Random House.

Shanghai Municipal Archives: Series A36-1-136; Series A36-1-248; Series A36-2-072, Series C1-2-338; Series C1-2-2257; Series C1-2-2723; Series C1-2-2724; Series C16-2-99.

Shanghai Number 31 Cotton Mill, Factory Archives: Labor and Wage Department, Series 56.

Shearer, David R. (1996) *Industry, State, and Society in Stalin's Russia, 1926–1934*, Ithaca, NY: Cornell University Press.

Sil, Rudra (1997) "The Russian 'Village in the City' and the Stalinist System of Enterprise Management: The Origins of Worker Alienation in Soviet State Socialism," in X.B. Lü and E.J. Perry (eds) *Danwei: the Changing Chinese Workplace in Historical and Comparative Perspective*, Armonk, NY: M.E. Sharpe.

Walder, Andrew G. (1986) *Communist Neo-traditionalism: Work and Authority in Chinese Industry*, Berkeley, CA: University of California Press.

Yuan, Lunqu (1990) *Zhongguo laodong jingjishi* [History of Chinese labor economics], Beijing: Beijing *jingji yanjiusuo*.

4 Industrial involution

Recruitment and development within the railway system

Lida Junghans

This chapter concerns railway work units and the workers who belonged to them at a "liminal" time in the early 1990s, when the policies of reform and opening were assured of neither durability through time nor diffusion through geographical or structural space. In 1991, reform policies had loosened many people from their fixed moorings in rural settings where their labor was redundant, but in urban China, and particularly in state sector China, work units and their employees remained relatively stable. Reform policies seemed unlikely to penetrate such strongholds of socialist conservatism as railway work units or to transform the social actions of the workers who belonged to them.[1]

Reform policies encouraged innovation and experimentation, apart from the dictates of the central plans which frequently bore little relationship to resources, needs, or desires on the ground. Beginning in 1979, agricultural production was shifted from people's communes to family farms, and reforms enabled farmers to contract with the state to produce quotas of crops to be sold to the state at a set rate. Beyond that commitment, farmers were permitted to invest their additional land and labor in cash crops, or to engage in sidelines, marketing and other productive activities, which they did with remarkable effect. In 1980, the Hong Kong border town of Shenzhen opened to investment from Hong Kong. Shenzhen, as a special economic zone (SEZ), was followed by Hainan Island and three other south-eastern towns, each with historic, linguistic, cultural, and kinship links to wealth in Taiwan or Hong Kong. In 1984, fourteen more special economic zones were opened along the length of China's eastern coast.

A spatial logic shaped these early reforms: Rural spaces where people relied on agricultural production for their livelihoods were *outside* of cities, where, in contrast, residency or work unit membership entitled people to basic necessities. The coastal towns that opened early to outside investment were literally on the edges of the nation's land, in close proximity to Hong Kong and international capital, with easier material and symbolic access to resources beyond the control of the centralized state. These early reforms put many people and many goods in motion, a phenomenon which placed railway workers in a position to witness and experience a distinct contrast between the flexibility and opportunities opened to some because of position in geographical or structural space, while their own formal opportunities changed very little.

I gathered the material in this chapter in Nanjing during the summer of 1991, before extended research on the lives of railway workers for fifteen months between 1992 and 1995. I made my first trip "behind the scenes" at the Nanjing railway station in the aftermath of torrential rains. In June and July of 1991, China and most of south-east Asia were inundated by floods. Forecasts warned that the Yangzi might overflow its banks and submerge the Xiaguan district. Over the river, just thirty kilometers west of Nanjing, national traffic flow was interrupted while emergency teams reinforced the tracks sufficiently to support constant heavy rail traffic again. Meanwhile national and provincial level authorities were deciding to dynamite portions of river dams, sacrificing some villages and farmlands to save cities and industrial infrastructure.[2]

On the day I visited the railway station, trains bound north and west were running again after a five-day hiatus. I went with a new acquaintance named Shu, to change the date of travel for a ticket I'd purchased to Beijing. Young Shu promised to introduce me to some of his old railway friends, leftover from the days when he worked in the station's propaganda department. This opportunity created another compelling reason for my visit to the station. We arrived at the station only to find that the window where I needed to return my ticket had closed fifteen minutes ahead of the posted schedule, and would not open again for several hours. Young Shu led us away from the crowds to visit an old friend so dear to him from his days working at the station that he called her his elder sister (*da jie*). We bumped into Shu's "elder sister" Wang Yunwen who was returning from the canteen. She led us to her office which was at platform level, facing the tracks. She was a member of the "Rear Logistics Department" (*houqin bu*), and was in charge of dispensing and keeping track of the supplies and equipment that station workers use. Her office was a cement cubicle with two wooden desks, a wooden wardrobe, a standing washbasin, a few chairs, with some charts and tables hanging on the wall. She sat us down in her office, gave me a glossy furniture magazine to look at, and dashed off to fetch us some lunch before the canteen closed for the day.

We stepped out of Wang Yunwen's office to watch passengers boarding the Shanghai-to-Xian train that had just arrived. A hard seat car was before us. Twenty-five or thirty people desperately crowded each of the doors of the train car. Bolder ones began to board the already crowded train through windows. We watched as a pair of young families from the countryside – two women, two men, and a couple of small children – pushed their babies up through the window into the arms of helpful strangers, and then tried unsuccessfully to follow them. Frightened, crying babies were handed back down to mothers who appeared distraught.

A very old, very small man and woman were struggling with all of their might to board the train, but the platform attendant was adamant about not letting the old man on. Finally, young Shu approached the attendant and persuaded him to "take care of" (*zhaogu*) the old man. Wang Yunwen returned from the canteen with covered tin rice boxes filled with bean sprouts, winter melon, and rice. As we ate, a man in a railway worker's uniform, red-faced drunk, slurring his words, walked in to wash his face in the office wash basin. Wang Yunwen scolded him for drinking so much at lunch and away he went. Then she invited me upstairs to the worker's recreation hall (*jule bu*) to join in lunchtime dancing with the workers. I declined, offended by the thought that while would-be travelers were under such duress, workers were dancing in their recreation hall, and certain that my appearance would create a spectacle I was not in the mood to be center of.

The railway workers

When I began to explore the possibility of focusing on the lives of railway workers, many Chinese friends warned me that railway workers would be a difficult, if not impossible, subject for a foreigner like me to pursue. The railway was "half-militarized" (*ban junshihua*), which meant that the system, closely allied with the military and the cause of national defense, was conservative. Many of its members, too, had come into the ranks after serving in the army, and thus were also thought to be conservative, old-fashioned, and well-disciplined.

How, then, should we understand the facts of drunkenness and dancing at the railway station while elsewhere in the city, labor was being mobilized to forestall disaster? The cavalier and irresponsible behavior of workers on the job supports recent public perceptions of railway workers as disreputable.[3] And, indeed, behavior that ranges from the merely negligent to the aggressively surly has characterized workers in service professions in many socialist settings. Chinese reformers themselves regard the Maoist era's "iron rice bowl," with its guarantees of security, and the egalitarianism of "eating out of one big pot" as responsible for instilling attitudes of irresponsibility, passivity, and dependence (the *dengkaoyao* syndrome) among workers.[4] By doing away with these provisions, reformers expressly aimed to improve the quality of workers and of the products they produce. They located the practices that needed reform in the misguided policies of the past. But the constellation of material goods and provisions associated with a permanent position in the state sector was also linked to an array of customary practices related to hiring, placement, and remuneration throughout Chinese industry. These features may not have been visible in official documents or organizational charts, yet they may have had more to do with the flavor of work unit culture than did the material benefits such placement promised.

It is also true that in the summer of 1991, competition between Dengist economic liberalizers and Maoist traditionalists in Beijing made local-level authorities reluctant to act definitively, even in routine matters, lest their decisions be dissonant with the values of whatever faction would win the power struggle in Beijing. Many reform processes that had been put in motion before 1989 were forced to follow a holding pattern until the new party line could be divined. The apparent absence of work discipline I encountered at the station may have had something to do with the station's leadership, more committed to its steady hold on power than to dynamic pursuit of profit or customer satisfaction.

The scene also provides symbolic expression of the social order in an indeterminate period of Deng Xiaoping's leadership: two years after the killings at Tiananmen Square in 1989 and seven months before the elderly Deng's fateful trip to the South. Deng's inspection trip by special train in January of 1992 to Shenzhen is widely interpreted as his conclusive endorsement of market reforms and as the signal that a new logic would shape work and life throughout society thereafter. The scene above proved anomalous during my subsequent seasons of fieldwork. Most railway workers I came to know were good citizens who carried out their work responsibilities with precision, competence, and pride. The scene I described above should not be taken as a typical moment in a smooth, continuous trajectory of reform era change, yet neither was it as "unthinkable" to local people as it was to me. In the following section, I explore some of the structural and cultural factors that have shaped the social order underlying the scene.

The administrative order of railway work in Nanjing

The Nanjing Railway Sub-Bureau (*Nanjing Tielu Fenju*) belongs to the Shanghai Railway Bureau[5] and is one of fifty-seven sub-bureaus nationwide. The Nanjing Sub-Bureau includes ninety-three stations and 749 kilometers of track. It also includes two hospitals, three worker training institutes, eight middle schools, and nine elementary schools for the children of railway employees. Additionally there are two construction and engineering teams (in the process of re-inventing themselves as construction and engineering companies during my fieldwork); two architecture and design units, three rock quarries, two forest management groups, a materials supply corps, as well as nineteen "base-level" units whose workers carry out the specialized tasks that railroads require: rolling stock maintenance, electrical engineering, freight and passenger service; signaling and dispatching. Finally, the Railway Sub-Bureau supports a centralized office for compiling contemporary data and writing local railway history. In all, the 41,891 workers employed within the Nanjing railway region are divided among eighty base-level units, some of which have only a tangential connection to railway transport (NTFN 1991: 39).

I owe all my data regarding the census and organization of this domain to the 1991 Nanjing Railway Sub-Bureau Yearbook, a *Neibu* (classified) volume I was not officially authorized to see. The Yearbook contains two charts that lay out the organization of Party work in the Nanjing Railway district. Beneath a disciplinary committee is a group to investigate cases and a group to carry out inspections. There is a Party school; a leadership group to investigate special topics, namely, politics and law; secrecy; war veterans' issues; the political history of leading cadres; administration; the implementation of policies toward intellectuals; communication with outsiders; railroad political atmosphere, and work style. Additionally, party organizations oversee propaganda, research, retired cadres, politics and law, secrecy (*baomi bangongshi*), arts and literature, as well as political thinking. Finally, the labor union manages propaganda and education, production, quality of life, women's issues, and sports, while the youth league carries out youth work and study groups. All of this ideological work is carried out by Party committees that are part of every station, every work team, every school, clinic, and quarry.

During my interviews with the primary authors of this compendium, the four-person staff of the Sub-Bureau History Chronicles Office (*Shizhi Bangongshi*), one railway writer described this immensely complex organization at every level of the system in terms of a machine gone crazy with redundant productivity. The machine he was referring to was the Chinese Communist Party which, in its administrative mode, appeared to have a strong tendency to produce complexity and reiterations. The Chinese Communist Party attempted to blanket its domain with rules, activities, and supervisory personnel, leaving nothing to chance. This tendency to master all spaces by the insertion of some device of control is reminiscent of the *horror vacuii* of the medieval manuscript illuminator, who feared that leaving any part of his page unadorned would give the devil opportunity to work.[6]

Within the railway, certain tasks are not negotiable. All railway stations need signal operators, switchmen, yard workers, mechanics, engineers, freight shipment clerks, ticket agents, station masters, engine drivers, and so forth. Although there are relatively few tasks in the railway organization that must be carried out by Party members, the railway counts a very high proportion of Party members among its personnel (see Table 4.1).

Of 41,891 employees in 1990, 32 percent (16,147) were members of either the Chinese Communist Party or the Communist Youth League (CYL membership grooms people under the age of twenty-five for party membership), whereas figures for 1986 show that Party members constituted 4.2 percent of China's population. The eight-fold difference in Party membership in railway organizations compared to the general population combined with the large number of offices at sub-bureau headquarters devoted to issues of secrecy and discipline suggests that the disciplinary/surveillance role of railway work units is well developed.

Table 4.1 Party and Youth League affiliation among Nanjing Railway employees

	Total	*CCP*	*CYL*	*Party affiliation (%)*
Nanjing Railway employees	41,891	9,363	6,784	32
Cadres	8,643	4,274	1,053	60
Workers	33,248	5,089	5,731	30

Source: *Nanjing Tielu Fenju Nianjian [Nanjing Railway Sub-Bureau Yearbook]* (1991), Nanjing: Nanjing Railway History Compilation Group.

An economics lesson with Chinese characteristics

A few days after our visit to the railway station, Xiao Shu took me to the home of an old friend of his named Wu, a philosophy professor in the local Party institute for training railway cadres. Professor Wu described a series of thorny problems that would make reform within the railway system especially difficult. To illustrate the principles underlying railway work organization, he sketched a diagram that showed that modes of production consist of relations of production (ownership relations, the relationships between people, and distribution relations) and forces of production (the workers, their tools, and raw materials). Surrounding these terms, up and down, and in the margins, he jotted another series of terms to capture the cultural specificity of China's problems – the "Chinese characteristics" often referred to, yet seldom spelled out in official declarations.

These were: *daigou*, or generation gap, which he glossed as "the difference between consciousness and attitude of workers today compared to the 1950s;" *xueyuan*, or blood ties; *jinqin fanzhi* or inbreeding; *qundai guanxi*, literally "apron string connections," figuratively used to indicate relationships through one's female relatives; here the term indicates the complicated kin relations that inflect work relations; and *wanhan baogan* "ten thousand things guaranteed within," a phrase used to describe the heavy burden of obligation carried by railway work units. I would like to add one more term which emerged repeatedly as friends would explain *danwei* logic to me – *feishui bu wang wai liu* "don't let your fertilizer run off into other people's fields."

Together, these terms provide a fairly comprehensive "emic" view of the conflicting values that shape the way things work in China's railroads. These practical logics are exterior to the closed world of economic theory, and are largely invisible to it, but to local people, they went a long way toward explaining why things were the way they are and how they got that way. These idiomatic expressions describe common-sense understandings of the world, confirmed through lived experience, and generative of behaviors that, in context, make sense. They constitute a *habitus* (Bourdieu 1990). The expressions reveal a dynamic centripetal pull inward toward the familiar, literally and figuratively, as well as a common-sense tendency to avoid people or entities external to the sphere of loyalty created by mutual belonging. By exploring these terms in ethnographic detail we gain an understanding of an interesting paradox that emerged in many analyses of socialist societies – namely the active production of atomized communities within a setting that explicitly celebrated collective values.[7] We are also able to understand the formidable obstacles to effective reform from the railway workers' situated view.

Generation gap

In the years of occupation and war that preceded the establishment of the People's Republic, much of China's rail system was destroyed. As the People's Liberation Army extended its domain during the civil war from 1946 to 1949, soldiers were mobilized as "railway columns" (*tiedao zongdui*) to repair strategic lengths of track in support of the war effort (ZTJ 1990: 11). These efforts were later held up as signs of the good stewardship that the Chinese Communist Party and its army provided to national infrastructure, and by extension, might be expected to provide to the nation as a whole.

In the first decade of Communist Party rule, the railway system was a choice destination for members of the PLA now that their revolutionary battles were won. For in the 1950s, the railway was conceived of as a tool of national defense as much as a tool of trade. What had been a specific branch of the military, the railway columns, split off and became a branch of railway organization instead. Demobilized soldiers from the PLA made lateral moves into positions of administrative authority and railwaymen who had joined the profession before 1949 were gradually divested of major responsibilities, but for the most part they were kept on for their expertise and experience.

In principle, there were no restrictions other than those of good class background on who might begin a career in the railway system, but in fact, it took good connections for a person to land an iron rice bowl with the trains. Higher than average pay and better than average benefits, as well as access to the rare privilege of travel or to goods and information from distant places, gave workers who belonged to the railway system greater prestige and security, not to mention cultural capital, than their peers outside the system enjoyed.[8] Military officers regarded the railway system as a desirable place for their children, thus a significant proportion of people in good railway jobs had genealogical links to the powerful and prestigious People's Liberation Army.

During the Cultural Revolution, when expertise became suspect, people with more oppressed family backgrounds found their way into jobs with the system.[9] Many well-trained engineers had to undergo scrutiny, and many lost their positions to workers who may have been poorly trained in mechanics, but were highly skilled in appearing "red." But the most powerful legacy that remains in the railway system today from Cultural Revolution times relates to the massive relocations of people it forced.

When the Cultural Revolution ended in 1976,[10] many urban sons and daughters were living as peasants, having been "sent down" to the countryside in the late 1960s or early 1970s. Returning to the city without a residence permit and a job meant that the sent-down son or daughter would be a liability that no family could afford. Competition for desirable urban jobs had always been stiff, but it became extraordinarily high during the late 1970s and the first half of the 1980s. The right of a railroad worker to bequeath his or her position to kin had been practiced since 1953 as a kind of insurance for families dependent on a worker in the case of death or injury.[11] But beginning in 1979, the *dingti* system of replacing one worker for another led many able, experienced, and well-trained older workers to take early retirement so that their children might inherit their secure state sector jobs. To national planners, this trend was not in the best interests of the system as a whole; the *dingti* system was abolished in 1986, but a cognate practice continued informally under the name of *neizhao*, or internal hiring,[12] and was prevalent throughout the state sector.

Blood ties

Most railway workers I met or surveyed entered their railway jobs through the process of *dingti*, *neizhao* or *fenpei*.[13] The *fenpei* process channeled graduates of railway-run middle schools into railway jobs or railway technical training institutes, thus thickening the web of kinship connections within the system. Another entry route followed by a striking number of young men who had been born between the late 1950s and late 1960s was by lateral transfer from the military or *diaodong*. In 1985, the ranks of the army were swollen with young men who had joined in order to leave the rural places the Cultural Revolution had exiled them to. In that year, the military reduced its forces by 20 percent. Losing so many well-trained, and potentially restive young men into the ranks of the "waiting for work youth" (*daiye qingnian*),[14] was not in the best interests of social stability. Soldiers were therefore encouraged to transfer to railroad work.

Additionally, three decades before contemporary marketizing trends gave state-run enterprises a mandate to "diversify," the railway system had created a wide array of subsidiary enterprises, many only distantly, if at all, connected to the business of running a railroad. The reason for creating these subsidiary enterprises was not to produce monetary profits – the rationale that underwrites much contemporary diversification. Instead, the railway's subsidiaries, such as laundries, barbers, and snack vendors, were established to produce a different kind of profit. They were created for the primary purpose of "taking care of" the unemployed children and kinfolk of permanent workers. The "care" represented by employment in a sub-sidiary railway enterprise had material and symbolic dimensions: It provided respectable and secure work, a *danwei* as a unit of belonging, and it increased the income of the household. Without such "care," permanent workers in stressful positions of responsibility could not be expected to work with the requisite "peaceful heart and steady concentration" (*anxin tashi*) needed for the operation of dangerous and valuable equipment. Profit is thus conceived in terms that differ from those of neo-classical economics.

Inbreeding

These historical legacies have created a railway system staffed by workers who are not simply interchangeable cogs. The system that was often described to me as semi-militarized is also remarkably "familialized." The relatively incestuous patterns of hiring from the military and from kin networks produced the situation Professor Wu referred to with the four character expression from biology, *jinqin fanzhi*, which, character by character, is "close kin breed." And just as narrowing the gene pool is thought to diminish the quality and health of biological species, the practices of job inheritance and internal recruitment were said in the early 1990s to have had serious effects on the quality of the work force. According to one researcher:

> Experienced and skilled staff and workers were retiring earlier, and the new workers lacked training. Among families, *dingti* and *neizhao* were regarded as a "salvation" to secure positions for the least capable children. Other children capable of getting jobs through state assignment programs or individual applications did not have to rely on their parents for jobs. School students who wished to take over their parents' jobs appeared to be those who were poorly motivated to strive for high educational achievement.
>
> (Bian 1994: 66).

Interestingly, of five interview subjects Bian uses to illustrate these familial recruitment strategies, two are Tianjin railway workers.

Apron string connections

One of Bian's interview subjects, Ms. Zhou, was a train conductor recruited through *neizhao*:

> I graduated from a senior-high school that was managed by the rail-road bureau of Tianjin. The majority of students in that school were from families whose members worked in the railroad system; so was I.

My father was a senior worker in a railroad factory. Everybody knew railroad jobs were better – a lot of prestige, higher salaries, and many benefits. It was easier to get an apartment in the railroad industry too. I easily got assigned to the railroad bureau because I was from a "railroad family." It was considered a kind of *neizhao*, a tradition in the railroad industry. But it was harder to get a good assignment *within* the bureau. I got help from the chief of the bureau's labor office, who was a good friend of one of my mother's brothers. I was extremely happy to be assigned as a conductor in the Tianjin to Shanghai fleet; that was the best line managed by the bureau.

(ibid.: 68)

The concept of apron string connections, or nepotism, explains Ms. Zhou's good fortune in being assigned to be a conductor on the prestigious Tianjin to Shanghai route. The help of her mother's brother's well-placed friend secured her the position. Among my friends and acquaintances in the railway system, Shen Yong was exceptional for being the only college graduate among railway workers I knew, and for being one of the least well connected. As a bright and hardworking boy from rural Jiangsu he tested into a keypoint school and from there tested into the Lanzhou Railway Engineering Institute. With his engineering degree, Shen Yong was automatically classified as a technical cadre. He was not, however, a member of the Communist Party, and generally avoided party activism and organizations. This lack of kinship connections combined with his utter lack of interest in cultivating useful connections resulted in his assignment to the smallest and poorest of the railway yards in the territory of the Nanjing Bureau. Shen Yong, who did computer analyses of his work unit's productivity, was supervised by an older cadre who literally did not know his alphabet (a standard system in railway engineering usage). He stands as a good illustration of someone with absolutely none of the connections that Professor Wu lamented were so rife throughout the system.

Ten thousand things

Wanshi baohan, "ten thousand things guaranteed within" describes the comprehensive nature of what the work unit provides. Another synonym for the *danwei*'s range of activities, *wanshi bu qiu ren* translates as "for ten thousand things one need not seek a person [from outside]." With this term, the important exclusionary effects of the *danwei*'s comprehensive qualities are indicated. For ten thousand needs and services, one need not seek outside help. Those close to one, sheltered by the same overarching umbrella, can provide all one would ever need.

Part of the purpose of creating a system of virtually all-inclusive *danwei* was to eliminate the need for market relationships because they were, in the eyes of China's communist architects, morally and politically suspect.

Ironically, however, it seems that the collectivization of urban China into cellular *danwei* actually succeeded in *creating* suspicion and competition throughout the nation's institutional landscape. *Danwei* themselves, as corporate actors, tended to avoid contacts with other *danwei* unless a friendly relationship had been forged. Forging mutually beneficial relationships between *danweis* produced *guanxi hu* or "connected units."

There was very little interdependence among the *danwei* of a city or between large-scale agricultural collectives.[15] Instead, *danwei* tended toward self-sufficiency. This tendency was celebrated as "Chairman Mao's great principle of self-reliance" (Donnithorne 1972: 606). As such, it reached its apogee at moments of extreme Maoist fervor – the Great Leap Forward (1959–1961) and the Cultural Revolution (1966–1969). But even in times when non-Maoist economic values dominated, such as 1962–1965[16] and the present, post-Deng era, the legacy of minimizing interactions with individual and institutional outsiders remains.[17]

In Maoist times, self-reliance was an avowedly collective concept. Individuals or individual families who attempted to be self-reliant were vigorously opposed in official pronouncements. "Self-reliance implies the ability to improvise out of one's own resources, rather than rely on planned co-ordination and state investment grants" (ibid.: 607). The flip side of this virtuous self-reliance is revealed with the notion of *feishui bu wang wai liu*, a concept not included in Professor Wu's presentation, but which emerged in many conversations about the *danwei* system and serves as a bridge between the *danwei* as a provider of things to itself and the *danwei* as a provider of employment to people.

Husband your own fertilizer

"Don't let your fertilizer leak out into others' fields" (*feishui bu wang wai liu*), a cardinal principle of Chinese agriculture, conveys the sense that one will not benefit by letting one's resources run off to enrich someone else's land. This logic shapes *danwei* behavior with regard to both goods and personnel – both are hoarded, lest their value be wasted on someone with whom one has no connection.[18]

Zhang Zhong, a worker-intellectual retired from the Puzhen Railway Car Factory explained how the principle worked in his factory.

> Now that there are so many petty commodities on the market, our factory has opened up a series of little shops that supply everyday objects and some luxury items. The idea is that we'll earn our workers' money instead of having some outside business enjoy it. Similarly, if there is some support function that our factory needs and we ourselves don't have the capacity to accomplish it, we'll give the task to our auxiliary factory (*fushu chang*). We won't let other people earn our money.

When I asked others about this phenomenon, many cited the example of China's postal service. Mail is delivered to the gatekeepers of *danwei*, or collected from the large green cylindrical receptacles that stand on city streets, by men and women who ride distinctive bicycles. These bicycles are large and clunky, painted green, and fitted with durable canvas panniers. The vehicles are produced in factories run by the postal service. In a nation of bicycle riders, post office bikes are widely recognized as second-rate, inferior to the brands of bicycles that people ride, given choice. But this inferiority is understood as an inevitable outcome of the practice of procuring supplies from within. The postal service's bicycle factories have a captive audience for their products. There is no fear that they will lack customers, and so no need to improve the quality of their vehicles.

This tendency to supply from within converges with the tendency to hire from within. And both generate concerns about quality. The quality of workers, the quality of their commitment to doing good work, and the low morale among younger railway workers were tangled together in Professor Wu's late night lesson.

Conclusion

To return now to the crowded scene at the station during flood season: How do the sketch of railway administrative structure and the terms Professor Wu used to explain the cultural complexity of Chinese relations of production help us understand the lack of disciplined work or service that day in the railway station? And what implications do that scene and those terms have for understanding the panorama of everyday life in post-Mao China?

At the rail station that day, people in their proper place were rewarded by the low pressure and scant expectations of their productivity or service. People out of their proper place – i.e., people traveling without the protective talisman of a letter from a *danwei* authorizing them to be on the road, away from where they are registered to be – ran the calculated risk of encountering Kafkaesque difficulties in a landscape overlaid with invisible yet palpable grids of bureaucratic control. Institutional structures such as the *danwei* system were created to enhance government control over individuals, yet their paradoxical effect produces demographic and material conditions conducive to traditional familistic values and destructive of more abstract bases for solidarity.

Professor Wu's economics lesson shows that both railway workers and railway units are encumbered by complicated genealogies that slow down any straightforward rationalizing process. The genealogy of the *danwei* as an institution and the genealogies of many of the individual workers who belong to it reveal strong ties, at both levels of analysis, to the military and to kin groups. These cultural forms generate particular loyalties and logics that challenge the ability of any regime to control what happens on the ground.

The architects of China's planned society and economy consciously intended to *eliminate* horizontal relationships created through market exchanges when they designed the *danwei* system.

> Since the role of markets in carrying out a principle of fairness was suspect in the minds of the leaders, they naturally felt that it would be a superior method to have the state carry out allocation through administrative arrangements, especially since this latter mode can epitomize the care and concern that the party-state has for the working masses.[19]
>
> (Lu 1993: 57)

Elizabeth Perry has argued that the very institution of the *danwei* was itself divisive, creating a gulf between the haves and have-nots of Chinese socialism that has fueled major strike waves in every decade of China's history since 1949 (1997: 13, 44). In a similar vein, Lü Xiaobo (1994) has analyzed the "rising waves" of corruption that have emerged with the increasing decentralization of economic decision-making in the PRC since the late 1970s. He presents persuasive evidence to argue that the revolutionary origins of the *danwei* system and its subsequent development go a long way toward explaining the "unhealthy" and "irregular" tendencies that have emerged in the reform era. Institutional causes embedded in history, rather than individual behaviors explain this phenomenon. The construction of *danwei* as corporate entities came to enact what I think of as "state Hobbesianism." That is, by containing people, *danwei* create segments of the included and the excluded. The creation of regions of inclusion and exclusion in a context of competition over scarce goods and opportunities fosters jealousy and protectionism, and spoils the opportunity for the cultivation of social trust. *Danwei* appear to have been distrustful and competitive by nature, and that nature, like all nature, was not merely given, but was produced by environmental influences, in this case the environment produced by the PRC's shifting but always centralized political economy, as well as by inherited dispositions, in this case, the cultural idioms of kinship, friendship, and reciprocity through which social relationships are made meaningful in the Chinese context.

The belief that outside the protective walls of the *danwei*, life is "nasty, brutish, and short" seems to be a self-fulfilling prophecy of China's socialist regime. This legacy invested the environment in which market transactions were beginning to take place with a very uneven quality.[20]

Notes

1 Han Dongfang, a Beijing railway worker who co-founded an independent labor union in the late 1980s and played an important role in the protests of 1989, is exceptional. Han presently runs the worker support group out of Hong Kong. In

my research I did not attempt to get close to workers who actively protested their conditions, out of concern not to increase official discomfort with my interest in understanding "normal" conditions of railway workers.

2 An FAO document from 1999 lists China's 1991 flood season among the eighteen most devastating flood disasters in the world since 1421. Unfortunately, China and its rapidly developing neighbor states have since experienced worse flooding in terms of economic value and human lives lost. These losses are directly linked to land degradation associated with economic development.

3 This, according to a 1988 Beijing survey, which found that the eight professions with the worst reputation among the public were, in order, tax agents, business regulators, grass-roots officials, reporters, medical professionals, police, railway workers, and mid-level officials. See Ge Yaoliang, "*Guanyu woguo shimin zhengzhi gaige yishi he xintai de fenxi*" [An analysis of psychological state and opinion of Chinese citizens on political reform], *Qiuce yu Xinxi*, 1989, no. 1, pp. 36–40. Cited in Lü (1994: 34).

4 Rofel (1989, 1999) analyzes the reform era critique of Maoist work practices as it reorganizes the order of things in Hangzhou's silk factories. Anagnost (1997) considers how the State uses the "quality" idiom to reimagine the subjects it rules, even as it reimagines the reasons that authorize it to do so.

5 China's railway system is divided into twelve administrative regions that correspond more closely to China's eight military regions than to the borders that divide the country into twenty-one provinces, five autonomous regions, and four independent cities. A cadre at the Guangzhou station, describing the organizational hierarchy encompassing his station, observed that the Guangzhou Railway Bureau Chief (*Guangzhou Tielu Juzhang*) was effectively more powerful than the Governor of Guangdong Province (*Guangzhou Shengzhang*) because the Bureau Chief's jurisdiction covered not one but three provinces – Guangdong, Hunan, Hainan Island, as well as Hong Kong and Macao. This observation hints at the obvious: neither provincial governors nor railway bureau chiefs are mere functionaries who serve as transmission belts for directions from central authority. Provincial or institutional domains provide distinct situational advantages for the masters of the turf.

6 In his intriguing study of leisure time, Shaoguang Wang notes that in the early 1960s, the Party began to develop a new thesis of leisure: "Spare time could not be a 'political vacuum'; it was filled by either 'proletarian ideas' or 'bourgeois ideas.' Because of this ideological innovation, leisure became increasingly politicized" (1995: 154). Wang's account suggests that the *horror vacui* analysis is not overdrawn.

7 Istvan Rev is one of many scholars who have explored this issue in Eastern European contexts. In his 1987 work he demonstrates that the rationality of national planning created conditions that forced peasants to dissimulate. Good examples of atomization and alienation with Chinese characteristics are in literature, such as Liu Binyan's famous reportage, "People or Monsters," and Wang Anyi's "The Destination."

8 In listing the average annual incomes of residents of the metropolitan area, the 1990 Yearbook of Nanjing divides work-units first by jurisdiction: Central, Provincial, and City and below. Annual salaries decrease with decentralization, from averages of 2,423, to 2,387, to 1,984 *yuan*, respectively. Divided by occupation, salaries have a greater spread: from a high of 2,906 for "whole people" workers for the Transport and Communications systems, to a low of 1,248 for the average worker on a collective farm (NJNJ 1990: 605–606). Additionally, the supply of uniforms and access to housing, travel and schools gave railway workers distinct material advantages.

9 See Billeter (1985), Kraus (1982), Shirk (1984), and Watson (1984) for

expositions of class and class-status in post-revolutionary China. Perry and Li's remarkable (1997) monograph shows how class categories were strategically used by factions of the Shanghai working class during the Cultural Revolution.

10 Official periodization labels the years 1966–1976, the Cultural Revolution. However, Lynn White III (1998: 11–16) provides a very satisfying explanation for why we should treat this periodization with suspicion. Rofel (1989) makes a similar case.

11 According to Dittmar and Lü:

> As early as 1953 "the revised draft of the labor insurance regulations" intro-duced the idea of occupational inheritance. In the years that followed, many circulars and directives were issued on this matter; it is notable how many restrictions and qualifications the government placed on the practice. The policy seems to have been essentially reactive rather than active in the sense that most of the documents were replies by central authorities to local or ministerial authorities on the matter. This has prompted some scholars to suggest that the regulations represent a codification of practices long estab-lished at the grass roots under local sanction.
>
> (1996: 261, note 34)

12 Korzec (1992) provides a brilliant analysis of these practices and argues that largely because of them, the Chinese reforms are doomed to failure.

13 *Fenpei*, literally, "distribute," is used for inanimate objects, like supplies, and for people. A more colloquial English language equivalent would be "assign," but that word loses the flavor of China's planning culture, wherein people discuss their own trajectories in passive terms, indicating that they too are resources, allocated according to the mandates of central planning.

14 "Waiting" for work, because there can be no unemployment in China, only delays in distribution of people into the units they belong in.

15 Economists have charted the oscillating tendencies toward centralization and decentralization in China since 1949. Centralization correlates with bureau-cratic power and complexity; decentralization signifies a local (not individual) self-reliance that obviates the multiple managerial layers that Mao found so problematic. The Great Leap Forward (1959–1961) and the Cultural Revolu-tion (1966–1969) were moments of radical decentralization. But throughout these ebbs and flows, regardless of the degree of centralization, the identity and membership in local collectives – *danwei* and collective farms remained power-ful.

16 In this period, following the Great Leap Forward, Liu Shaoqi advocated local specialization and other economists encouraged methods of supply that would cross administrative boundaries in the interest efficiency and rationality (Don-nithorne 1972: 610–611).

17 The cultural construction of risk, and the placement of the conceptual line that divides insiders from outsiders are both undergoing radical change as China marketizes. In her 1998 ethnography of the Shanghai stock market, Ellen Hertz provides very insightful analyses of these shifts.

18 It explains individual behavior as well. Shang Aiyi who shopped and cooked for my husband and me a few times a week, scolded me once for giving away a large collection of empty soy sauce, vinegar, and beer bottles to a person, a total stranger to me, collecting rubbish. "Giving to a stranger is giving wasted," she explained (*Ba dongxi songgei moshengren jiushi bai song dongxi*). Even though the empties were garbage to me, if there were value to be found in them, the value should go to someone connected to me, and thus worthy. And thus deepening my connection...

19 This array of provision is often telegraphically rendered as, "*shenglaobingsi,*

yishizhuxing," which translates as: birth–old age–illness–death, clothing–food–dwelling–travel."

20 This is a great deal like "amoral familism" (Banfield 1958). But like the Schneiders showed in their ethnography of Sicily (1976), a wider historical frame reveals not a culture of amoral familism, but a reasonable response by a local community to exogenous political challenges in the name of the nation. Herzfeld explores this theme in many works (most explicitly in 1992: 53). Skinner (1971) examines similar phenomena in village China in macro-structural terms.

References

Anagnost, Ann (1997) *National Past-Times: Narrative, Representation, and Power in Modern China*, Durham, NC: Duke University Press.

Banfield, E.C. (1958) *The Moral Basis of a Backward Society*, New York: Free Press.

Bian Yanjie (1994) *Work and Inequality in Urban China*, Albany, NY: State University of New York Press.

Billeter, Jean-François (1985) "The System of 'Class-Status,'" in Stuart Schram (ed.) *The Scope of State Power in China*, London: School of Oriental and African Studies.

Bourdieu, Pierre (1990) *The Logic of Practice*, Cambridge: Polity Press.

Dittmer, Lowell and Lü Xiaobo (1996) "Personal Politics in the Chinese *Danwei* Under Reform," *Asian Survey*, 36(3): 246–267.

Donnithorne, Audrey (1972) "China's Cellular Economy: Some Economic Trends since the Cultural Revolution," *The China Quarterly*, 52: 605–619.

Hertz, Ellen (1998) *The Trading Crowd: An Ethnography of the Shanghai Stock Market*, Cambridge: Cambridge University Press.

Herzfeld, Michael (1992) *The Social Production of Indifference: Exploring the Symbolic Roots of Western Bureaucracy*, New York: Berg.

Korzec, Michael (1992) *Labour and the Failure of Reform in China*, New York: St. Martin's Press.

Kraus, Richard (1982) *Class Conflict in Chinese Socialism*, New York: Columbia University Press.

Liu Binyan (1983) "People or Monsters?" in Perry Link (ed.) *People or Monsters? and Other Stories and Reportage from China after Mao*, Bloomington, IN: Indiana University Press.

Lu Feng (1993) "The Origins and Formation of the Unit (*Danwei*) System," *Chinese Sociology and Anthropology*, 25(3), entire issue.

Lü Xiaobo (1994) "'Small Public' vs. 'Big Public': the *Danwei* Regime and Institutional Corruption," paper presented at Association of Asian Studies annual meeting in Boston, 24–27 March.

Lü Xiaobo and Elizabeth Perry (1997) "Introduction: The Changing Chinese Workplace in Historical and Comparative Perspective," in Lü Xiaobo and Elizabeth Perry (eds) *Danwei: The Changing Chinese Workplace in Historical and Comparative Perspective*, Armonk, NY: M.E. Sharpe.

Nanjing Nianjian [Nanjing Yearbook] (1990) Nanjing: Nanjing Gazetteer Publishing Group.

Nanjing Tielu Fenju Nianjian [Nanjing Railway Sub-Bureau Yearbook] (1991) Nanjing: Nanjing Railway History Compilation Group.

Perry, Elizabeth (1997) "From Native Place to Workplace: Labor Origins and Outcomes of China's *Danwei* System," in Lü Xiaobo and Elizabeth Perry (eds) *Danwei: The Changing Chinese Workplace in Historical and Comparative Perspective*, Armonk, NY: M.E. Sharpe.

Perry, Elizabeth and Li Xun (1997) *Proletarian Power: Shanghai in the Cultural Revolution*, Boulder, CO: Westview Press.

Rev, Istvan (1987) "The Advantages of Being Atomized: How Hungarian Peasants Coped with Collectivism," *Dissent*, 34(3): 335–350.

Rofel, Lisa (1989) "Hegemony and Productivity in Post-Mao China," in Arif Dirlik and Maurice Meisner (eds) *Marxism and the Chinese Experience: Issues in Contemporary Chinese Socialism*, Armonk, NY: M.E. Sharpe.

Rofel, Lisa (1999) *Other Modernities: Gendered Yearnings in China after Socialism*, Berkeley, CA: University of California Press.

Schneider, Jane and Schneider, Peter (1976) *Culture and Political Economy in Western Sicily*, New York: Academic Press.

Shirk, Susan (1984) "The Decline of Virtuocracy in China," in James Watson (ed.) *Class and Social Stratification in Post-Revolution China*, Cambridge: Cambridge University Press.

Skinner, G. William (1971) "Chinese Peasants and the Closed Community: An Open and Shut Case," *Comparative Studies in Society and History*, 13(3): 270–281.

Walder, Andrew (1989) "Factory and Manager in an Era of Reform," *The China Quarterly*, 118: 242–264.

Wang Anyi (1989) "The Destination," in *Best Chinese Stories, 1949–1989*, Beijing: Panda Books.

Wang Shaoguang (1995) "The Politics of Private Time: Changing Leisure Patterns in Urban China" in Deborah Davis, Richard Kraus, Barry Naughton, and Elizabeth Perry (eds) *Urban Spaces in Contemporary China: The Potential for Autonomy and Community in Post-Mao China*, Washington, DC: Woodrow Wilson Center Press and Cambridge University Press.

Watson, James (1984) "Class and Class Formation in China," in James Watson (ed.) *Class and Social Stratification in Post-Revolution China*, Cambridge: Cambridge University Press.

White, Lynn T, III (1998) *Unstately Power: Local Causes of China's Economic Reforms*, vol. I, Armonk, NY: M.E. Sharpe.

Zhongguo Jiaotong Nianjian [Chinese Transportation Yearbook] (1994) Beijing: Transportation Yearbook Publishing House.

Zhongguo Tielu Jianshe [Chinese Railroad Construction] (1990) Beijing: Chinese Railway Publishing House.

5 Serving the state, serving the people

Work in a post-socialist department store

Amy Hanser

Rising up in the heart of the city, the Harbin No. X Department Store was a setting easily associated with socialism. The store itself was a prize of the revolution, originally a foreign-owned and managed store that was nationalized even before the founding of the People's Republic in 1949. Physically, the store was vast, a massive ring of eight towering floors of cement covering an entire city block. On one inner wall, a colossal mural of a hard-hatted worker reminded store employees to be vigilant against fire as they crowded into the store every morning. Each day the store opened its doors to a highly operatic broadcast of the store song, steeped in revolutionary fervor and sung in CCTV military chorus style, entitled "Soar, Harbin No. X!"

> Great ambitions to expand, like the surging ocean!
> The spirit to engage struggle, like the lofty mountain!
> Genuine smiles win the customers' love!
> Exquisite merchandise is exchanged for a golden reputation!
> Glorious Harbin No. X! Glorious Harbin No. X! Go create a splendid
>   new era!

Although composed for the opening of the store's new building in the early 1990s, the song was infused with the language of the Chinese revolution and extolled the contributions of China's workers to a glorious future.

Harbin No. X and the organization of sales work in this state-run store raise a number of questions about workplace culture in China's context of rapid social change. What are the legacies of socialism in the Chinese workplace? What are the consequences for workplace culture and the labor process? And most importantly, how might workplace culture serve as a resource for workers as they negotiate daily work demands?

In this chapter, I argue that the state-run Harbin No. X Department Store was a workplace bearing the indelible marks of state socialism, in terms of employment practices, labor process, and work culture. I first show that close ties to the local Party-state enabled Harbin No. X to essentially maintain an "iron rice bowl" of secure employment for its workers.

Store managers, preoccupied with local state agencies instead of the sales floor, left sales clerks relatively free from managerial intervention. The resulting work culture was characterized by a "negative class consciousness" – a critique of managerial authority – and assertions of worker control and professionalism. The store's work culture was also reflected in egalitarian service interactions that proceeded on a basis of customer–worker parity.

I should emphasize that I am not arguing that service work at Harbin No. X was the same as that found in pre-reform China – it was not – but rather that the organization of work and the quality of interactions in the store were clearly shaped by pre-reform, state-socialist social relations. Indeed, as this chapter will show, work culture can structure a durable set of dispositions deeply embedded in the practices of the managers and workers who make up a work organization (Schoenberger 1997). French sociologist Pierre Bourdieu pointed to the "harmony" between objective social structures and subjective orientations. An organization only comes to life if, "like a garment or a house [it] finds someone who ... feels sufficiently at home in it to take it on" (Bourdieu 1981: 309, cited in Powell and DiMaggio 1991: 26). In other words, largely unspoken values, dispositions, and practices deposited in individuals and groups help explain why social structures, housed in work institutions, endure. Those institutions are reproduced through the daily practices of individual social actors who feel "at home" in them.

The Harbin No. X Department Store, with a history shaped by the social and economic organization of pre-reform China, offers an opportunity to consider questions of cultural durability in the workplace. It was a retail setting in which important elements of a socialist organization have proved resilient through the course of economic reforms – certain "objective" employment practices, as well as a more "subjective" workplace culture, prominent features of which I characterize as socialist. The attitudes, values, and practices of Harbin No. X work culture all made up the "tool kit" (Swidler 1986) that Harbin workers relied upon to structure their daily work activities in the store.

I base this chapter upon data gathered in China between 2001 and 2002, when I conducted participant observation in several department stores and market places in the north-eastern city of Harbin. At the Harbin No. X Department Store (a pseudonym), I spent over two months working as an uniformed sales clerk in the women's department. I also conducted interviews with workers, store managers, merchandise suppliers, and other industry experts and conducted archival research on institutional changes to China's retail sector. This chapter draws most heavily upon my sales floor experiences at the department store and with the workers who made their "home" there.

A socialist work unit

The Harbin No. X Department Store of 2001 retained many institutional orientations rooted in China's pre-reform, planned economy era. Having enjoyed a privileged position within the state hierarchy prior to 1979, Harbin No. X's links to and dependencies upon the local city government and party organs continued through the reform period. This situation allowed the store to retain the central elements of the pre-reform employment system. Economic reforms had, of course, dramatically altered the way the store engaged in the business of retailing. In the early 1990s, the store shifted from turning over all its profits to the state and instead was taxed at the standard rate for state-owned enterprises. From the 1980s, workers were shifted from flat monthly wages to a commission sales system. In 2001, workers' health and retirement benefits also underwent change. Store workers were enrolled in social welfare programs sponsored by the city government and into which they were required to make individual, monthly contributions. As a result, the store no longer shouldered the full social welfare burden for its workers.

However, the store had remained a traditional, state work unit in a number of key respects. Unlike newer department stores in China which often employ only young women under the age of thirty, many of Harbin No. X's sales clerks were middle-aged workers who had worked at the store for ten or even twenty years. Workers still effectively enjoyed an "iron rice bowl," and although sales clerks had technically shifted to a contract system, they expected to work at the store until they retired or perhaps left in pursuit of better opportunities. Store managers claimed they were unable to fire workers, unless the individuals engaged in illegal activities, and they could not recall a single instance of having let a worker go. Managers also believed that, given the high rates of unemployment in Harbin, city government would not allow the store to add to the pool of unemployed. As one top manager at the store explained,

> When people enter a state enterprise, it is [still] expected to be a lifetime relationship. If you try to fire someone, the labor bureau (*laodongju*) will probably intervene ... You might tell someone they have to leave, and they'll say back to you, "Well, I'm just not leaving."

The inability to fire workers was just one example of how managers felt little sense of authority or control in the store. Indeed, reforms had done little to truly separate enterprise from state, and municipal commerce officials still maintained *de facto* control over the store. Although store ownership had been converted to stock, the government retained a formal 33 percent stake in the enterprise and in practice controlled the 33 percent interest retained by the store itself (the remaining shares were owned by staff and management). City officials also controlled the store through its general manager, an external Party cadre appointed by the municipal commerce bureau who was expected to approve every managerial decision of any importance. As a result, the managers below him, many of whom had worked their way up the store hierarchy from sales clerk positions, expressed little interest in the major business affairs of the store. "Store management doesn't have a say (*bu shuo de suan*)," one manager explained to me after I witnessed her tell another manager that an important store matter could not be decided until the general manager returned from a business trip. "The city commerce committee still sends down a plan (*xia jihua*)," another manager commented. "We basically have to respond to the demands of those above us."

Continued links to the local Party-state meant that despite mounting financial woes, managers felt confident the store would not go bankrupt. Although Harbin No. X owed the local government loans exceeding 500 million *yuan* (over US$60 million) (Ji 2002) and experienced serious cash flow problems in the slow summer months, store managers repeatedly assured me that the state would not allow the store to fail. The upshot of continued state involvement in the store was that not only did managers feel they lacked control over the store, but they also felt sufficiently insulated from the market to safely ignore much of the daily business on the store's sales floors. Workers, secure in their jobs, were largely left to their own devices.

A socialist work culture

Secure employment combined with an inattentive management made the sales floor into a relatively autonomous domain for workers. It was also a space bearing the clear marks of China's experiences with state socialism, and sales clerks at the state-run retailer cultivated a work culture infused with the stated, if not realized, egalitarian values of socialism.

Work culture in a service work setting can provide workers with the resources to stake claims and challenge managerial control on the sales floor. In her study of American department stores, Susan Porter Benson defines work culture as "the ideology and practice with which workers stake out a relatively autonomous sphere of action on the job" (1986: 228). Work culture "guides and interprets the tasks and social relations of work," becoming "an inextricable part of the work process itself" (Melosh 1982: 5–6). Benson describes how the sales floor became a space where workers asserted themselves collectively through self-organization of work, a sense of professionalism and selling skill, and strategies to handle both managers and customers (Benson 1986, Chapter 6).

Many of these elements could be found at Harbin No. X, ranging from the flouting of managerial rules to the collective development of selling skills and techniques. However, the work culture at Harbin No. X also bore the imprint of China's experiences with state socialism: workers frequently invoked socialist values and engaged in an explicit, almost Marxist, critique of inequality in the workplace and especially of managerial authority over workers. This critical worker consciousness is a key reason I characterize work culture at Harbin No. X as "socialist."

Ethnographies of life under state socialism identified a critical consciousness grounded in both the ideology and material relations of the state socialist system. Michael Burawoy and János Lukács have argued that the transparency of state power under state socialism produced "a heightened consciousness of the discrepancy between ideology and reality, between proclamation and experience" (1992: 82). Whereas under capitalism, the sale of a worker's labor power takes place through the obscuring mediation of the market, under socialism, labor and its products are clearly appropriated by state. This results in a kind of "negative class consciousness" that enables people to criticize the state and social reality for failing to live up to ideological claims (Burawoy and Lukács 1992: 114).[1] In Eastern Europe, the lived experience of state socialism, and the political rituals that punctuated it, formed the basis for a highly skeptical orientation towards the socialist state and the power it wielded (Drakulic 1991; Verdery 1998). In the Hungarian steel mill where Burawoy labored as a furnaceman, farcical political performances – such as the "cleaning" of a dirty industrial workplace for the Prime Minister's visit – highlighted for workers how much everyday reality departed from state propaganda (Burawoy and Lukács 1992).

There was evidence of a similar orientation in pre-reform China, where decades of state-orchestrated class struggle and revolution-making – the Cultural Revolution in particular – generated an extensive, and explicit, toolkit with which to critique authority relations in the workplace. Factory workers would use work hours and work unit goods to meet personal needs in an effort to "reclaim time and material goods from the enterprise in a situation where compensation was perceived to be insufficient" (Walder 1986: 215). This was a reversal of the usual power relationship between the socialist state and its subjects, and the creation, in the words of Mayfair Yang, of a "sphere of oppositional tactics" that *"redistributes* what the state economy has already distributed" (1994: 204, emphasis in original).

In China, anthropologist Lisa Rofel has situated this "negative class consciousness" in the cohort of Chinese workers who came of age during the Cultural Revolution and for whom "the radical questioning of authority as well as the politicization of everyday life became ... commonsense knowledge" (Rofel 1999: 166). In Rofel's study, this oppositional "politics of authority" was most clearly expressed on the factory shop floor, where workers resisted attempts to impose new, production-oriented controls by taking extended cigarette and rest breaks and disregarding managerial attempts at stricter discipline (see also Rofel 1992). Rofel holds that this mindset was historically contingent, tied to the era in which a specific cohort of workers came of age, rather than the result of a general, state socialist organization of production as Burawoy and Lukács argue.

But at Harbin No. X, an oppositional consciousness was not only or even primarily embedded in a particular generation. Younger workers as well as the seasoned Cultural Revolution generation could present an almost structural critique of their relationship to store management and the socialist state more generally. Workers demonstrated an acute understanding of the inequalities created under China's socialist planned economy and during the reform era. Much like the Chinese industrial workers described by Ching Kwan Lee (2000, 2002), Harbin No. X sales clerks drew upon cultural resources cultivated by state socialism to critique the state's building (or even un-building) of a failed or compromised socialism. But unlike laid-off industrial workers, employees at Harbin No. X experienced a socialist and egalitarian work culture that was grounded in the daily rhythms of work and revealed itself through routine work practices, discussions among workers, and in the course of interactions with managers. The result was a set of deeply held dispositions – a kind of socialist "habitus" – from which workers actively endeavored to make Harbin No. X an organization in which they felt at home.

Politics of authority on the sales floor

The Harbin No. X sales floor was a crucible of "negative class consciousness" forged daily through life on the sales floor. This space of autonomy and worker self-direction enabled sales clerks to engage in a "politics of authority" that both challenged managerial power and asserted worker authority and professionalism on the sales floor.

The women's clothing department at Harbin No. X occupied the store's second floor and was composed of aisle upon aisle of blouses, skirts, and pant-sets. In the winter, a large down coat area sprung up in the center of the department, where clerks worked in two- or three-person sales teams selling a single brand of merchandise. I found myself assigned to the Ice Day counter, where I joined an existing team of three: Big Sister Zhao, in her early forties; Big Sister Lin, in her late thirties; and Little Xiao, in his late twenties. Both Zhao and Lin had been at the store almost twenty years, Little Xiao for almost ten. We worked together from behind a stretch of glass counters stuffed with colorful coats (Figure 5.1).

Starting from the early 1980s, reforms had gradually altered the wage system at Harbin No. X, and stagnant wages and storewide bonuses had been replaced with standard base pay and team-based sales commissions. My co-workers equally divided a 1 percent sales commission on their monthly sales, which could double, triple, or even quadruple the basic monthly wage of 400 *yuan*. These wages were issued by the store, though the suppliers of our merchandise actually paid the costs. Given the low

Figure 5.1 Sales counter at the Harbin No. X Department Store (source: Author's photograph).

basic wage, workers actively pursued sales commissions, and on the sales counters I worked, I never witnessed workers restricting sales upon reaching a collectively recognized sales limit, what has been termed in the American literature on department stores a "stint" or "good book" (Dalton 1974; Benson 1986: 248).

A department manager and two assistant managers were in charge of daily operations in the department, and upper-level managers conducted periodic, though infrequent, inspections. Workers were subject to fines – for being late, for a sloppy work area, for chatting with one another – but in practice such penalties were infrequently applied. Management was a rare presence on the floor, and when a manager did pass, he or she was likely to focus on superficial and incidental problems like a forgotten bucket of soapy water or a sloppy work area. Workers could run errands, visit friends at other counters, or even take a nap (if well concealed) without ever being discovered. Much like the "socialist" labor processes observed elsewhere in the world (Burawoy and Lukács 1992; Warhurst 1998), this high level of autonomy also gave workers the freedom to organize their work activities, work space, and merchandise as they saw fit. The result was an idiosyncratic, but highly efficient, self-organization of work activities.

High levels of worker autonomy on the sales floor made sales clerks especially skeptical of managerial power, so it is perhaps unsurprising that open critiques of authority were most frequently roused by the relatively rare appearance of upper-level management. When upper management *did* appear – usually in some formal "inspection" sense – workers were likely to denounce the power relation between workers and management, revealing the politicized nature of work and authority on the sales floor in the process.

Just such a critique came out quite unexpectedly one day when I was quizzing Little Xiao about service inspections. A group of men from "upstairs," where management offices were located, had just passed. "Is the store stricter about inspecting service than when you first came here?" I asked Little Xiao. "This matter..." Little Xiao's voice trailed off. Then he launched the conversation in another direction: "You know, there are about 3,000 people working at this store, but only about half of them are actually salespeople who produce anything of value. We are just carrying along the rest of them. Those folks upstairs, they simply don't have anything to do, they're just whiling away the time (*tamen xianzhe*)." Xiao's comments pointed to the injustice of non-producing members of the store asserting authority over those who were truly productive. This critique was quickly directed against the realities of life under state socialism. "Those people are just where they are because they have *guanxi*, whereas the rest of us don't and can't really do anything about it. It's because of how things worked under socialism," Little Xiao continued. He used his hands to indicate that organizations that should be pyramid-shaped are instead structured like straight-sided buildings. Xiao criticized both domination by bureaucrats (who are not themselves productive) and the social realities of state socialism.

I got an earful of complaints on another occasion when, once again, a few members of upper management appeared on the sales floor. I was chatting with Xu Li-mei and "Snow Lion" Wang, sales clerks at neighboring counters. When two women wearing Harbin No. X's blue blazers passed near our counter, Li-mei and Wang straightened up, making it clear that these women were upper management inspecting sales person behavior. Wang joked that since I was present, he and Li-mei probably would not be fined. "This isn't chatting (*lauker*)," he pointed out, "it's cultural exchange (*jiaoliu*)."

"How much do they fine you, anyway?" I asked. Snow Lion Wang explained that the fine issued by upper management for chatting was 40 *yuan*. When they "write you up," a slip of paper is filled out and then the next day when you come to work you are handed the slip and expected to pay on the spot. "It's pretty brutal," Wang noted, "seeing as we don't earn that much money." According to Wang, he once was fined 70 *yuan* for being "one minute" late for work. (This was an infrequent fine only applied by upper management; department management levied a 5 *yuan* fine for lateness.) "I decided after that to get up earlier in the morning so I won't be late again, even if I have to come in running, huffing and puffing," he said.

Wang continued with his comments, his voice rising in volume. "Everyone has a say over us (*shei dou guan women*)," he said, and started rattling off a list: the department management, the store management, the human resources department, customers, newspaper reporters, and Setting Sun Red (*Xiyang Hong*), an organization for the retired. "It seems like just about everyone but the traffic police!" he quipped. At this point, Little Xiao arrived and joked that Wang was "telling the bitter history of a revolutionary family" (*tongsu geming jiashi*), a reference to the Cultural Revolution-era opera, "The Red Lantern" (*hongdengji*).

That the rhetoric of the Cultural Revolution – along with the analytical concepts of Marxism – continued to find critical, if at times ironic, usage on the sales floor hints at the close connection between workers' critiques of authority and the legitimating discourse of Chinese state socialism.[2] As Burawoy and Lukács (1992) argue, critiques of state socialism made from *within* state socialism are often based on a notion of justice and democracy that is promised, but not delivered, by the socialist state itself. Ironically, socialist ideology provides the bar against which to measure reality – and criticize that reality for coming up short.

Workers' skepticism was heightened by the increasingly anachronistic political rituals in which Harbin No. X's management still engaged. The emptiness of these rituals was apparent by my third day on the job. That morning, the entire store staff attended an hour-long political education meeting in their respective departments. I arrived to find the clerks of the women's department streaming over to a large staircase where they set up small, army-green folding stools that had been issued for such political meetings. The gathering felt more like a party than a political education session, however. A group of women behind me joked raucously among themselves until Manager Zhang dispatched Assistant Manager Yu to the top of the staircase. As Yu climbed the stairs with a sour expression on her face, workers whispered warnings to the troublemakers. Despite Yu's presence, workers paid little heed to the speaker, a sales clerk reading out a prepared document. At times, the chatter rose to a level that made the speaker hard to hear. Some of the women massaged each other's backs or chatted quietly, others tried to get down a little breakfast. For most of the meeting I could distinctly smell cigarette smoke. No one took notes. Upstairs on the third floor, a similar meeting was being held, and the volume of their address system was set so high that it was difficult for us to hear clearly what was being said on our own floor.

As a result, the content of the meeting was hard to follow. Manager Zhang first announced that this was a political theory (*lilun*) study session. The document read aloud had been prepared by the store's propaganda department and covered a large range of things: Jiang Zemin's "three represents" (*san ge daibiao*) and its basis in Marxism-Leninism, as well as exhortations to maintain the country's socialist spirit. There was also some discussion of market issues and China's coming entry into the World Trade Organization. Wal-Mart was explicitly identified as a threat.

My co-worker Big Sister Zhao took out her pen and carefully wrote out this list of issues on the palm of her hand. The people sitting around her chided, "Why are you bothering to write this down?" "For fun," she replied, unruffled, but her co-workers were offended that Zhao was taking any of this seriously.

On one level, workers and management alike recognized that these events paid lip-service to ideals and principles that the state and the Chinese Communist Party had, in practice, largely abandoned. Yet, the visibility of management in orchestrating these events made them seem like co-authors of the charade. These events slotted neatly into workers' negative opinions of their "higher-ups" (*shangji*), feeding a critique of managerial authority that drew in part upon experiences of the inequalities of state socialist society.

This ethic was especially evident in criticisms of managerial favoritism and the use of personal connections (*guanxi)* to secure good positions or promotions within the department store. *Guanxi* can be viewed as an oppositional force, acting counter to universalizing forces of the bureaucratic, socialist state (Yang 1994), but for that exact reason, the existence of *guanxi* practices makes the state vulnerable to criticisms based on notions of impartial fairness. In fact, workers perceived the use of instrumental ties in the workplace, rather than skill or merit, to be *part* of the socialist planned economy, and not in opposition to it. The use of *guanxi* served as yet another basis upon which to critique store management.

At Harbin No. X, concerns about favoritism were also linked to market-induced changes to the workplace. With pay composed of uniform base salaries and variable sales-based commissions, a clerk's earning potential was powerfully influenced by the type and brand of merchandise he or she sold. Favoritism was no longer expressed through the direct distribution of non-wage benefits but rather had been re-situated in a new hierarchy of good and bad merchandise and corresponding sales positions.

When I asked Big Sister Lin how sales positions were distributed, she explained that work assignments depended on whom managers looked favorably upon; the process was, to some degree, a matter of *guanxi*. Little Xiao agreed. When I asked him if workers could request or apply for a specific sales position, Xiao said, "You can, but it's no use. Unless you have *guanxi* or money, you won't be able to influence the decision." For this reason, sales clerks' earnings were not perceived to be a good measure of ability or effort, but rather a sign of the attractiveness and saleability of the merchandise and, by extension, the strength of one's connections with store or department management. Xiao portrayed an inequality produced, in part, by commission sales and the market economy as a negative legacy of socialism.

The failure of the store to fully realize an effort-based system of rewards, coupled with the legacy of China's "virtuocracy" (Shirk 1982) which demanded deliberate and instrumental expressions of revolutionary zeal and loyalty to the party-state (Walder 1986), could make overt displays of hard work laughable, much as the lingering rituals of the socialist state like the one described above seemed pro-forma and devoid of real meaning. For example, one morning after shuffling back to our counter from the daily group meeting (itself more form than content), Little Xiao started working on our "books," our records of daily sales. As Xiao sat working over the numbers with a calculator, other sales clerks passing by repeatedly joked at what a hard worker Xiao was. "Just got here and you are already pouring over the books," said one woman, and when Snow Lion Wang passed he quipped, "So hard at work, you really are a model worth studying (*zhide xiang ni xuexi*)!" In fact, much like the Chinese state that originally promoted the image of the model worker (Chen 2003), management and their priorities at Harbin No. X were the targets of a steady flow of worker criticism that was part of daily life on the sales floor. This is not to say that workers did not exert themselves – the pursuit of commissions insured they did – but appearing to display your hard work where management might observe you was nevertheless a source of merriment and skepticism.

Worker authority on the sales floor

Challenges to managerial authority had a flipside on the Harbin No. X sales floor, namely a powerful assertion of worker authority, expertise, and selling skill. I witnessed no open challenges to store management on the sales floor, and workers recognized the formal hierarchy that allowed management to fine them and allocate their sales positions. All the same, scarce managerial presence meant sales clerks would regularly flout store rules and regulations. On my counter, Little Xiao would periodically light up a cigarette, stepping out from behind the sales counter so customers would not know he was a clerk. On one occasion Xiao even performed this maneuver in front of a floor manager.[3] And on my very first day on the Ice Day counter, Big Sister Zhao handed me a stick of mint gum, a common after-lunch procedure, saying as she did that we were not supposed to eat anything behind the counter. The trick was to pretend that there was nothing in our mouths. A customer lingering by the counter interjected, "Is that a good thing, pretending not to be eating? What if we see you?" Zhao replied slyly, "Well, then we're not pretending not to be eating, are we?"

However, workplace autonomy at Harbin No. X extended far beyond the freedom to circumvent formal store rules and even beyond flexibility in dealing with customers – the kind of autonomy we might expect with service work (Leidner 1993; Sherman 2003). For example, each sales team

tailored their stocking arrangements to their own needs, habits, and preferences. As sales clerks, they were keenly aware that well-organized stock
could greatly enhance their ability to sell. Stock issues also highlight
another set of relationships within the store: that between factory sales
representatives (*changjia daili*) and sales clerks. In a technical sense, sales
clerks in the store had two bosses: (1) the store management, who loosely
monitored their daily work and service performance; (2) and representatives from manufacturers, who actually paid commissions and salaries,
funded advertisement campaigns, shouldered the costs for outfitting a sales
area, and, importantly, supplied merchandise. Manufacturers would naturally seek to channel the best and most popular merchandise to venues
where they believed it would sell the fastest, and as a result, they did not
treat all stores and did not supply all sales counters equally. Harbin No. X
workers recognized that, in this respect, they were highly dependent upon
the manufacturers of the goods they sold.

But at the same time, sales clerks at Harbin No. X repeatedly asserted
themselves with *changjia* reps in ways that reflected their authority and
expertise on the sales floor. My co-workers regularly made lists of the merchandise they hoped our manufacturer would re-supply us with. If dissatis-
fied when new shipments arrived, clerks might hassle the "*daili*," or sales
rep. On one occasion, Big Sister Zhao was particularly stern with our sales
rep, an affable, middle-aged man from the company headquarters in
Jiangsu province. Zhao informed him that on the previous day (her day
off), she had visited a clothing market in Harbin and found an Ice Day
wholesaler selling a style of men's coat our counter had never carried and
another style of which we had only received a single box. Big Sister Zhao
even quoted the prices of the coats and their product numbers. The sales
rep seemed a bit surprised but assured her that he would try to make sure
we got these goods. Zhao did not conceal her annoyance at his oversight.
To her satisfaction, later that day, several boxes of merchandise arrived.

My fellow sales clerks understood very well that having the right merchandise was crucial to maintaining sales levels and maintaining brisk sales
was the basis for healthy commissions. When the various sales reps from the
down coat company would stop by, Xiao, Zhao, and Lin would discuss
popular colors and styles with them in the hope that more of these items
would be channeled our way. It was from one of these conversations that we
incidentally learned that our counter had the best Ice Day sales in the city.
This provided more ammunition in our haggling for more and better stocks.
"We have hardly anything left, and we were still able to sell twenty-three
coats today!" Little Xiao exclaimed one day to the sales rep, who immediately agreed that we needed to restock but noted that there was little left in
the company's own Harbin storage facility – new shipments were on the
way. "Whatever I can get I'll send to you," he assured us.

Sales clerks also recognized that they served as a vital source of current
market information and were often the only source of information about

how well competitors' merchandise was selling. Passing that information back to the manufacturer was a self-interested move – clerks wanted to improve sales by getting better merchandise – but it was also an assertion of expertise, professionalism, and authority. Sales clerks at Harbin No. X were so confident of their expertise that they would routinely offer marketing advice to manufacturer representatives. My co-workers advised our sales rep that women's coats should include one size larger, because many older women were unable to squeeze into our largest size. Long coats, they added, should be made a little longer – many people had been asking for longer coats. And one afternoon Little Xiao began lecturing a young sales rep on the company's publicity campaign, complaining that advertising had been too thin. "I've never heard of Ice Day before, and I'm selling the stuff!" he exclaimed.

This sense of authority enabled workers to assert themselves in other ways, such as resisting attempts to impose new routines or work practices upon them. For instance, Ice Day coats were all labeled with a cardboard tag at the base of which was a detachable stub listing the color, style, and size of the coat. Because collecting the stubs was a new procedure, we frequently forgot to rip them off before a customer walked away with his or her purchase. One afternoon, one of our sales representatives pressed Big Sister Zhao and Little Xiao over our failure to collect them, saying, "How can we calculate your wages if we don't have the tabs?"

"You have to pay us!" exclaimed Zhao. "What do you expect us to eat if we are to sell your coats, the Northwest Wind (*xibei feng*)? You can't live off the Northwest Wind, you know!"

Little Xiao joined in. "Sometimes we are simply too busy to have a chance to rip off the tags."

Zhao added, "Some customers dislike it (*you fan'gan*) when we rip off the tags, they don't like it." The harried sales rep eventually left for another sales counter, and though we all made a greater effort to collect the tabs, no one seemed overly concerned about doing so.

The egalitarian service encounter

Work culture at Harbin No. X, then, was composed of not only a critique of managerial power but also a sense of authority, expertise, and professionalism among workers. The dignity this generated carried over into interactions between sales clerks and their customers. In stark contrast to China's newer service settings, sales clerks engaged in egalitarian service interactions. These were not the surly service encounters of China's pre- and early-reform years but rather involved a set of interactions characterized by high levels of parity and mutuality between customer and clerk.

In many ways, Harbin No. X was broadly an egalitarian setting. Because managers did relatively little to regulate the sales floors of Harbin No. X, the store was an open, permeable, and even democratic space, and the world "outside" spilled into the store. Rural families in town for a day of shopping and working-class urbanites in blue or white work smocks enhanced the store's populist and proletarian feel. Many people carried on other, non-store business activities inside the store as well – fruit sellers, telephone card peddlers, even a roving tailor and a friendly pornography salesman.

Workers themselves were not so distinct from "the masses." Lax policies governing uniforms meant that, through the winter months, workers were only required to don a blue blazer, allowing them to adapt their work clothing to individual tastes and comfort. Permed and dyed hair sat piled atop heads, and female sales clerks skittered about in impossibly tall high-heeled shoes and stylish, tight pants. This diversity of appearance allowed the streets of Harbin to be reproduced within the store walls. As one store manager pointed out to me, the store was very *dazhonghua*, or "massified."

Without management dictating the contours of the customer–clerk relationship, Harbin No. X clerks and shoppers performed one of great parity. Workers and customers would even make explicit the lack of social distance between them. For example, when trying to sell a man's down coat to a young Southern man, Big Sister Zhao urged him to purchase navy blue, explaining that it had "*laoban qi*" and would give him the "air of a boss." The young man joked with us that he was not a boss at all, only a *dagongzai* (slang for "male worker"). In another instance, a customer complained to us about how his son wanted a new winter coat every year in order to keep up with fashion. Zhao diagnosed this as "*guizu bing*," or "aristocracy syndrome," to which the man immediately replied that his own economic situation was not so good. "You folks aren't so bad off," he continued, gesturing to my colleagues, "You can earn a bit more [than basic wages] in this line of work." At times, workers would point out their own wages to customers as a way of establishing a sense of empathy or rapport. One clerk joked that if there was a problem with a coat after the customer washed it, she would give the customer the money for the coat. "Out of my wages!" she exclaimed.

At the same time, sales clerks sought to establish themselves as professionals. Customers and clerks did not, of course, enter into these interactions as complete equals, especially as sales clerks' salaries were closely bound to customer purchases. However, while customers expected sales clerks to respond to their requests and needs, they did not expect clerks to enact extreme deference to customer wishes (though they also did not anticipate pre-reform levels of surliness). Sales clerks, for their part, constructed a knowledge hierarchy that elevated them above customers and allowed them to issue judgments and pronouncements on customers' tastes, choices, and product knowledge.

For example, Little Xiao chided a customer fussing over a loose thread on a coat: "It is impossible not to have a loose thread or two on these coats! The coat isn't made with a single length of thread!" Clerks could also be quite aggressive about redirecting customers' choices (often to fall in line with what we had in stock), and customers were sometimes cowed into accepting these authoritative instructions. Big Sister Zhao exclaimed to a customer wanting a smaller-sized coat that if the woman wore a size smaller her bottom would be hanging out (*lou*) and it would be unattractive (*bu hao kan*). The customer purchased the recommended size.

Clerks would repeatedly resort to such tactics, and customers rarely dared to openly challenge clerk interpretations of consumption norms. In fact, those that did not conform to clerk standards of customer and consumer behavior were sometimes described as deviant or even "sick-in-the-head." An amusing exchange occurred when Little Xiao introduced a coat with netting sewn into the lining to an older customer. The customer, unfamiliar with this innovation to allow for better ventilation, was suspicious. "But won't dust get into the coat then?" the woman worried. "How much dust can you possibly have on your body?!" Little Xiao cried. "The coat does not have a problem, it's your ideas (*gainian*) that are the problem (*you wenti*)," he added. In another case, Little Xiao became irritated with an elderly man who was confused by the distinction between down and feathers. After Xiao attempted a careful description of the distinction between down and feathers, the customer was still baffled. Xiao threw up his hands in defeat and exclaimed, exasperated, "I don't know how else to explain it to you, unless I pull out a dictionary and show you the words!" As the man shuffled off Little Xiao turned to me and complained loudly, "That guy is sick-in-the-head (*you bing*)! He understands less Chinese than a foreigner!"

The level playing field upon which clerks and customers engaged one another was further exemplified by the degree of give and take between actors and the doses of mutual disrespect they served up to one another. On the part of the clerk, disrespect at times took the form of gruff dismissal of fussy or troublesome customers. One time, some customers responded with suspicion to Little Xiao's claim about merchandise quality. Xiao rejoined, "Go have a look around! (*Liu yi quar ba!*) I tell you there is no need to doubt the quality, and you don't believe me. Go look elsewhere and if you find better, then buy that."

Customers, of course, dished out such disrespect as well as they received it. The most common way of doing this was to simply ignore a clerk who was rattling off a sales pitch, but customers might do other things, like ask to see an item and then leave while the clerk went to fetch it. Sometimes they would even have us write out a receipt and package up the item and then never return.[4] Sometimes this disrespect was expressed as distrust in the clerk's honesty. For example, one customer cut a sale pitch short by exclaiming "*La dao ba*! Give it a rest!" Big Sister Zhao responded evenly, "Do you mean that you think that what I said is incorrect?"

Ironically, it was clear to me that both sides felt they should be treated with respect. For example, in response to a customer who had just described our merchandise as "*ke'chen*," a somewhat coarse word in local dialect for "ugly," Little Xiao turned to me and said with gravity: "With the steady improvement of people's quality (*suzhi*), this kind of language will disappear." He continued: "Our treatment of customers is already very friendly. There is no need for customers to use such language with us." At the same time, customers also expected a degree of respect from clerks (and likewise might attribute bad service to the poor "quality" of the individual). For example, when Big Sister Zhao muttered something under her breath in response to a particularly annoying customer, he wheeled around and confronted her. "What was that?" Zhao then repeated what she had said: "I said, I wasn't able to explain clearly to you." The man, satisfied that he had not been insulted, moved off, at which point Zhao turned to me and said with irritation that the man was a "*waihang*," or "non-expert."

My claim that sales clerks at Harbin No. X engaged in service interactions marked by parity and mutuality is subject to an important caveat, however. Clerks' treatment of rural people was colored by pronounced urban–rural status distinctions. It was not uncommon for people who were clearly from non-urban backgrounds, especially migrant workers, to be summarily categorized as outside "the norm." For example, the relation between a middle-aged man accompanied by an attractive young woman, both of whom were definitively labeled "peasants" by my colleagues, was debated intensely after they left. "Certainly not father–daughter nor husband–wife relation, and not relatives," Little Xiao decided. "*Er hun guanxi*," said Big Sister Zhao, "second marriage [meaning extra-marital] relations." "Whatever their relationship," replied Xiao, "it is not normal (*bu zhengchang*), and they've just come to Harbin to piss all of us off (*chou de'se*)." In another case, a group of deeply-tanned young men, probably casual laborers from the countryside, were quickly labeled deviant. "They aren't like us normal people," Big Sister Lin explained to me quietly. "We feel uncomfortable just looking at them." These "abnormal" rural shoppers, marginalized as they are in China's urban centers, were neither directly confronted with these judgments nor did they challenge the reserved manner in which they were served. And as the presence of rural customers shows, the egalitarian nature of customer–clerk interactions in the socialist department store was nevertheless bounded by pre-reform urban–rural social divisions that have persisted into the present.

Conclusion

Given the trend in China towards less worker control over the labor process – as many chapters in this volume attest – what explains the high degree of worker autonomy and authority on the Harbin No. X sales floor? And how resilient might sales clerks' work culture prove, given widespread managerial efforts to impose more modern, "advanced" forms of workplace discipline, such as that described in Chapter 7 by Calvin Chen?

Secure employment – partly a result of organizational inertia, and most certainly enabled by the local state – served as the crucial buttress to worker empowerment at Harbin No. X. While workers had to dodge occasional fines and penalties, they had little need to fear losing their jobs. Managers, for their part, preferred to avoid confrontations with workers whom they could expect to retain for many years. But whereas *danwei* structures produced insularity and inefficiencies in the Nanjing Railway work unit Lida Junghans investigated in Chapter 4, at Harbin No. X, a legacy of work unit socialism instead fostered a vibrant and industrious, if perhaps undisciplined, workplace. For at the same time that managers felt little sense of control over or interest in the store, sales clerks worked for commission-based pay that made them inclined to perform their work efficiently and effectively.

I would further argue that the actual form that workplace culture took at Harbin No. X was deeply shaped by the enduring legacy of Chinese socialism. The Harbin No. X Department Store was, in many ways, a "socialist" department store. Workers sustained a vital sales floor culture characterized not only by a "politics of authority" that critiqued managerial power but also by active assertions of worker authority, professionalism, and skill. The sense of professionalism and pride sales clerks took in their work, fostered by sales floor autonomy and years of work experience, was strengthened by a "negative class consciousness" that highlighted worker, not manager, contributions in the workplace. In this way, workers' culture served as a durable repository for values linked with social life under state socialism and its legitimizing ideology. The empowering elements of Harbin No. X's workplace culture become especially apparent in the relative parity displayed between customer and sales clerk. The sales floor was a space of egalitarian service interactions and, as such, stands in stark contrast to an increasingly dominant service paradigm in China that extracts sales clerk deference in the name of customer satisfaction.

In the context of economic reforms and the shift to a market economy, however, this critical worker consciousness and egalitarian work culture increasingly come unhinged from the larger historical framework that marked it not only as oppositional but even as "vanguardist." A workplace culture that maintains a perceived continuity with the socialist past is marked, and marks itself, as belonging to the past. Like the "straightforward" Polish workers associated with socialism in Elizabeth Dunn's research (1999), Harbin residents frequently described the sales clerks at Harbin No. X as "honest" and "frank" (*laoshi*), characteristics that also marked them as belonging to the simpler, less sophisticated socialist era. In an increasingly marketized society, being *laoshi* also differentiated these working-class clerks from more "modern" and prosperous groups. Much like the divisions among cohorts of workers that Mark Frazier describes, we see here the lines for a new division between older, "socialist" workers and younger ones more willing to submit to capitalist discipline.

Notes

1 Burawoy and Lukács label such class consciousness as "negative" because it is only critical of the existing system; a "positive" class consciousness would also include an alternative vision of social organization (1992: 114).
2 Even customers might tote the language – and the implicit critical perspective – of the Revolution into the store. For example, when Big Sister Lin told one young man that our coats used fabrics imported from the United States, the man scoffed, "*Chongyang meiwai*!" ("Worship foreign things and toady to foreign powers.") This slogan was a recurring theme under the Gang of Four – thanks to Tom Gold for pointing this out.
3 The cigarette maneuver was not only an assertion of Xiao's freedom and autonomy on the sales floor, I believe it was also an assertion of his masculinity in a strongly feminized workplace. Chinese women are much less likely than men to smoke, and in Harbin women were rarely seen smoking in public.
4 In most department stores and other retail settings in China, clerks must write out a receipt for customers, who then go to a separate cashier location to pay and return, with a stamped receipt, to collect their merchandise.

References

Benson, Susan P. (1986) *Counter Cultures: Saleswomen, Managers, and Customers in American Department Stores, 1890–1940*, Urbana, IL: University of Illinois Press.

Bourdieu, Pierre (1981) "Men and Machines," in K. Knorr-Cetina and A.V. Cicourel (eds) *Advances in Social Theory and Methodology: Toward an Integration of Micro- and Macro-Sociologies*, Boston: Routledge and Kegan Paul, pp. 304–317.

Burawoy, Michael and Lukács, János (1992) *The Radiant Past: Ideology and Reality in Hungary's Road to Capitalism*, Chicago: The University of Chicago Press.

Chen, Tina M. (2003) "Female Icons, Feminist Iconography? Socialist Rhetoric and Women's Agency in 1950s China," *Gender & History*, 15(2): 268–295.

Dalton, M. (1974) "The Ratebuster: The Case of the Saleswoman," in Phyllis L. Stewart and Muriel G. Cantor (eds) *Varieties of Work Experience: The Social Control of Occupational Groups and Roles*, New York: Halsted Press, pp. 206–214.

Drakulic, Slavenka (1991) *How We Survived Communism and Even Laughed*, New York: W.W. Norton & Co.

Dunn, Elizabeth (1999) "Slick Salesmen and Simple People: Negotiated Capitalism in a Privatized Polish Firm," in Michael Burawoy and Katherine Verdery (eds) *Uncertain Transition: Ethnographies of Change in the Postsocialist World*, Lanham, MD: Rowman and Littlefield, pp. 125–150.

Ji, Yongkai (2002) "Entry into the WTO: The Opportunities and Challenges Faced by Large-Scale Retail Businesses and Countermeasures," unpublished manuscript in the author's possession.

Lee, Ching Kwan (2000) "The 'Revenge of History': Collective Memories and Labor Protests in Northeastern China," *Ethnography*, 1(2): 217–237.

Lee, Ching Kwan (2002) "From the Specter of Mao to the Spirit of the Law: Labor Insurgency in China," *Theory and Society*, 31: 189–228.

Leidner, Robin (1993) *Fast Food, Fast Talk: Service Work and the Routinization of Everyday Life*, Berkeley, CA: University of California Press.

Melosh, Barbara (1982) *"The Physician's Hand": Work Culture and Conflict in American Nursing*, Philadelphia, PA: Temple University Press.

Powell, W.W. and DiMaggio, P.J. (eds) (1991) *The New Institutionalism in Organizational Analysis*, Chicago: The University of Chicago Press, pp. 63–82.

Rofel, Lisa (1992) "Rethinking Modernity: Space and Factory Discipline in China," *Cultural Anthropology*, 7(1): 93–114.

Rofel, Lisa (1999) *Other Modernities: Gendered Yearnings in China After Socialism*, Berkeley, CA: University of California Press.

Schoenberger, Erica (1997) *The Cultural Crisis of the Firm*, Cambridge, MA: Blackwell Publishers.

Sherman, Rachel E. (2003) "Class Acts: Producing and Consuming Luxury Service in Hotels," PhD dissertation, Department of Sociology, University of California, Berkeley.

Shirk, Susan L. (1982) *Competitive Comrades: Career Incentives and Student Strategies in China*, Berkeley, CA: University of California Press.

Swidler, Ann (1986) "Culture in Action: Symbols and Strategies," *American Sociological Review*, 51: 273–286.

Verdery, Katherine (1998) *What Was Socialism, and What Comes Next?* Princeton, NJ: Princeton University Press.

Walder, Andrew G. (1986) *Communist Neo-Traditionalism*, Berkeley, CA: University of California Press.

Warhurst, Christopher (1998) "Recognizing the Possible: The Organization and Control of a Socialist Labor Process," *Administrative Science Quarterly*, 43(2): 470–497.

Yang, Mayfair (1994) *Gifts, Favors and Banquets: The Art of Social Relationships in China*, Ithaca, NY: Cornell University Press.

6 Capital's incorporation of labor rights and corporate codes of conduct in a Chinese dormitory labor regime

Pun Ngai

With its increasing incorporation into the global economy over the past two decades, China has become the "workshop of the world," not only providing a huge pool of cheap labor but also trained engineers and skilled professionals for global production. Substantial numbers of China's burgeoning labor force are migrants from rural areas who work in transnational or private companies located in urban, peri-urban and rural areas. The majority of labor migrants have been contained in a dormitory labor regime in which factory premises consist of production sites as well as workers' dormitories, resulting in tight surveillance over migrants' work and leisure time (Smith and Pun 2003). Since the mid-1990s, there has been a surge in the use of company codes of conduct in China for improving labor standards. These codes are adopted by transnational corporations (TNCs), often big brand-name American and European retailers, which impose them on their Chinese contractors and subcontractors (Frenkel 2001; Tan and Liu 2003; Chan and Wang 2003; Pun 2005a).

Classic neo-liberal arguments hold that codes of conduct at the company level, combined with increased legal rights at the societal level, will usher in a process of rationalization and institutionalization of industrial relations which will then lead to a decline of despotic or authoritarian labor regimes in the new millennium (Schak 1997; Guthrie 1999). By contrast, scholars who subscribe to the thesis of East Asian authoritarian labor regimes argue that globalization causes a "race to the bottom" in terms of labor standards. Labor relations in China are therefore unlikely to be improved by legal or institutional change, and China will remain confined to a stage similar to the "primitive accumulation" of early capitalism (Hsing 1998; Lee 1998; Chan 2001; Pun 2005b). This chapter engages in this debate by providing an in-depth study of code of conduct *practices* in a workplace in Southern China. My hope is that a look at the actual implementation of codes of conduct will give us a deeper understanding of labor politics in China and help us to go beyond these dichotomized propositions.

This chapter is based on a case study of a Hong Kong-owned garment factory in the Pearl River Delta. Rather than reflecting the viewpoints of

Chinese agencies that research or monitor codes of conducts in TNCs (Liu 2003), of labor organizations or NGOs involved with codes of conducts (CIC 2000; LARIC 2000; NLC 2000; China Labor Watch 2002), or of TNC representatives who implement such codes in China, this chapter will be firmly anchored in a workers' perspective.[1] Workers, who are at the receiving end of these codes, are well placed to observe their concrete implementation in the workplace, and as this chapter shows, they are decidedly less optimistic about them than outside observers.

From a workers' perspective, codes of conduct and the numerous human rights or labor rights departments that are being set up inside transnational or regional company headquarters in China constitute a *capital-initiated initiative toward the formalization and incorporation* of labor rights in China (Pun 2005b). Until recently, the sole lawful organization for the protection of labor rights was the All-China Federation of Trade Unions. Labor relations in China were entirely under state control, and therefore best understood in a state corporatist framework (Chan and Nørlund 1998). By rationalizing and ameliorating labor relations, TNCs seek to preempt regulatory action by the corporatist state; at the same time, internal, top-down regulation aims to subsume workers' interests under the capital imperative and dilute workers' collective power. This process of incorporation may result in the improvement of certain aspects of workers' working and living conditions; however, the fact that workers' rights are granted exclusively from above undercuts the long-term hope for labor empowerment and strengthens China's undemocratic and paternalistic labor regime.

Managing codes of conduct

The first company codes of conduct on labor standards in China and other developing countries in Asia were launched in the early 1990s in the textiles, clothing and footwear industries, in response to anti-sweatshop campaigns, global consumer campaigns, and students' movements in North America and Europe (Sajhau 1997; Ascoly 2000). For Levi Strauss, Nike, Reebok, The Gap, and other TNCs that produce famous brand-name products for global consumers, codes of conduct became part of a strategy to secure sales in the global market.

Codes of conduct and labor standards obligate a transnational company to uphold certain standards in its own operations and apply the same standards to its suppliers or trade partners. Such codes are voluntary and in most cases drawn up by the company itself. Code clauses are often measured against ILO conventions, in particular those concerned with human rights in the workplace. Key clauses in company codes address seven major areas: no forced or bonded labor, no child labor, no discrimination in employment, living wages and benefits, normal working hours, no hazards to safety and health, and decent working environment. Only a few company codes cover the clauses on freedom of association and the right to collective bargaining.[2] There are huge variations in the application of TNC company codes in China.[3] TNCs like Levi Strauss, Reebok, and Sears, Roebuck and Company (SR) created specific codes concerning forced labor and human rights for their Chinese suppliers and subcontractors, largely because of their poor records in these two areas. For example, in addition to its "Import-Buying Policy and Procedures" that is applicable to both US and China subcontractors, SR produced an additional code on forced labor titled "Policy on Goods Made by Forced Labor in China" (Sajhau 1997).[4] The Gap also requires their Chinese suppliers and trade partners to sign a vendor compliance agreement under which they must conform to the company's codes of conduct. In most cases, subcontractors or suppliers are monitored by the companies' representatives on a regular basis, and sometimes independent auditors will be paid to audit the companies' conduct so as to enhance credibility.

The trend towards codes of conduct in China began with an eye-catching piece of news reported by the *Washington Post* in 1992, stating that Chinese prison laborers had been exploited to produce Levi jeans (Sajhau 1997). Stunned to hear the news, Levi Strauss immediately reacted by setting up a labor standards code entitled, "Business partner terms of engagement and guidelines for country selections," to protect its corporate image (Women Working Worldwide 2000). Afraid of trailing behind, other major TNCs, especially in retail industries, set up their own company codes of conduct. The race to apply ethical codes in China reached its climax in 1999, when the CEOs of Phillips-van Heusen, Reebok, and Levi Strauss launched a concerted action by writing a letter to President Jiang Zemin, requesting a meeting to explore the possibility of "working together" to improve labor rights in China (Emerson 2000).[5] The companies' concern is, of course, their public image, which is a decisive factor in determining whether the public purchase their products and hence their survival in conditions of severe global competition. This also explains why corporate codes are mainly adopted by brand-name retailers, especially clothing and footwear companies that sell not only their products but also an image to their customers.

Launching codes of conduct in a workplace

To understand the actual implementation of codes of conduct in the workplace, I studied one garment supplier, China Galaxy Garments (China Galaxy) in Southern China.[6] This company produced casual wear as well as sportswear for several famous American and European brand-name corporations. It adopted three sets of corporate codes, including Disney's. Intense observation for two years (2002 and 2003) included frequent exchanges with the company director and interviews with production managers and shop floor workers. I also visited dormitories in order to have a comprehensive understanding of the implementation of the codes of conduct and how workers made sense of them.

Founded in 1997, China Galaxy is a subcontracting factory in Guangdong province. Originally located in Shenzhen, China Galaxy soon moved to Dongguan (located between Shenzhen and Guangzhou) because of cheaper land and labor and because the local state provided a better investment package, including lower taxes, reduced management fees, and a lower rent for a larger factory compound. With a workforce of 600, China Galaxy is a typical Hong Kong-owned enterprise, controlled by a Hong Kong director who has the sole authority over the operation and management of the factory. China Galaxy lies at the end point of the global subcontracting chain, producing garments for Hong Kong buyers who receive orders from American and European corporations. Its entire output is for export and as yet the company has shown no interest in exploring China's domestic market. China Galaxy's main office in Hong Kong coordinates marketing, production orders, materials provision, and shipping with the China-based manufacturing process.

Managers repeatedly mentioned a reputation for on-time delivery and good personal relationships with Hong Kong buyers as the best strategy for securing orders. Buyers often change companies but circulate within the same sector; therefore, it was individual rather than firm-to-firm relationships that persisted. Other strategies included establishing a good reputation in the locality, having close personal contact with other entrepreneurs in the sector, and informally sharing work with other companies to keep production going. Building personal networks, rather than improving the company's profile, lay at the heart of the business strategies of China Galaxy.

Both production and dormitory premises were rented from the local district government which charged the company a management fee of 15 percent of the labor cost per head. Production facilities and working environments were poor, but given its low public profile, the company felt little need to upgrade its outward appearance. Management was aware of the international pressure to improve the working and living conditions and displayed a simplified version of the Disney code of conduct on the wall. At the same time, they stressed that profit margins were too tight to allow for improvements that caused extra costs or reduced labor productivity. In consequence, code implementation was often reduced to window-dressing: "I know how to deal with the ethical code persons from my many years of work experience. I can make judgments about the balance of power between buying departments and sections responsible for codes of conduct to see where the real power lies," said the Hong Kong Director.

The management of China Galaxy admitted that the factory was not up to the standard of the Disney code and other codes of conduct. Workers were generally unaware of the codes and showed little interest in their detailed provisions. The Personnel Department said that each worker had been provided with a written Chinese copy of the Disney code and claimed that the provisions of the code were introduced to the workers during morning pre-start meetings. However, when I interviewed the workers and checked whether they had received a copy of the Disney code, most of them said that they could not remember. Some of the workers clearly had never heard about the code. One worker actually asked me to explain the code provisions in some detail, so that he could answer my question correctly. When I explained some of the provisions to him, he looked puzzled and seemed not to believe that workers could possibly enjoy such rights. Another worker mistook the Disney code for China Galaxy's own regulations and showed me the regulation handbook. Only a few foremen knew that the Disney code was a set of regulations stipulated by the TNC to improve working conditions, reduce labor turnover, and safeguard product quality.

When I asked the Personnel Department why none of the production workers could tell me what the code of conduct was about, the secretary replied that the workers were not interested in knowing the code provisions, and thus lost whatever the company distributed to them. Despite these excuses, only one-paged summaries were given to the workers or posted on notice boards in the workplace, canteens, or dormitories, indicating that China Galaxy was not prepared to implement the code whole-heartedly and was still testing the effectiveness and seriousness of the monitoring system. In contrast to the Personnel Department, production managers on the shop floor openly admitted that the code of conduct was frequently evaded. When production orders put them under time pressure, they had no choice but to sacrifice labor rights and demand excessive overtime in violation of the code. Severe global competition for low-cost products and just-in-time production structurally constrained the implementation of the code of conduct and resulted in a hypocritical and insincere implementation of company codes of conduct.

Working hours and wages

The workers in China Galaxy worked extremely long hours, usually starting at eight in the morning and working until ten in the evening. If there were rush orders, they could be requested to work until midnight. Twelve hours of work each day was normal; rest days were provided only in between orders or during the low season. This meant that workers worked between seventy-two and seventy-seven hours each week, far in excess of the hours allowed by Chinese law (forty hours a week and thirty-six hours overtime in the course of a month). In open violation of the Chinese law, the factory remained in operation on National Day (1 October, which is a statutory holiday), despite the fact that the Disney code promises to obey local regulations and guarantees workers at least one day off in seven.[7] When asked to compare the working hours with the situation two years ago, most workers saw little progress, though a few said that they were given more holidays than before. Although the Disney code states that overtime work is voluntary, the workers' handbook states that workers who cannot do overtime have to apply to the supervisors for a written exemption. The workers also confirmed that they could refuse overtime only for very pressing reasons, especially during the high season.

When I visited the workers in their dormitories, they were often more willing to talk about such pressures. One worker said, "We were taught to answer whoever came to inspect the factory that the working hours were eight and overtime was voluntary. Do you believe that we can choose to work overtime or not?" In another attempt to erase traces of their long working hours, China Galaxy changed their clocking system so that workers clocked their card only when they entered the factory (Figure 6.1). Workers had to clock their card three times: when they came to work in the morning at 8 a.m., in the afternoon at 1 p.m., and in the evening at 6 p.m. However, clocking records did not show the total number of working hours, because they did not register when the workers left the shop floor.

Figure 6.1 Morning shift at China Galaxy (source: Author's photograph).

Almost all corporate codes state that payment for overtime work follows national or local law. According to Chinese laws, workers receive 150 percent of normal wages for overtime on normal workdays, 200 percent during rest days, and 300 percent during statutory holidays. Most workers, in particular those in the cutting, sewing, packing and quality control sections were paid on a piece-rate basis. Other workers and apprentices were paid on an hourly basis, while management staff received monthly salaries. Piece-rate workers were paid the legally prescribed overtime premium on normal work days but not the higher rates for rest days and statutory holidays. Even on Sundays and after 8 p.m., overtime wages were only 1.5 times the standard rate. The workers interviewed, for their part, did not have a clear understanding of what constituted overtime and were under the impression that overtime was only paid in the evenings, and not on Saturdays or Sundays.

TNCs and their representatives often argue that it is the workers themselves who opt for overtime in order to earn higher incomes. We paid particular attention to this issue and repeatedly asked the workers to express their views. Most of them answered that if they did not work overtime, their salary would be too low to support them. A female worker said, "We earn as much as 900 *yuan* a month with overtime work in the evenings and weekends. Without overtime work, we only earn half that amount." In this company and other companies I visited, workers said "Yes, you may say we prefer long working hours. We sell our own labor to earn money. We travel a long distance to *dagong* (work); if we can't earn good money, what's the use of having a holiday on Sunday?" The average wage for production workers was 950 *yuan* each month inclusive of overtime work, with maximum wages of up to 1,500 *yuan* in the high season – high when compared to other foreign-invested companies in China (see Chan 2001). The paternalistic dormitory labor regime provided an absolute lengthening of working hours and an intensified extraction of labor power through absolute control over labor time and living space. The only reward was higher payment which was particularly important to rural migrant workers.

Freedom of movement

The Disney code stated that the provisions of the workers' contract would be based on local legislation. A standard labor contract, according to Section 19 of the Chinese Labor Law, should contain at least the following clauses: contract term, work description, labor protection and working conditions, labor remuneration, labor discipline, conditions for the termination of the contract, and responsibility for contract violation. China Galaxy asked all workers to sign a contract at the end of the probation period but this was not a standard labor contract. The contract contained only the name of the production unit; the obligation to abide by factory regulations, follow work arrangements, and accept a change in position without arguing; the obligation to ensure a safe work environment and respect safety regulations; a warning that workers who did not follow regulations or caused loss of production would be dismissed; and a statement that wages, insurance, and overtime premiums would be paid in accordance with the Labor Law.

When I asked the workers about their contracts, most of them could not show their copy, since copies were kept in the Personnel Department. Only one or two knew that they had signed a one-year contract and that the company could not arbitrarily dismiss them. Most workers had no clear ideas of the contract clauses; moreover, none of them knew that they were covered by the social security insurance as stipulated by Chinese Labor Law.

Although no cases of forced or bonded labor were found, China Galaxy tightly controlled its workers who came from more than five provinces. Despite the code's prohibition of punitive wage deductions, the company kept the workers' identity cards and enforced a system of deposits, including 20 *yuan* for a company's card, 30 *yuan* for a set of uniform, 20 *yuan* for work tools if applicable, and 50 *yuan* for dormitory accommodation, making up a total of 120 *yuan*. In addition to the Disney code, China Galaxy had its own code, which was far more detailed and disciplinary. Upon hiring, every worker received a handbook listing more than fifty provisions. The details in terms of deductions and punishments are shown in Table 6.1.

Workers' accommodation

Nearly all workers in China Galaxy were rural migrant workers from the provinces of Guangdong, Hunan, Hubei, Jiangxi, Anhui and Sichuan, except one local who was the accountant and housekeeper of the company. Housing for these migrant workers was difficult to arrange and expensive, according to the housekeeper, though only very basic facilities were provided. The three-storey dormitory building was just adjacent to

Table 6.1 Deductions and punishments at China Galaxy

Types of offenses	Deductions (yuan RMB)
Late arrival: less than 10 minutes	5
Late arrival: between 11 and 30 minutes	10
Late arrival: 30 minutes to 1 hour	Equals absence from work for half a day
Late arrival: 1 hour or more	Equals absence for a whole day
Late more than three times	Sanctions doubled
Half-day absence	30
Full-day absence	50
Absence from work for 3 days and above	Termination of contract

Figure 6.2 Dormitories at China Galaxy (source: Author's photograph).

the production building, facilitating a just-in-time labor system for just-in-time production. Dormitory rooms housed twelve to sixteen workers in crowded conditions, with little light and ventilation and absolutely no private or individual space. No kitchens, toilets, or bathrooms were provided in the rooms, so that the workers had to share common toilets and bathrooms at the end of the corridor. The management admitted that living conditions were poor but blamed the local government for not providing enough space for dormitory use. The dormitory building was built to accommodate five hundred workers only, but China Galaxy employed more than 600 (Figure 6.2). In one of the dormitory rooms, the toilet walls were black with moisture and covered all over with plastic sheets, and the broken window panels had been replaced by plastic in order to prevent air from entering the room. The general state of both the bathrooms and toilets was quite bad, in some places filthy, indicating long-term neglect.

One of the corporate codes adopted by China Galaxy provided a whole list of regulations on workers' housing, which China Galaxy was required to follow. The details are as follows.

Corporate Code on Housing Facilities:

1 Dormitory facilities meet all applicable laws and health and safety regulations, including regulations on fire safety, sanitation, risk prevention, and electrical, mechanical and structural safety.
2 The living space per worker in the sleeping quarters meets both the minimum legal requirement and the local industry standard.
3 Workers are provided with their own individual mats or beds.
4 Dormitory facilities are well ventilated. There are windows to the outside or fans and/or air conditioners and/or heaters in all sleeping areas for adequate ventilation and temperature control.
5 Workers are provided their own storage space for their clothes and personal possessions.
6 There are at least two clearly marked exits on each floor, and emergency lighting is installed in halls, stairwells and above each exit.
7 Halls and exits are kept unobstructed for safe and rapid evacuation in case of fire or other emergencies. Fire drills are conducted at least every six months.
8 Directions for evacuation in case of fire or other emergencies are posted in all sleeping quarters. Fire extinguishers are placed in, or accessible to, all sleeping quarters.
9 Hazardous and combustible materials used in the production process are not stored in the dormitory or buildings connected to sleeping quarters.
10 Sleeping quarters have adequate lighting.
11 Sufficient toilets and showers, segregated by sex, are provided in safe, sanitary, accessible and private areas.
12 Facilities to boil water are available to dormitory residents.
13 Dormitory residents are free to come and go during their off-hours under reasonable limitations imposed for their safety and comfort.

Despite these obligations, the management showed little genuine concern about dormitory conditions. Lacking space and resources to improve accommodations, the company tightened disciplinary controls. "More fines, more supervision, and more inspections can be enforced, of course," explained the facilities manager. The workers were expected to discipline themselves and maintain proper living conditions.

Registering codes of conduct

Since China Galaxy obviously failed to meet its corporate codes, it was advised to employ a "social compliance officer" to improve the implementation of the codes' provisions in the workplace. A young university graduate was assigned to the Personnel Department to build up a monitoring system. Believing that good monitoring depended on a good filing system, which would allow the company to show its past performance to TNC auditors, the social compliance officer designed a series of forms: Worker Contract Records, Overtime Records, Workers' Training Procedures, Code Test Records, Workers' Assessment Forms, Workers' Complaint and Handling Records, and Dormitory Management Guidelines. Code implementation was largely about documentation: to show figures and data to buyers and monitors was to demonstrate the company's efforts to improve its records; the more detail in the files, the better the company looked to outside observers.

The need for documentation becomes obvious when we examine the monitoring and auditing processes. Most monitors or auditors simply visited the factory for a few hours during daytime, though some inspections were unannounced. Monitors and auditors thought of themselves as white-collar specialists and tended to rely on paperwork rather than interviews with workers. Auditors from the West or from Hong Kong actively advised companies such as China Galaxy on how to "improve" their filing systems. For instance, on the issue of working hours and wages, the auditors suggested that China Galaxy change its register in such a way that it showed net monthly wages for a forty-hour week that corresponded to the legal minimum wages. Although workers received a monthly wage slip, the slip did not list explicitly the number of regular and overtime working hours worked in a month. It also failed to include detailed information on the piece-rate and payment of statutory holidays. The workers were thus still unable to calculate and determine themselves whether they had or had not received correct wages.

Despite many obvious infractions, the company director was particularly satisfied with China Galaxy's success in institutionalizing the code, especially with the suggestions given to him by the auditors. The filing system seemed to resolve the contradiction between code obligations and production. Documentation, registers, and records demonstrated compliance with the codes of conduct and the Chinese Labor Law: unannounced inspections could be easily dealt with if piles of files were shown. Instead of the intended rationalization of the production process in the workplace, the code of conduct resulted in the institutionalization of paperwork, with little impact on working conditions.

Conclusion

This in-depth study of codes of conduct in a typical workplace in Southern China has shown how capital incorporates the sphere of labor rights in China. It provides a case for critically reviewing the increasingly widespread belief that codes of conduct will lead to the rationalization of workplace management in China. Codes of conduct aim to demonstrate the company's commitment to internationally required labor standards, but only secure the company a firmer place in the global production chain. As the director of China Galaxy explained, compliance with TNC codes was part of the company's "market behavior." The code resulted in the provision of certain labor rights, but at the same time, it was a first step in the incorporation of labor rights into the sphere of capital, dictated by global market logic and worked through a joint-venture supplier.

It is true that the company did devote certain resources to setting up systems and procedures for controlling labor standards, but it showed no genuine concern for labor rights, not to mention workers' representation or participation. Codes of conduct implementation looked "rational" enough, but the granting of labor rights from above only resulted in furthering the typical East Asian authoritarian factory regime in which the management played a paternalistic role in "protecting" their workers from labor exploitation but preempted all attempts at workers' self-organization. The implication is that codes of conduct are neither about the rationalization of workplace management nor about the alleviation of despotic or paternalistic factory regimes, but rather about the hybridization of these two opposed forces, and ultimately about capital's incorporation of labor rights.

Acknowledgments

The author would like to thank Anita Chan and John Unger for reading the previous version of this chapter. I am particularly grateful to Mark Selden for his comments on this chapter. Part of the field studies of this chapter was financially supported by Hong Kong Research Grant Council on a research project, "Living with Global Capitalism: Labor Control and Resistance through the Dormitory Labor System in China" (2003–2005).

Notes

1 Workers were never invited to participate in the process of drawing up, implementing and monitoring the corporation code or the international code.
2 Reebok, The Gap, and Switcher are among the few companies that include freedom of association in their company codes. In the past few years, Reebok has begun to set up trade unions among its suppliers, in accordance with China's Trade Union law.
3 Some codes consist of general principles applicable to all business partners of the TNC, including material providers, manufacturers, and retailers. Some are much

more detailed and distinguish between the internal policies that apply to the company itself, and external policies that apply to suppliers or trade partners. Codes are selectively implemented, depending on local labor laws and working conditions.

4 This particular code includes a clause in all contracts with Chinese subcontractors concerning the non-use of forced labor and highlights the possibility of carrying out unannounced inspections of the plants of Chinese subcontractors and the termination of trade relations with any supplier using forced labor.

5 This attempt failed when the Chinese government, which considers labor rights protection an internal affair, showed no interest in talking to the CEOs of the three companies.

6 The name of the company and all the workers hereafter are fictitious.

7 According to the China Labor Law, workers should have two days off out of seven.

References

Ascoly, Nina (2000) "About the Clean Clothes Campaign: A Brief Overview of the CCC's Development and Areas of Activity," paper presented at Forum on Industrial Relations and Labor Polices in a Globalizing World, 9–11 January, Beijing.

Chan, Anita (2001) *China's Workers under Assault: The Exploitation of Labor in a Globalizing Economy*, Armonk, NY: M.E. Sharpe.

Chan, Anita and Nørlund, Irene (1998) "Vietnamese and Chinese Labor Regimes: On the Road to Divergence," *The China Journal*, 40: 173–197.

Chan, Anita and Wang, Hong-zen (2003) "Raising Labor Standards, Corporate Social Responsibility and Missing Links – Vietnam and China Compared," paper presented at Labor Standards in China Conference, 21–22 March, University of Michigan.

China Labor Watch (2002) "Reebok's Human Rights Standard and Chinese Working Conditions," at http://www.chinalaborwatch.org/reports/reebok.htm.

(CIC) Hong Kong Christian Industrial Committee (2000) "Nike, Show Workers that Your Commitment to Human Rights is Genuine," *Change*, February at http://www.cic.org.hk/ce_00feb.htm.

Emerson, Tony (2000) "A Letter to Jiang Zemin: The Quixotic Tale of three American CEOs and their Ill-Fated Mission to Change China from Inside," *Newsweek International*, 29 May.

Frenkel, Stephen (2001) "Globalization, Athletic Footwear Commodity Chains and Employment Relations in China," *Organization Studies*, 4: 531–562.

Guthrie, Douglas (1999) *Dragon in a Three-piece Suit: The Emergence of Capitalism in China*, Princeton, NJ: Princeton University Press.

Hsing, You-tien (1998) *Making Capitalism in China: The Taiwan Connection*, Oxford: Oxford University Press.

LARIC (2000) "Independent Monitoring vs Workers' Representation on Labor Practices," *China Labor Bulletin*, 55, July–August: 1–4.

Lee, Ching Kwan (1998) *Gender and the South China Miracle: Two Worlds of Factory Women*, Berkeley, CA: University of California Press.

Liu, Kaming (2003) "Implementation of Codes of Conduct in China: Current Status and Predicaments," paper presented at Labor Standards in China Conference, 21–22 March, University of Michigan.

National Labor Committee (NLC) (2000) "Made in China: The Role of U.S. Com-

panies in Denying Human and Worker Rights," at http://www.nlcnet.org/
report00/introduction.html.

Pun, Ngai (2005a) *Made in China: Women Factory Workers in a Global Work-place*, Durham, NC: Duke University Press.

Pun, Ngai (2005b) "Global Production, Company Codes of Conduct, and Labor Conditions in China: A Case Study of Two Factories" *The China Journal*, 54: 101–113.

Sajhau, Jean-Paul (1997) "Business Ethics in the Textile, Clothing and Footwear (TCF) Industries: Codes of Conduct," *ILO Bulletin* II-9, at http://www.ilo.org/public/english/dialogue/sector/papers/bzethics.

Schak, David C. (1997) "Taiwanese Labor Management in China," *Employee Relations*, 19(4): 365–373.

Smith, Chris and Pun, Ngai (2003) "Putting the Transnational Labor Process in its Place: The Dormitory Labor Regime in Post-Socialist China," paper presented at 21st International Labor Process Conference, University of the West of England, Bristol, UK, 14–16 April.

Tan, Shen and Liu, Ka Ming (2003) *Kuaguo gongsi di shehui zeren* [Transnational corporate social responsibility in China], Beijing: shehui kexue wenxian chuban-she.

Women Working Worldwide (2000) "Company Codes of Conduct," at http://www.poptel.org.uk/women-ww/company_coc.htm.

7 Work, conformity, and defiance

Strategies of resistance and control in China's township and village enterprises

Calvin Chen

The astounding growth and increasing competitiveness of Chinese industry, especially in the last ten years, are no longer a surprising development. With China's displacement of the United States as Japan's top trading partner in 2004, more scholars, business people, and policy-makers are calling attention to understanding the trajectory and consequences of China's booming economy (Zaun 2005: C8). While analysts have long recognized the difficulties of market-oriented transition, others have noted that China's transformation into the world's workshop is inevitable, in part because of its inexpensive yet productive labor force. Yet this factor alone does not and cannot explain China's industrial success.

In order to better understand the emergence of Chinese industry, we not only need to closely examine how production is organized and executed in Chinese firms, but also the critical role played by rural-based enterprises in China's explosive industrial growth since 1978.[1] In 2004, rural enterprises employed over 135 million workers, nearly a third of the total rural workforce and nearly 20 percent of China's total workforce (*Chinese Statistical Yearbook* 2004: 122–123). Those numbers continue to grow rapidly each year with major repercussions for both the Chinese and global economies. While current studies of rural enterprises have highlighted critical components and aspects of their growth, they tend to emphasize the role of local cadres in rural industrial development, especially how they connect potential clients with factories in their jurisdictions (Oi 1999). However, they shed little light on how these enterprises manage the day-to-day affairs of production and how they create and sustain organizational stability. As Jacob Eyferth points out in the Introduction, building a stable workplace requires attention not only to the production process, but also to how social meanings are constructed and impact interactions among the workforce in the factory.

This chapter attempts to address these issues through an examination of how workers in rural enterprises navigate the difficult terrain of the factory on a daily basis. It focuses on worker responses and tactics in the face of heightened managerial control over the content and process of industrial work. The argument is based largely on data gathered through participant observation and personal interviews conducted in China's Zhejiang province in 1997 and 1998 at two firms, "Phoenix" and "Jupiter." Phoenix, a firm located in Wenzhou, is a privately-owned enterprise established in 1984 that primarily produces low-voltage electrical products; in contrast, "Jupiter," a firm situated in Jinhua, was originally established in 1975 under collective ownership, and today turns out a vast assortment of goods that range from textiles and furniture to audio speakers and electrical relays.[2] Both enterprises are among the largest and most successful firms in their sectors, counting thousands of workers on their payrolls. In 1998, Jupiter already employed a workforce of 14,000 while Phoenix reached a workforce of over 13,000 in 2004. Although these two firms can hardly be seen as representative of all rural enterprises, they do serve as an important lens through which we can understand more broadly the enterprise as a community where issues of individual opportunity, collective welfare, and higher purpose are articulated, debated, and resolved.

In my analysis, I follow the lead of James Scott, who, in his masterful *Weapons of the Weak*, reminds us that acts of defiance and resistance do not always have a collective or organized character to them. Rather, "they require little or no coordination or planning; they often represent a form of individual self-help; and they typically avoid any direct symbolic confrontation with authority or with elite norms" (Scott 1985: 29). I argue that while enterprise managers retain enormous leverage over the industrial workplace, workers in rural factories can and often use "weapons of the weak" – for example, work slowdowns and rumor mongering – to thwart or blunt managerial imperatives. This contrasts with the idea of worker resistance, which I see as a more sustained and organized effort to defy and defeat managerial designs and one that involves more direct and riskier behavior. While the use of informal and organized tactics has not yielded overwhelming success (workers at Phoenix and Jupiter have lost and still lose most of their battles with management), their use of informal tactics has forced enterprise leaders to take worker interests seriously, rethink the costs and benefits of new production and management techniques, and adjust company policies, even as increasing market competition prompts company leaders to search for more efficient production approaches.

My findings also suggest that these informal strategies of defiance may have a positive impact on the transformation of workplace relations and reduce labor strife in rural enterprises. In the following sections, I analyze the evolution of labor relations at Phoenix and Jupiter during the post-1978 reform period and examine the connections between weapons of the weak strategies among workers and shifts in production and control strategies among enterprise management.

Labor relations in the early years

The early histories of Phoenix and Jupiter were notable for a remarkable absence of informal strategies of resistance. Instead, during the first stage of development, what I call enterprise survival,[3] labor conflict was low and a high degree of cohesion and harmony among members of the enterprise was commonplace. For Phoenix, this stage began in 1984 and ended in the late 1980s; for Jupiter, it started in 1975 and ended in the mid-1980s. In contrast to factories where severe disagreements often broke out, both Phoenix and Jupiter were able to contain disputes and prevent them from turning into major confrontations. This approach emerged from the founders' heavy reliance on kinship and native-place networks for staffing, which affected how authority was structured and exercised.

Although the factory's managerial structure was clearly hierarchical, it was simple rather than bureaucratic. Authority – the decision-making power over work content, scheduling, and pace – rested in the hands of the enterprise founders and an inner circle of "heroic cadres." The founder determined the content and direction of work on a daily basis; in his absence, his lieutenants kept operations running smoothly and efficiently. All of the remaining factory personnel were expected to follow their example. As in late nineteenth-century industrializing America, factory founders were personally involved in almost every facet of factory activity. They "saw everything, knew everything, and decided everything" (Hymer 1979: 25). Their ability to monitor events and personnel on the shop floor was facilitated by the small size of their workforces and their work areas. In this initial stage, Jupiter employed fewer than sixty workers while Phoenix had fewer than thirty in 1975 and 1984, respectively. Almost all Jupiter's employees were from the same village while Phoenix's personnel were nearly all from one extended family. Although I could not find any exact data on the size of the original workshops, respondents emphasized that spaces were cramped, simultaneously serving as office, workshop, and warehouse.

The personal presence of the founders on the shop floor served to inspire workers and strengthen the bonds between members of the factory community. Industrial work was backbreaking and dirty, yet when workers saw their superiors working side by side with them, they gained a new sense of dignity and self-respect. High levels of trust and reciprocity, a spirit of cooperation, the collective sharing of benefits, and reliance on persuasion gave the management system legitimacy in the eyes of employees. On the whole, it was a system that was flexible enough to accommodate differing levels of skill, ability, and commitment yet strong enough to focus diverse interests and viewpoints towards the common purpose of enterprise-building. This stands in stark contrast to Lida Junghans's study of railway work units in this volume where blood ties led to "inbreeding" and increasing dysfunction.

Fostering camaraderie and "human feeling" (*renqing*) also eased the transitions of workers into the new world of industrial work. A plant manager at Phoenix, widely regarded as one of the most caring and upstanding men in the managerial ranks, explained his approach this way:

> I don't like to use a tough, cold approach. If I have a problem with a worker, I call that person into my office and we talk. I discuss the problem and ask how the worker feels. It's a discussion, not a scolding. I would never discuss anything in the workshop. The worker would "lose face" [*meiyou mianzi*] and this would cause serious emotional problems. I try to treat people in such a way that if they leave the factory, they leave on good terms. It's impossible to work without some "human feeling" ... If you think the worker is here to serve the factory and the factory has no need to serve the worker, the factory will eventually fail. You can't go around ordering people to do whatever you want them to do.

Under this paternalistic approach, workers were less likely to use informal tactics to derail managerial directives because they did not yet see their relationship with superiors in adversarial terms. Although the operations of the factory relied heavily on the personal discretion of managers, this did not mean decisions were always arbitrary. Work rules were few in number, circumscribed in scope, and primarily focused on safety concerns. In production areas where grease or oil could be found, for example, managers at Phoenix prohibited smoking to guard against the outbreak of fire. In other instances, female workers were asked to tie up their long hair to prevent it from being caught in running machinery. Workers were not fined if they violated these rules, but they were reprimanded and cautioned. Management hoped that embarrassment and the danger of injury would be sufficient to elicit a change in behavior.

While I stress the significance of close ties between workers and managers, I do not want to romanticize them. In his classic study *Work and Authority in Industry*, Reinhard Bendix cautions that "intimate personal contacts can be every bit as unbearable as the impersonality of the market place" (Bendix 1956: 37). Moreover, "paternalistic benevolence and ruthless oppression often made use of exactly the same managerial devices" (ibid.: 51). Hence, flexibility and informality did not mean dissatisfaction was non-existent. In fact, workers often grumbled about unpaid back wages and the long overtime hours they were asked to work. When they approached factory managers with these concerns, most were counseled to be patient. Wages would be eventually paid out, they were told. Relatives and friends, they argued, would not betray the trust of one of their own, although it appears that in some instances, they nearly stretched this trust beyond its breaking point. Consequently, most workers stayed on the job so that they would not end up with nothing if they left (*baizuole*) while giving their relatives another chance to make amends. This development parallels Minchuan Yang's findings of initial kinship-based cooperation among factory members in a Sichuan village (Yang 1994: 157–179). Like the factory in Yang's study, Phoenix and Jupiter were able to maintain a high level of social cohesion during this period because competing socio-economic interests within the firm had not yet emerged.

Still, the tensions and frantic pace engendered by tight deadlines often set everyone on edge. It only took one flippant remark or one dirty look to ignite a confrontation that threatened to upend the social stability of the workshop. Despite the close ties of kinship and friendship that bound members together, rifts occasionally surfaced. When pent-up grievances arose, major arguments and in some cases fistfights ensued. However, what is noteworthy about both firms at this time is that employees were more comfortable expressing their dissatisfaction directly to their superiors, both individually and collectively. Although no one expected to win a favorable resolution every time, members of the enterprise were confident they would at least receive a fair hearing and did not feel so alienated that they needed to use less formal tactics to correct perceived injustices.

Informal strategies of defiance in rural enterprises

Most of the workers I interviewed in the late 1990s complained that labor relations within the enterprise worsened after the initial stage of enterprise survival and that work-related problems were harder to resolve than in the early years, when management defused tensions through informal means rather than bureaucratic regulations. As a result, workers have increasingly relied upon informal strategies – slander and foot dragging, among others – to blunt managerial imperatives. These tactics are not readily noticeable unless one spends a considerable amount of time watching the dynamics of the shop floor. However, during my time at Phoenix and Jupiter, it was obvious that these techniques of protest were a response to the management's decision to simultaneously rationalize and expand production. This launched the stage of enterprise expansion, a period which lasted from the late 1980s through the early 1990s for Jupiter and the early 1990s through the mid-late 1990s for Phoenix.

Enterprise management at both firms believed that greater specialization would lead to a more efficient division of labor, allowing employees to apply their skills for maximum effectiveness. Improved coordination of the enterprise's various activities would reduce redundancies and lock in even greater efficiency. To enterprise management, these changes meant more than a convergence with reforms in state-owned enterprises; they were hoping to join the ranks of elite Chinese companies and approximate the standards used by advanced Western firms. Through various study visits to other domestic and foreign-owned firms, managers concluded that reforms were critical to maintaining their long-term competitiveness. However, workers saw these changes as an attempt to construct what Ching Kwan Lee calls a "localistic despotism," a hierarchy built on impersonal rules and control over class and native-place identities (Lee 1998: 135).

In spatial terms, production was reorganized in a more linear fashion so that neat rows of workstations or an assembly line dominated the work-space. Where new machinery, most notably conveyor belts, was intro-duced, workers became part of the *liushuixian*, or assembly line, which limited them to performing specific tasks in larger teams, meeting produc-tion quotas established by management. Along with this new production arrangement, enterprise leaders implemented a contract system, in which workers contracted with management for the fulfillment of production tasks; they also introduced performance-based wages, which they hoped would ease worker anxieties and boost production. This development was similar to the output-based compensation system introduced in China during the 1950s as described by Mark Frazier in this volume. Enterprise leaders hoped this policy would result in expanded output with minimal social fallout.

Still, some managers considered rewards insufficient: without fines and sanctions, they argued, workers would never break bad habits. Many of the managers I met expressed exasperation with their workers. When many of them, after touring other companies, saw how disciplined and focused workers at other firms were, their positive views of their own workers turned negative. Said one administrator in Jupiter's central offices: "Most of the workers are peasants and don't have strong educational backgrounds. Although many have worked here for some time, you must be tough on them or else they become spoiled. They'll slack off." Indeed, some managers believed that by demanding changes in personal habits, they were not only improving the productivity of their workforces, but more importantly, molding "useful and productive citizens."[4] These man-agers saw themselves as following in the footsteps of their counterparts at other successful firms where iron discipline was instilled through military-inspired training exercises. While my respondents could not explain why managers were so committed to this particular vision, it was clear that at least some of the managers were inspired by martial valor and interpreted the Party–state's economic "call to arms" literally. In other words, man-agement saw this control system as a means of instilling focus and discip-line in workers while they were on *and* off the shop floor, a development they hoped would add stability to the factories as well as the broader community.

Both firms eventually adopted work regulations that laid out a sliding scale of fines for various violations. Minor infractions, like failing to wear identification badges, sloppy dress, or combing one's hair during work time, usually resulted in fines of 2 to 5 *yuan* out of a monthly wage of 500–700 *yuan*. More serious offenses, especially those involving work safety or product quality, drew heavier fines. For instance, one of

Phoenix's transformer panel plants specifically held quality control inspectors responsible for product quality. "If anything goes wrong," one young inspector stated, "there is a tracking number as well as the inspector's name on the certification. There is absolutely no way [we] can avoid the responsibility. If the product fails, the inspector is fined 100 *yuan*."

At other plants, poor product quality drew collective punishment, with all workers on the entire assembly line fined, forced to fix the defective items, or both. When I worked briefly on a Jupiter line assembling audio speakers, a client angrily returned a large shipment of defective speakers and demanded that the products be redone. All line workers and workshop directors were fined 50 *yuan* and forced to work overtime for two weeks to remake the products to the original and correct specifications. Even factory managers were held responsible for such deficiencies. One division administrator told me that it was common in such instances for the manager to be fined 200 *yuan*. To make matters even worse, some managers insisted on publicly displaying the name of the guilty party, the rule they violated, and the amount of the fine on a blackboard. One vice-manager at Phoenix emphasized that through the open posting of violations, "Everyone can see this and learn from it. It's embarrassing to have your name on the blackboard for everyone to see, so workers will try to avoid another violation. A 5 *yuan* fine is not too heavy but it will remind them to be careful."

While such a tough factory regimen did propel the volume and quality of production to new heights, workers complained that the new production orientation ran counter to the norms of worker initiative and control to which they were accustomed in the previous stage of enterprise survival. It usually engendered stiff worker opposition wherever and whenever it replaced older forms of factory organization. Some workers directed their frustration at the "floating population" (*liudong renkou*), non-local workers hailing from such provinces as Anhui and Jiangxi. Because migrant workers shared few common experiences with locals, they were often viewed by local managers and workers with suspicion and often blamed for causing unpopular changes in policy. Others were so incensed they complained directly to management, although such displays of hotheadedness were rather rare.

At a Phoenix control switch plant where the new production method was applied, workers remained suspicious even as the manager extolled the possibility of higher wages as well as the benefits of being "responsible for just a few tasks." Some workers saw this as a ploy to cut their wages, retorting in response, "What if some people are slow or lazy? If our pay is tied to the whole group, some of us will receive lower pay because someone else isn't working." Despite some positive results at the beginning of the experiment, this format only lasted two months before the reversion to individual remuneration, causing the manager to lament that "We just don't have a sense of teamwork or collective effort here. They only care about themselves."

I was present at Phoenix in 1997 when management tried to push through these changes. As the experiment proceeded, I watched how workers moved from wide-eyed astonishment over the dramatic change in work organization to occasional mutterings about its irrationality to bitter complaints about its overall ineffectiveness. In the earliest stages, the complaints were diffuse, anonymous for the most part. Most of the grievances were aired only among workers as they struggled to meet their daily production quotas. However, as the inability of some workers to keep up created bottlenecks in the assembly line, the protests became harsher and the workshop atmosphere increasingly tense.

Still, the threat of fines and the imposition of tighter controls made it more difficult for workers to openly defy their superiors. Consequently, most workers voiced their dissatisfaction indirectly, irregularly at first and then seemingly at every opportunity, seeking to garner some sympathy from management. Most grumbled anytime the managerial staff appeared on the shop floor. Some couched their complaints as "suggestions" while others expressed their concerns in groups. Moreover, the complaining was not only constant, but over time involved more and more, if not all, members of the assembly line. This tactic not only provided collective protection from potential managerial retribution, but more importantly, it amplified the volume of worker discontent, forcing managers to take notice and respond.

When this approach failed to restore the old system, a surprising development occurred. The thrust of their criticisms shifted from how the new system hurt them personally to how it inhibited the factory's potential for efficiency and growth.[5] The unrelenting, continuous daily grumbling for two months, coupled with worker unwillingness to "go the extra mile" made the completion of work orders an arduous task and finally forced the plant manager to abandon the system, albeit with a heavy feeling of disgust. Although he felt that the workers had not given his new approach a fair chance, there was no denying that neither output nor efficiency had improved. In fact, it had decreased. This development, combined with the amorphous groundswell of discontent, eventually precipitated his capitulation.

It is important to note that concerns about these new procedures were not limited to workers; in fact, divisions often arose among members of the managerial staff. In contrast to upper-level management, numerous plant-level managerial staff at both Jupiter and Phoenix viewed the new approach with unease. Factory-level managerial staff wanted to maintain as much flexibility as possible in tackling production demands. To them, rules were an unnecessary constraint. One vice-manager at a Phoenix plant charged that "they [upper management] just pass down regulations to us from above and don't know if they are helpful. They should come work here for a while before going back [to their offices], then they'll know something about managing." This statement highlights a belief that factory policies should mesh with the informal social norms that undergird the workplace. In many plants, the staff simply went through the motions and read the work rules to workers; few issued handbooks to incoming employees or demanded that they become familiar with the contents as a condition of continuing employment. They were content to present them orally and post them in a public space whenever they found it convenient or whenever they remembered to do so. On one of my early visits to one of Phoenix's smaller plants, an official from the central office explained:

> We used to give workers a handbook but we stopped last year. What we do now is tell them orally. We give them a brief introduction to the guidelines when they arrive. If they make a mistake, we correct them and explain to them what the proper method is. The old method seems so rule-oriented and impersonal: it lacked any "human feeling" [*renqing*]. We like this way of doing things better.

Workers in these factories were also nonplussed when I asked about work regulations. "We're not fined here and it's pretty loose," related one female assembler at Phoenix. "When I first came here, they didn't give us a handbook or explain the rules ... If we do something wrong, they just tell us not to do it again." A young male quality control inspector at another Phoenix plant echoed these views: "We don't have a lot of rules here ... they only want us to be clean and on time. [For example], we can't spit and must make sure our workspace is tidy."

Shop floor managers, and especially workshop directors, many of whom had started their careers as production workers, were often reluctant to fine workers for infractions. In fact, many staff members sympathized with workers since they remembered the demanding conditions under which they had previously labored. One workshop director expressed strong reservations about her duty to punish:

> We hardly ever fine workers now. Although I have the authority to fine them, I usually don't dock their pay when pay day arrives ... I just don't feel good about fining them. I used to be an assembler myself and I still remember how bad it felt to be fined. Everyone works hard for their money so I'm reluctant to take it away from them. I guess I'm just not ruthless enough.

In contrast, the head of quality control at one of Phoenix's plants worried about the long-term impact of punishment upon the worker. For him, "the real problem with discipline is deciding how much is enough ... our goal should be to discipline and teach, not to destroy them. With a salary of only 800 *yuan* per month, a 15 to 30 *yuan* fine would really make them take notice."

Others were less philosophical and more concerned about their personal relationships with workers. Another workshop director emphasized to me that "I don't like to fine them because we're still friends after all. I see them often after work, and I feel awkward saying they violated such and such a rule. Most of the time I just tell them to be careful about the rules." Workers could easily sense when members of the managerial staff were reluctant to fine them and were deft at manipulating these feelings to their advantage. Of course, when management forced the issue, the workers acquiesced but they often followed up with other actions. Employees, for example, often spread rumors about managerial staff, snubbed them, or excluded them from social activities. These tactics were often used to devastating effect, as evidenced by the response of this female workshop director at Phoenix:

> When you correct female workers, they accept it and you think everything is just fine. But then they begin to gossip behind your back and say how I'm unfair and other terrible things … If I did something wrong, they should tell me and I'll try to change, but if they say things behind my back, there's nothing I can do … So I just make a few comments and leave it at that. It's not worth it because everyone just ends up angry … What's the point anyway if I win? It's harder to get along with them later on.

These rumors sometimes contained sexual overtones. One rumor at a Phoenix plant suggested that a particular supervisor was intimate with a superior and gained her promotion on the basis of her "looseness" rather than her ability or hard work. In other instances, rumors and personal put-downs were used to irritate and snub managers who had violated informal norms and made work especially difficult for workers. At a different Phoenix plant where electrical switches were produced, I saw how a group of female assemblers harassed a male supervisor each time he conducted an inspection. One worker would begin by asking, "What's the matter with you today? The inspection is taking too much time!" Another would then join in with "He's probably tired. I bet it's because he was up all night having sex!" At this point, the entire group would break out in uproarious laughter, much to the embarrassment of the supervisor who then stormed out of the room.

When I asked the group of young women why they engaged in what seemed to me a risky venture, they were rather nonchalant. They declared that it was all in good fun and more importantly, that these periodic snubs prevented the supervisors from becoming too overbearing. Furthermore, they seemed totally unconcerned about how this would affect their job situation because they could hide behind a screen of relative anonymity. That is, if they encountered any problems, they simply blamed someone else for telling them the supervisor was engaged in such activity and deflected any accusation that they intended to malign his character. What is perhaps most interesting about this particular case is that the workers involved seemed to understand how far they could go without triggering a serious backlash.

In plants where strict adherence to work rules was demanded, the "factory regime," as Michael Burawoy (1985) calls it, was experienced as oppressive and fanatical. Although "despotic" factory regimes were mostly associated with the manufacture of the most advanced products, leaders at both enterprises hoped that all employees would eventually see the benefits of rationalization. One of the toughest managers at Phoenix justified his view in the following manner:

> Some people have criticized me for my strict approach to management. I impose stiff fines and some people say I should also give out rewards for good work. But my rules should be seen in the same way as traffic rules. Do you reward each person individually for stopping when the light is red? How much would you give him? The reward comes on a broader level. When everyone follows rules, everyone arrives at their destinations quickly and easily. It's the same in the workshops.

For him, the only way benefits could be reaped was to divorce production demands from social values whenever possible. Anytime these concerns came into direct conflict, production unquestionably won out, even if the fallout resulted in an unmitigated social disaster. Indeed, those most committed to enforcing the rules often became isolated individuals, excluded from the dinners, card games, and gatherings organized by the other employees.

Of course, strict factory regimes did not stop employees from attempting to dilute the thrust of such managerial approaches. Workers sometimes disrupted the flow of work by turning work rules against managers, for example, by refusing to assemble products unless all the components met the stated standards for quality. Others stuck carefully to their "job descriptions" and would not help with other tasks when deadlines were pressing or the factory was understaffed. Under established work rules, they were not obligated to perform such assignments nor could they be fined for refusing to do so. In this way, workers made their dissatisfaction obvious without opening themselves up to the possibility of managerial retribution. In short, the formal work code was turned on its head to advance informal protests.

In other instances, harsh factory regimes actually accelerated a turn towards kinship and native-place networks for redress. For example, disgruntled employees utilized their connections with high-ranking enterprise officials like the founder, president, or division general manager to pressure lower-ranking managerial staff into acceding to their demands. One Phoenix employee, a native of the area, noted with special delight that he was a distant relative of the company founder. If any problem with superiors arose, he only needed to inform his relatives and the problem would be resolved. Family strife was so dreaded that personnel often scrambled to prevent it. While migrant workers did not have access to similar connections, they could still ask *tongxiang* (people from the same region) who occupied more influential positions at the enterprise to take action on their behalf. Although these networks were not as effective as those of locals, it created a splintered workplace where disputes were often mediated through informal channels instead of the formal mechanisms of the enterprise (Lee 1998: 109–136; Pun 1999).

For workers, the institutionalization of an inflexible, rules-bound system represented not only an utter disregard for their financial welfare, but more importantly, an assault on their dignity. Public shaming in particular was a sore point, leading one shop director to conclude that "you have to give workers some 'face' (*mianzi*). If they think they've been humiliated, they won't listen to you next time." The number of rules violations never decreased significantly during this period, indicating that workers cared little for the views of their superiors and even less about internalizing them. Rather than subscribing to managerial demands, workers upended prevailing authority relationships in ways that reaffirmed their own dignity without threatening their employment.

Trade unions and the formation of a new enterprise culture

Recognizing that heightened employee discontent threatened to undermine organizational stability, Phoenix and Jupiter established unions in the mid-late 1990s as part of a larger effort to create a new enterprise culture (*qiye wenhua*) that would embody the camaraderie and rapport of the past. In demonstrating their commitment to addressing worker concerns and mediating disputes, enterprise leaders hoped to create a new "enterprise family" where common purpose and collective well-being would supersede personal status and goals. They took membership in kinship and native-place networks, both exclusive modes of association, and redefined them to be more inclusive in the hope that loyalty and trust would be restored. Management believed unions could be effective in two ways: first, they could help them get a clearer idea of worker concerns and morale; second, and most importantly, unions could help implement new policies that would ease worker anxieties and enhance their security.

This policy began with expanded outreach. At Phoenix, for example, union representatives periodically hold open drop-in sessions, usually one Saturday morning or afternoon per month, where employees can voice any grievances they have about work. Attendance at such sessions varied, mostly because Saturdays were not convenient for workers who had to work overtime, attend to family matters, or were simply too exhausted from their regular work regimen. The workers who did show up were often reticent about expressing their true feelings and did not want to be punished for unwelcome comments. Even when Phoenix installed suggestion boxes so that employees could express their views anonymously, few used this opportunity to raise serious concerns. Enterprise and union officials were clearly exasperated when workers used the suggestion boxes to complain about specific supervisors, vent when they had a bad day, or simply used them as a receptacle for their litter. More recently, they have set up electronic posting boards on their networked computers where complaints can be aired. The trade union chairman told me that this is "most democratic" and allows him to respond much more quickly to employee grievances. For him and others, these channels of dialogue are more than cornerstones of a new openness: they serve as a means of heading off discontent before it disrupts the social harmony they aim to achieve.

Despite mixed results, these efforts have been applauded by many in the enterprise. Still, most employees are not convinced that the union can provide them with critical backing when it matters most. For example, although union representatives have pushed for improved wages and job security, few workers have benefited from these efforts. Employees recognize that the union, while formally the advocate of worker interests, is heavily dependent on management. Ultimately, enterprise leaders, not union representatives, decide whether or not to fund union-sponsored events or implement new policies. Furthermore, with the exception of the union chairman, union representatives hold other positions within the enterprise, almost all in management. In other words, if the union pushes too hard on behalf of workers, union representatives could potentially suffer major repercussions, including lower compensation and job loss. To be fair, leaders at Phoenix rarely resorted to such action, but it was clear who held the upper hand. Hence, workers rightly perceived a conflict of interest in their union: the union is supposed to be on the side of workers, but it serves at the behest of management.

Nevertheless, the union continues to gather information on what workers want and works towards the fulfillment of their desires. Perhaps the most promising union activities involve efforts to extend and equalize the distribution of benefits. For example, shortly before my stay at Phoenix, the labor union successfully lobbied for the extension of subsidized meals to workers in addition to managerial staff. It built a reading room/library and has plans for fitness/weight rooms, in hopes that this would help reduce work-induced stress and aid workers in resisting the temptations of late-night card and *mahjong* playing. At Jupiter, the enterprise periodically handed out a range of daily necessities like packets of detergent, bars of soap, towels, and cooking oil. Some of the more profitable plants even initiated far-ranging plans to provide housing and even pensions to workers whose tenure at the factory exceeded fifteen years. While all of this is reminiscent of the old *danwei* system,[6] it also highlights the persistence of a moral economy perspective among workers at Phoenix and Jupiter. Many workers believed that given their sacrifices on behalf of their "enterprise family," they deserved a greater share of the profits. For older workers, it seems their views are influenced by expectations of reciprocity that derive from their membership in kinship and social networks; for more recent workers, it seems their views stem from expectations that management will uphold their end of the informal "social contract," one which grants fair remuneration in exchange for superior performance.

In addition, both enterprises have organized an array of events called *biwu*, or matches of skill. These events range from bicycle races, Chinese chess, and *karaoke*, to tug-of-war, typing competitions, and basketball games. Nearly all of these events have generated a positive buzz among enterprise employees: they are generally well attended and have re-injected enthusiasm and friendliness into the enterprise community. Under the direction of the union and former local party cadres, these activities are not only contests of individual prowess, but also contain elements of public spectacle and large-scale party. For instance, one singing contest at Phoenix generated more excitement than was first anticipated:

> Most recently we held a *karaoke* competition. Over ninety people originally registered for the contest, so we held tryouts and cut the number of contestants down to thirty. Each contestant sang two songs so the competition lasted from 7:30 p.m. to 1 a.m.! Almost everyone stayed until the end to lend moral support to the representative from their factory. People bought so many flowers that local flower shops were completely sold out. Some participants couldn't even hold all the bouquets given. It was fantastic because of the festive atmosphere and the goodwill of everyone involved.

For management, these seemingly ordinary events are not mere diversions or entertainment: they are opportunities to reinforce identification with the enterprise. While these events are competitive, they are conducted with enterprise unity, not individual glory, in mind. For many employees, such events present opportunities to meet new people and even develop new organizational or computer-related skills. For them, the enterprise is becoming a more engaging, caring workplace. On the other hand, some employees see these events as diverting attention away from more pressing concerns like better wages, job security, and promotion opportunities. After revisiting Phoenix in 2004, my sense is that more workers believe the company is moving in the right direction, even though they often think the pace of change is too slow. Under such circumstances, they remain very savvy in responding to enterprise policies. They use formal institutions whenever they can, but will press with informal tactics if those mechanisms fail to produce the results they want.

Conclusion

This chapter focuses on the evolution of labor relations in two rural enterprises in Zhejiang province in the post-Mao reform period and the day-to-day experiences of workers on the shop floor. Increased competition from rival firms, changes in production methods, and the incomplete development of enterprise institutions have resulted in a constant tug-of-war over what constitutes industrial work and how it should be carried out. While this situation is not likely to change anytime soon, it is noteworthy that informal strategies of worker defiance have emerged against managerial designs for increased control over the industrial workplace. Of course, workers and managers are constantly engaged in battles where victory by either side is never fully assured. Although complaining, slander, foot-dragging, and social exclusion may not seem like effective tools in these contests, they can be powerful weapons, even if wielded by those who are relatively weak. These tactics have produced just enough turmoil within the enterprise that high-level management has been forced to soften some of its policies and adopt a "kinder, gentler" approach.

To be sure, the overall effectiveness of informal strategies depends heavily upon a factor outside of their control, enterprise management itself. Managerial staff members who are deeply embedded in social networks operating throughout the factory are much more susceptible to these tactics. This may not be a negative development, for it suggests that weapons of the weak may have more than a marginal impact in reducing inequities in China's rural enterprises. The prevalence of these acts reminds us that the legitimacy of formal institutions goes beyond aligning financial incentives and material rewards with effort. Legitimacy also hinges greatly on the extent to which issues concerning worker dignity and fairness are addressed. These are not easy issues to resolve, especially since most rural-based enterprises are more concerned about simply staying financially afloat. However, if the recent experiences of Phoenix and Jupiter are indicative of future trends, these enterprises must, sooner perhaps rather than later, grapple with how best to adjust workplace institutions to the needs of its members. How they resolve this vital issue may be as crucial in determining the well-being of workers and the long-term success of rural enterprises as turning a profit.

Notes

1 Until a few years ago, TVEs, non-urban enterprises, were either collectively owned or privately operated. Their reclassification as *minyin qiye* or "people-run enterprises" means they are now predominantly, if not totally, privately run.
2 Phoenix and Jupiter are fictitious names I created to protect the identities of the firms and the respondents I interviewed.
3 My use of developmental stages and core tasks is drawn from the work of Ken

Jowitt. For a fuller discussion of this framework, see "Inclusion," in Ken Jowitt (1992), especially pp. 88–91. Also see Chen (forthcoming).

4 Calvin Chen, "Assembling Peasant Factories," PhD dissertation, University of California, Berkeley, 2000, p. 157. These efforts to alter worker orientations in China are reminiscent of actions taken by English entrepreneurs in the early stages of the Industrial Revolution. See Pollard (1965), especially pp. 160–208.

5 This contrasts with laid-off workers of state-owned enterprises who have used Maoist rhetoric in their efforts to secure unemployment and welfare support from the state. See Ching Kwan Lee (2000: 41–59).

6 For an overview, see Lü Xiaobo and Elizabeth Perry (1997).

References

Bendix, Reinhard (1956) *Work and Authority in Industry*, New York: John Wiley and Sons.

Burawoy, Michael (1985) *The Politics of Production: Factory Regimes Under Capitalism and Socialism*, London: Verso.

Chen, Calvin (2000) "Assembling Peasant Factories," PhD dissertation, University of California, Berkeley.

Chen, Calvin (forthcoming) "Leninism, Developmental Stages, and Trans-formation: Understanding Social and Institutional Change in Contemporary China," in Vladimir Tismaneanu, Marc Morjé Howard, and Rudra Sil (eds) *World Order Without Leninism*, University of Washington Press.

Chinese Statistical Yearbook 2004, Beijing: Chinese Statistical Press, pp. 122–123.

Edwards, Richard (1979) *Contested Terrain: The Transformation of the Work-place in the Twentieth Century*, New York: Basic Books.

Hymer, Stephen (1979) *The Multinational Corporation: A Radical Approach*, Cambridge: Cambridge University Press.

Jowitt, Ken (1992) "Inclusion," in *New World Disorder: The Leninist Extinction*, Berkeley, CA: University of California Press.

Lee, Ching Kwan (1998) *Gender and the South China Miracle*, Berkeley, CA: University of California Press.

Lee, Ching Kwan (2000) "Pathways of Labor Insurgency," in Elizabeth Perry and Mark Selden (eds) *Chinese Society*, New York: Routledge, pp. 41–59.

Lü Xiaobo and Perry, Elizabeth J. (eds) (1997) *Danwei: The Changing Chinese Workplace in Historical and Comparative Perspective*, Armonk, NY: M.E. Sharpe.

Oi, Jean (1999) *Rural China Takes Off*, Berkeley, CA: University of California Press.

Pollard, Sidney (1965) "The Adaptation of the Labour Force," in *The Genesis of Modern Management: A Study of the Industrial Revolution in Great Britain*, Cambridge, MA: Harvard University Press.

Pun, Ngai (1999) "Becoming Dagongmei: The Politics of Identity and Difference in Reform China," *The China Journal*, 42: 1–19.

Scott, James C. (1985) *Weapons of the Weak: Everyday Forms of Peasant Resistance*, New Haven, CT: Yale University Press.

Yang, Minchuan (1994) "Reshaping Peasant Culture and Community: Rural Industrialization in a Chinese Village," *Modern China*, 20(2): 157–179.

Zaun, Todd (2005) "A Growing China Becomes Japan's Top Trade Partner," *New York Times*, 27 January: C8.

8 Labor on the "floating native land"

A case study of seafarers on PRC ocean-going ships

Minghua Zhao

The beginning of the twenty-first century has seen the People's Republic of China (PRC) emerging as a major maritime power with one of the largest fleets in the world. While this has generated great interest in Chinese shipping, little is known about seafarers and their ships. This chapter examines the dynamics of the workplace in one important sector of the country's transport industry, merchant shipping, against the background of economic reform since the 1980s, when China transformed itself from a planned economy to a "socialist market economy." Empirical data are drawn from the author's interviews with senior managers in a number of major state-owned shipping companies in China during several research trips between 1998 and 2001, interviews with Chinese seafarers aboard six PRC container ships[1] in Hong Kong and some major European ports during the same period, and recently completed studies of political commissars on Chinese merchant ships and the seafarers' labor market in China.

The Chinese shipping industry[2]

Although shipping has a long history in China, the country's emergence as a major maritime nation is a recent phenomenon. In 1949, when the communists came to power, over 85 percent of the fleet (in gross tonnage) had been moved to Taiwan, Hong Kong, and other Asian countries, including virtually all large ocean-going ships (Wang 1982: 529). Many vessels were intentionally destroyed or grounded by the Kuomintang troops on the realization that they could not possibly take these ships away from the mainland before the arrival of Mao's People's Liberation Army. New China was therefore left with only 10 percent of the national fleet, mostly old, small ships in private ownership (Chinese Shipping Society 1989: 1). International trade was carried primarily by ships hired from other countries and ships jointly owned by China and two socialist countries – Poland and Czechoslovakia (Sun and Zhang 2002: 6–8). Towards the end of the 1950s, the lifting of the American-led embargo improved the environment for international trade. This, together with the end of the disastrous Great

Leap Forward, led to a rapid development of the Chinese economy, which in turn led to the decision to set up a Chinese state-owned ocean fleet. In 1961, the state-owned China Ocean Shipping Company (COSCO) was formed. Starting with only four small ships, the fleet grew rapidly in the next four decades, especially through the purchase of second-hand ships in the 1970s and the order of new ships in the 1990s. In 1998, the mainland had become the fifth largest ship owner in the world. If Hong Kong is included, China ranks third only behind Greece and Japan, well before Norway, Germany, the UK, and other traditional maritime powers (UNCTAD, cited in ITF 2002; ISL 1998: 30).

China's shipping industry is dominated by three state-owned companies (Table 8.1). These companies used to have clearly defined territories, concentrating on ocean, coastal and river trades respectively. Now, with the disappearance of the planned economy, companies are free to trade where they wish, although in practice each of these main players still dominates in its traditional sphere (Ministry of Communications 2000).

Private shipping has developed rapidly in the past twenty years. However, until recently most of the private companies owned only a single ship and traded intra-regionally rather than internationally. Foreign ship owners have also made some advances into the country's market. By 1999, eighteen foreign ship-owners had set up branches in Shanghai, Guangzhou, Shenzhen, and other major port cities. Joint ventures in vessel ownership and operation are still uncommon, but foreign operators from Japan, Norway, and Switzerland have made inroads in maritime education and training in Shanghai, Guangzhou, and other major port cities.

The expansion of the fleet has led to a rapid growth of the labor market for seafarers in China. The number of Chinese seafarers is estimated at 338,000, about one-third of whom are employed on ocean ships, consisting of 6 percent of the world's total seafaring workforce (Lane *et al.* 2001; Zhao and Shen 2001). No women are employed on deep sea cargo ships, although women seafarers are found in passenger vessels where they play the traditional "women's role" as cleaners, waitresses, cabin stewardesses, and other careers. Traditional maritime nations such as Britain, Germany, Japan, and Norway have long been unable to recruit enough seafarers from their own countries to crew their ships. The world fleets have therefore increasingly been crewed with seafarers sourced from developing

Table 8.1 Top three shipping companies in China

Place	Company	Dead weight tonnage (1,000)
1	China Ocean Shipping Group (COSCO)	1,587.27
2	China Shipping Group (CSCO)	795.13
3	Changjiang Shipping Group (CSC)	357.21

Source: Ministry of Communications (PRC) *et al.* 2000.

countries, especially from Asia and Eastern Europe. The Philippines provided the fleets with the largest number of seafarers (about 25 percent of the world total). Because of its high-quality maritime education and its cheap labor, China has the potential to become the main labor supplier for the world fleets (BIMCO/ISF 1995; Grey 1999; Lee and Wonham 1999; Lane *et al.* 2001; Sharma 2002; Zhao and Amante 2003).

Institutional and technical changes in the workplace

The past two decades have witnessed a fundamental restructuring of the workplace for seafarers in China, in both institutional and technical aspects. Enterprise reform, hand in hand with the modernization of the fleet, has significantly changed the landscape of the Chinese shipping industry, especially since the 1990s.

Enterprise reforms

As in many land-based industries, enterprise reforms in shipping began in the mid-1980s and essentially introduced two new principles: the separation of ownership from management and the reduction of employment and welfare guarantees for workers. Reforms in the production process have encouraged managerial autonomy in a whole array of areas, from purchasing and pricing to labor recruitment and pay determination; profit and productivity are now key performance criteria. The reforms have also replaced collective with individual incentives at various levels, expressed in a battery of "responsibility systems" which aim to establish closer links between rewards and performance. The reform also involves the introduction of the Modern Enterprise System (MES) and the Group Company System (GCS), intended to transform China's largest state-owned enterprises into internationally competitive corporations. It is expected that these corporations, while still remaining in overall state ownership, will much more closely resemble typical Western corporations, with Boards of Directors accountable to shareholders rather than subject to the political authority of the Party–state. Second, reforms in employment relations have replaced permanent employment with contract labor (Hassard *et al.* 1999). While labor contracts terminated life-long employment for seafarers and granted management the right to hire and fire workers, the Economic Contract Responsibility System (ECRS), with its system of rewards and penalties, has linked individual income to targets controlled by managers ashore (Wan 1988, cited in Shen and Lee 2002).

The modernization of the fleet[3]

New technologies have been introduced to the PRC fleet primarily through the purchase of new vessels, in sharp contrast to the previous "peak" of fleet development in the 1970s, when growth was realized almost exclusively through the purchase of second-hand vessels (Sun and Zhang 2002). A senior Chinese fleet manager engaged in ocean shipping for twenty years recalls his experiences in selling and purchasing ships for a major Chinese shipping company:

> We have purchased many ships since the 1990s. They were new ships, big and beautiful and tailor-made for us by the Germans or the Japanese. Meanwhile, we have also sold many old ships. Some of these ships went to scrap yards, but many to small, private companies for short-sea trade.

Shipbuilding technology has allowed a rapid increase in ship size, matched by cargo handling equipment and port structure. As average ship sizes in the world container fleet have doubled from Panamax (3,000–4,000 TEU)[4] to post-Panamax vessels (6,000–8,000 TEU), ship size in the PRC fleet has increased from 1,500 TEU in the early 1980s to 5,440 TEU in 2002 (Figure 8.1). Ships are now running faster and calling at more ports in shorter voyages. In the mid-1980s, it would take a 1,500 TEU ship, then the largest in the PRC fleet, ninety days to complete the voyage from Shanghai to Antwerp, calling on eight ports en route. Now, a vessel of 5,440 TEU only needs fifty-six days to cover the same vast distance, calling on twelve ports on the way. More efficient cargo handling has

Figure 8.1 Modern Chinese container ship (source: Author's photograph).

dramatically reduced vessel turnaround time in port. As recently as the early 1990s, turnaround time for a 1,500 TEU container ship in the British container port of Felixstowe was thirty-six hours; in 2002, the time was more than halved, even though ships carry more "boxes." The rationale behind such fast turnaround is cost: "failure to run is failure to earn" as pointed out by many ship owners and shipping managers (ILO 2001).

Automation, adopted in the 1960s in OECD fleets, was introduced to the PRC fleet in the early 1980s. Integrated bridge systems are now a standard feature of new ships, with the bridge as the integrated control centre for navigation, propulsion, and communication. The introduction of computers to monitor propulsion resulted in automated engine rooms, with seafarers benefiting from daytime working patterns. The main effect of deck and engine room automation is a reduction of crewing levels and a change in work organization. Obviously, the physical workplace of seafarers, the ship, has changed significantly. This, together with the institutional change brought about by enterprise reform, has inevitably impacted seafarers' work and life.

Seafarers' experiences at sea

The ship is not only the seafarers' workplace but also their home and community. Land-based industries in China, as in some other developing countries, often use dormitory regimes to ensure "just-in-time labor" for "just-in-time production" (Pun Chapter 6 in this volume; Smith and Pun 2003). In shipping, however, ship owners do not need the modern factory system to tie seafarers up with their ships. After all, sailors have lived in their workplace ever since humans started their exploration of the seas. Seafarers typically spend two-thirds of their lives working and living in this physically confined, geographically mobile place, far away from friends, family, and the larger society ashore. Any study of seafarers' work will therefore have to include their life at sea.

Labor reorganization

Globalization has generated an ever growing volume of international trade, with a concomitant demand for maritime transport and, in turn, for seafarers. Although shipping is a capital-intensive industry, labor costs still comprise 50 percent of operation costs. It is therefore "rational" for shipping capital to reduce the crew to a minimum and make the remaining crew work harder, for example, through the adoption of new technologies, increased ship speed (more ports visits, faster turnaround), and increased ship size (ILO 2001). Technological changes promoted by profit-driven and cost-sensitive shipping companies have led to smaller crews, higher workloads, reduced opportunities to take shore leave, and the redefinition of skills.

Crew size reduction

In contrast to labor-intensive industries such as textiles, toys, construction, and mining, which employ large numbers of unskilled or low-skilled migrant workers from poor inland provinces (as Pun observed in Chapter 6), the operation of modernized ships demands an increasingly well-trained and productive workforce. Although Chinese seafarers are among the lowest paid in the world, the crew cost still is a significant part of the ship's operation cost at sea. Crewing levels in the PRC fleet have shown a significant reduction since the 1990s. A container ship of 3,800 TEU, for example, had a crew of thirty-eight in 1994; in 2002, crew size had been slashed to twenty-three. In the course of eight years, crews had been reduced by 40 percent, to a level only slightly higher than that of European or Japanese competitors.

Seafarers' chances to escape redundancy depend on their status as core or peripheral workers. Officers, the most skilled and functionally flexible employees, are among the core workers that companies retain. Seafarers with relatively low skills (able seamen, ordinary seamen, carpenters, motormen), those whose skills have been made redundant by technological change (radio officers), and those whose functions, although important to the well-being and welfare of the crew, are considered "non-productive" (cooks, stewards, doctors and political commissars), are most likely to be made redundant.

Given the fact that technology remains constant aboard the latest generation of ships, the reduced crew size suggests that the retained seafarers have to work harder to complete tasks that were previously handled by larger crews. Labor intensification has been reported by many seafarers, in spite of management's assertion that demand for physical labor has been much reduced as a result of ship automation and computerization. The following account is from a commissar on board a brand-new Japanese-built container ship. The man is fifty-four years old and has sailed on more than twenty ships since 1987:

> Now, with the increase in ship size and the automation level, the crew size has become much smaller. Before automation, a smaller ship would need more than 40 seafarers. Now, we have only 24, and we are going to lose another one soon. The worker seafarers (known as ratings in the international shipping industry) in particular have to work harder than before, because the ship is bigger and they have more chipping, painting and other things to do. At the same time, the ship spends so little time in port that seafarers have to race against time to finish the work, because the best time to do maintenance is when the ship is in port.

Officers are also affected by crew reductions. On vessels where the post of sailing commissar has been phased out, the captain has to take over the responsibility of crew management previously shouldered by the commissar. Many captains complained about the double burden of having to manage the ship *and* the crew – and many of them seemed to genuinely miss the companionship and comradeship of the commissar. "Technical cadre seafarers," officers in the deck and engine departments, are considered to have benefited most from ship automation and computerization. Nevertheless, these seafarers also reported an increased feeling of fatigue and loneliness in recent years. The reduced crew level cuts into both seafarers' health and their perception and experience of their workplace community. In the engine room, with fewer "hands" around, engine officers have to keep themselves more alert when monitoring the machines. The work in the engine control room is less arduous than before, but it can be stressful and lonely.

Fast turnaround

Containerization has revolutionized cargo transportation and handling, to the benefit of ship owners and cargo owners. Its implication for the quality of seafarers' working life, however, is largely negative. A general cargo ship takes fifteen days to load and unload in Shanghai, giving seafarers time to take shore leave and visit their families. With container ships, the same process takes only 24–36 hours, and seafarers find it difficult to take shore leave and virtually impossible to visit their families. The speed-up does not stop with containerization but also happens *within* the container sector. Research found that the average time a ship spent in port was 150.37 hours in 1970; in 1998, the ship touched upon the port only for 11.23 hours before sailing again (Kahveci 1999). The port office manager for a major Chinese shipping company reported at a European port,

> I joined the company in 1989. The average turnaround time of our ships then was 32 hours, with a total of about 500 moves [of boxes]. We now turnaround ships in about 21 hours, but that is approximately 1,700 moves. Sometimes, we can get here a ship with 1,500 moves and it might be in port for only 13 hours.

Until recently, loading and unloading was primarily dockers' work. Once the ship was in port, seafarers had time for shore leaves, visiting shops, pubs, or the seamen's centers. This has changed due to new technologies such as "simultaneous vessel loading" (ships are loaded and unloaded simultaneously rather than sequentially) and "twin picking" (cranes pick up two boxes in a single move; technologies that allow cranes to pick up four boxes in a single move are currently being developed). The key to improved productivity lies in seamless co-operation between dockers ashore and seafarers aboard. While the dockers operate the cranes, the seafarers are expected "to keep stevedores simultaneously supplied with the gear they need to continue working." "You need a team of people out on the ship, on the docks, helping with lashing and unlashing and supplying ship's gear." This has been constantly confirmed by dockers, seafarers, and shipping managers. Such intensification has in fact spilled over the ship and the docks and is flooding into offices, affecting managers there. The above quoted company port office manager said that since he finds it increasingly hard to cope with the increased workload caused by the increase of "boxes," the Chinese company has "kindly" purchased him a laptop computer so that he can work "in the evenings, over the weekends, and even on holidays."

In the recent past, work and life while "floating at the big ocean" (*fang da yang*) could be relatively relaxed. Aboard, large crews gave seafarers the opportunity to interact with one another and sufficient time to maintain ship. Ashore, seafarers could go to pubs, cinemas or even theatres – daily activities many land-based workers take for granted. Now, seafarers have more work to do, fewer mates to interact with, and less time to spend ashore. At the same time, seafarers find that they have less to see and do while ashore, because ports are increasingly receding from the city.

New ports

Ports that are located near city centers, such as Liverpool, Yokohama, and San Francisco, are now regarded as "historic ports." Modern ports generally are built at considerable distance from residential and shopping areas. These ports are automated, "unmanned," and devoid of public transport (ILO 2001). An international transport worker union inspector observes the changes in Northern California:

> With containerization also, you need a lot of room, and you need room where it's cheapest to purchase to build a container terminal. So this is out in the hinterland and very difficult and very expensive to go anywhere. As the industry has changed the terminal facilities have changed, and that's all changed with containerization. In San Francisco, we have the Embarcadero which is the street that runs along the water front which used to be full of ships and now that's all gone and the ships are all 15–20 miles away. They're not just far away from San Francisco, they are far away from anything – no municipal transport because there's no people nearby other than people involved in the terminals on shore who drive where they're going and drive home. There's no reason for the municipalities to out in a bus service. So these guys lead very isolated lives.
>
> (Kahveci 1999)

In Felixstowe, one Chinese captain noted on board a large container ship:

It really is a serious problem for us. Before, when the ship called at Hamburg, she berthed right in the Operation Zone set for Chinese vessels. The zone was close to the Seafarers' Centre and we stayed in port for two weeks. Now, we can't arrive in the port until very late on Sunday night. Monday, you are fully occupied with cargo handling, meeting the port people, immigration officers, and so on. Then, before you can touch the land, you have to sail away again, very early on Tuesday morning. The ship stays there only for 36 hours, and the container terminals are so big. How can you go to the city centre? And it's not a problem only in Hamburg. You have the same problem in Rotterdam, Antwerp, and so on.

Chinese managers and seafarers, like their counterparts of other nationalities, consider the distance from the cities and their service facilities "one of the most serious problems in recent years." One senior manager at Shanghai Seafarers Centre observed:

Until the mid-1980s, we had 50 ship visitors in our Centre. They spoke various foreign languages and could talk to seafarers from all countries. They visited many ships a day and took many foreigners here and served them with the facilities here. At that time, ships called at the port right there (pointing at the water front), we were close to ships and seafarers. Now, we still have the water front here but ships are gone. The new port is built in Waigaoqiao, which is dozens of miles away from the city. There are two bus lines serving that route. But it takes you at least two hours to and from the port; the traffic is getting really bad in this city. It is very difficult for us to visit them there, or for them to come to us here.

Moreover, seafarers' centers have been drastically streamlined in recent years. The Shanghai seafarers center, for example, had over forty ship visitors in the mid-1980s who spoke more than ten languages; in 2002, it had three ship visitors left who only spoke English and Chinese. A report by the International Labor Organization on changing work conditions for seafarers notes:

Fast turnaround times have limited the possibilities for social contact for seafarers beyond the ship board community while the simultaneous reduction in crewing levels has diminished both the extent and the quality of social contact when at sea on passage. Ships are not built primarily to accommodate seafarers on board. However, these are places where everyday life activities such as working, eating, sleeping, socializing take place in a limited environment where there is vibration, sea motion, engine noise, etc. A lack of shore leave means that many seafarers are trapped in this environment, for months at a time.

There is increasing concern that a lack of shore leave affects seafarers' mental and physical well-being as well as reinforcing isolation, fatigue, depression, and stress.

(Lane, in ILO 2001)

Indeed, shore leaves are so vital to seafarers that international regulating bodies like the International Labor Organization (ILO) and the International Maritime Organization (IMO) were outraged when the US government tightened port security control and banned seafarers of certain nationalities from having shore leaves after 9/11.

Seafarers' skills

"Modernization" of the ship has different effects on seafarers of different categories. While the work of engine officers has become less physically arduous than before – temperature and noise in the engine-room have been considerably reduced and night watch has been abolished – it has become more intellectually demanding, because modern IT facilities which monitor the engine room demand intensive brain input. At the same time, seafarers still need their traditional skills to fix the machines when they break down. New knowledge *supplements* rather than *replaces* traditional skills. By contrast, the skills of deck officers have been significantly reduced and *replaced* by the adoption of GPS (Global Positioning System), which has made traditional celestial navigation skills redundant. Nowadays, seafarers navigate "by operating a facility that feels much like a joy-stick in Play Station 2." Containerization has altered but not replaced traditional skills in cargo loading, stowing, and unloading. Most of these tasks are now conducted by computer-controlled machinery, but the new cargo handling technology has been designed in such a way that not only dockers but also seafarers are intensively involved in cargo handling, as already noted.

At first sight, the skills of ratings have not changed much. "Deck hands" still chip and paint, while "engine hands" are busy with wiping, oiling, and general maintenance. Changes come mainly from the social organization of shipboard work: larger ships and smaller crews mean that ratings have more bolts to tighten, more areas to chip and paint, and more machinery to maintain. Labor intensification is reported in the following quote from an ordinary seaman from Shanghai:

> Of course, people have to work a lot harder than before, because we have fewer hands nowadays. Before, you saw people drinking beer, playing chess or poker in the mess when they were off duty. It was a good occasion for people to chat and to see each other. Now, you rarely see people grouping together in the mess. They leave shortly after the meal. They have work to do, or they are tired and need sleep. So, they either return to work or to their cabins to sleep.

Polarization of conditions

On Western ships, "hierarchy touches almost every aspect of shipboard life. It is a subject that reveals deep-running social divisions and seems to offer a microcosm of society at large" (Lane 1986: 152). On these ships, officers have their own bars, cabins, and dining areas that are unquestionably better than those for ratings, and there is little informal interaction between officers and ratings. Even on American ships, where the hierarchy is believed to be less rigid and the relationship between officers and ratings is "often quite informal" and "easy-going," the officers and ratings are always "cordoned off into separate classes with officers socializing with officers and ratings mingling with ratings" (Schrank 1982: 4, 45).

In contrast, egalitarianism has been widely recognized as a hallmark of the Chinese ships. Under the planned economy, and indeed for many years after its demise, seafarers on board ship received similarly low wages, ate the same kind of food, lived in similar quarters, and shared the same recreation facilities regardless of rank and position. Since the mid-1990s, management has consciously increased the social and economic gap between seafarers of different ranks. On PRC ships, officers are traditionally called "cadre seafarers" and ratings "worker seafarers," reflecting the general social hierarchy under the planned economy. Early in 2000, one of the main shipping companies announced that seafarers should be called "senior" or "junior" seafarers, following European norms that were imported through Hong Kong. Although not yet widely adopted, the change indicates an ideological restructuring of the ship hierarchy and suggests that changes in the workplace are not necessarily driven by economic rationality but can sometimes be driven by ideology or "fashion."

Since the latest wage reform in state enterprises, in 2000, wage levels are closely associated with position. Age and seniority, which until recently were important wage determinants (Zhu 2001: 3, see also Frazier, Chapter 3, in this volume), have lost this function. Table 8.2 compares the monthly pre-tax wages proposed by a major Chinese container shipping company with a payroll collected from a large German container ship in March 2001. Chinese shipping is clearly moving towards a greater wage stratification, although inequality is still less pronounced than on the German ship.

Before the reform, there was no significant difference between wages paid to sailing seafarers and those paid to seafarers on leave, because fully paid leave was considered a compensation for overtime while at sea. This contrasts with practices in the global labor market, where seafarers are paid during their employment at sea only. Since the early 1990s, wages at sea have been linked to position, and the gulf between ratings and officers has increased. Wages on shore, however, remain linked to seniority and age: the captain who earns more than $2,000 aboard ship is paid $60 while on leave, while the able seaman who earns $611 aboard ship still receives $51 on shore leave. Since ratings have to take longer leaves (typ-

Table 8.2 Wage scales for Chinese and German seafarers: a comparison (2001)

Rank	Chinese	Index	German	Index
Captain	$2,011	329	$4,521	551
Chief Engineer	$1,857	303	$4,110	501
Chief Mate	$1,420	232	$2,800	168
AB	$611	100	$819	100

Source: SIRC Archive (2001).

ically twice as long as senior officers), the annual income gap remains significant. The "wages" paid ashore have actually turned into a retaining fee, effective in cutting labor cost and guaranteeing a stable labor supply. On the other hand, the labor-retaining strategy is also an indication of the legacy of the country's socialist tradition. The Chinese government, for fear of labor unrest, does not allow shipping companies to lay off workers in large numbers and obliges companies to pay their workers a subsistence income during their redundancy.

Hierarchy is also found in other aspects of seafarers' work and life, aboard and ashore. In recent years, seafarers in some companies were instructed to regroup seats and tables in the mess so that "officers sit with officers and ratings with ratings, as the foreigners do on their ships." This particular measure has met with strong resistance from seafarers, officers and ratings alike. "This is because," as explained by a shipping manager, "it does not fit into our Chinese culture and our habits, and it is not convenient for the organization of work." Mess tables aboard Chinese ships are usually divided by functions. Seafarers in the same department sit at the same table without distinction of rank, "so that when we have meals, we can talk about our work, our families, and other things." What is referred to as "Chinese culture" and "our habits" is actually the ritual of sharing food – a legacy of Maoist egalitarianism. This reform has so far been aborted.

Differentiation in terms of welfare and living standards is more successful ashore. In recent years, many captains and other senior officers have moved to spacious and well-furnished apartments built by shipping companies. Ratings or "junior seafarers" have only limited access to this kind of luxurious housing. Age and seniority have become minor factors in allocating the company's resources to seafarers; ranks and positions are becoming increasingly important in determining the wages and welfare packages for seafarers. The seafarers' community, if still less stratified at sea than their American, European, or Japanese counterparts, shows clear signs of polarization on land, in particular in their lifestyles, reflecting the country's movement towards a class society (Lu 2001).[5]

Political control and welfare on board

For seafarers, the ship stands for home, security, warmth, and life, indeed their "native land." This has traditionally lent legitimacy to the Chinese Communist Party's grip over the floating workplace, since the Party identifies "native land" with "socialism," "proletarian dictatorship," and control. Traditionally, control was exercised through the political commissar, who acted as the Party's representative on board ship. However, the function of the political commissar has undergone significant changes during the reform.

The traditional role of the commissar and the debate

China is now the only country whose ships carry political commissars. The post is a communist invention which can be traced to the commissar system in the USSR fleet and to Mao's Red Army (Lu 1993) and was introduced to China's merchant ships in the early 1950s. The initial intention was undoubtedly to deploy the Party's control over the workplace and to ensure that seafarers would be "correctly" informed of Party politics and ideology despite the geographic mobility of the vessel. Sailing commissars were usually recruited from the military and placed on board ship alongside with or even above the captain.[6] All commissars were, and still are, male. According to the "Guidance for Political Commissars on Ocean Going Ships," issued in 1975, the commissars were expected

> to see to it that the principles and policies of the Chinese Communist Party and the state laws and decrees be implemented among and carried out by the crew on merchant ships. They must take Marxism, Leninism, and Mao Zedong Thought as the guideline in their daily work. They must concentrate their main efforts on big issues, that is, on ideological and political work and on the constant raising of the ideological consciousness of the seafarers.

In the real world on board ship, more complex relations developed. In addition to his designated role, the commissar played an important part in providing welfare support to seafarers. Even though "political thought work" mainly served the aim of "ideological and political education," seafarers often report that talks with the commissar made them "feel better" or helped "solve some practical problems."

For half a century, the commissar regime was deeply rooted in the management structure of PRC shipping and the commissar accepted as a normal part of the Chinese crew. Since the mid-1980s, however, profits have replaced plan-fulfillment as the goal of production, and questions have been raised as to the usefulness of the post. Ship owners, managers, and maritime economists argue that it should be removed on the ground that it represents an unnecessary cost. Party officials, on the other hand, insist that the commissars are useful as part of the Party's organizational control over the workplace. Little thought is given in this debate to the social dynamics of the shipboard community.

The commissar's role under reform

Both designated roles and real functions of the commissar have undergone substantial change during the reforms. In an internal document issued in 1995, the Party committee of a major shipping company noted:

> Commissars must focus on the task of changing their mentality to adapt to the constantly changing market circumstances. They must promote the reform principles and policies and help implement the company's reform programs. They must emphasize the concept of competition in their education of seafarers and strive for better economic efficiency during the voyage.

One of the changes to which commissars have to adapt is the shift of decision-making power from commissar to captain, similar to the shift from Party Secretary to factory director in land-based factories. The captain now has the final say in most issues; the commissar is expected to "assist" rather than "lead" or "supervise" the captain. The *Handbook for Shipboard Political Commissars* exhorts commissars to "focus on how to assist the captain to complete the objective in production. Political thought work must be employed to ensure the fulfillment of the tasks in trading and shipboard production (COSCO 1997: 472)." The commissar is specifically instructed to look after the captain, for example, by taking "the initiative to have meals prepared and brought to the captain (ibid.: 476)."

The subordinate position of the commissar was clearly observed in our interviews on board ship. Conversation tended to be dominated by the captain, with the commissar playing a supporting role, for example, serving tea and consulting the "ship master" in words or glances when he felt it was his turn to speak. Most of our land-based interviews were conducted with captains or commissars on a one-to-one basis. This allowed actors more room to report their feelings and experiences. In these circumstances, more captains expressed content and satisfaction with their job; more commissars complained about the decline of their status. A commissar with twenty-two years' sailing history noted, "With the deepening of the reform, in our company, the ideological work has been increasingly weakened and seeking better economic performance has taken the lead. In other words, the political work has been devalued."

Changes in the workplace have given rise to a greater demand from the crew for advice from the commissar. Seafarers approach the commissar when they encounter problems concerning mental hang-ups and psychological setbacks, or problems in respect of task assignments and job transfers, or disputes on wages and bonuses, welfare and allowance, labor intensification and labor protection, arrangements for work shifts and work conditions, their health and general well-being, rewards and punishments meted out by the captain, miscellaneous kinds of conflicts between the captain and the crew, relations between the captain and the trade union, relations among the crew, and so on.

Given that trade unions in China are still under Party control and that Chinese seafarers are not allowed to contact world trade unions such as the International Transport Workers Federation (ITF), seafarers have no choice but to channel their complaints and problems to the Party's representative. A sailing medical doctor aptly describes this function of the commissar:

As the proverb goes, "The onlooker sees most of the game." So the captain sometimes needs a person as his adviser. Everything is OK as long as the captain is clean-handed. But should anything go wrong, there must be someone to intervene. At this juncture, the commissar should come out to get the nut cracked. He is expected to play a positive role in safeguarding the rights and interests of the ordinary crewmen.

In most cases, however, the commissar can only alleviate problems and frustrations by listening, talking, or expressing compassion to the seafarers that come to him for help:

Seafarers come to talk to me quite often. Frankly speaking, today's seafarers face quite a lot of difficulties. First of all, their wages are quite low, out of proportion to the efforts they have made. Second, working on board for a long time, they often have problems with regards to their families, their sons, daughters, and parents, and many complain about overdue leave. Some of these problems I can solve, but most are beyond my ability. However, when a seafarer comes to you with these problems, you have to receive them warmly. Many times, the point is not to find an immediate solution. What really matters is that you help them iron out their thinking and appease their emotions.

Such a buffering effect has proved important for the welfare and well-being of the crew, especially in the absence of a political mechanism that represents seafarers and fights for their rights and interests. The majority of seafarers are appreciative of this, sometimes comparing the support they receive from the commissar to the service provided by sailing chaplains on board some European ships. The analogy has also been observed by some trade union leaders, who believe that "what the priest or sailing chaplain can do for seafarers should also be done by the commissar." It is worth noting that the commissar combines functions that are separate on Western ships: part trade union representative, part chaplain, part personnel manager. If the post were to be abolished, seafarers would need access to other supporting networks such as ship visitors, port chaplains, and world trade unions in various parts of the world.

Conclusion

Seafarers are invisible workers. Their ships carry over 90 percent of world trade (ILO 2001), but little is known about their work outside the shipping community. Land-based Chinese often imagine that seafarers "take holidays at sea, sailing between the white clouds and the blue skies." Seafarers are viewed as "privileged workers in beautiful uniforms, well-paid and having opportunities to visit many countries" (Cai 2001). Indeed, the view contains a slice of truth: in Mao's time, ocean seafaring *was* a privileged occupation, offered only to those who were trusted by the Party, and seafarers received higher wages than most workers in land-based industries. As recently as the late 1980s, the job was still sought after by sons of senior government officials.

The evidence presented in this chapter indicates that institutional and technological changes have had a major impact on seafarers' experiences at sea, on the nature of seafaring, and on the overall attractiveness of the occupation. Overall, shipboard production has intensified, while social conditions for seafarers deteriorated. Seafarers from privileged families have long been replaced by sons of peasants, recruited from the country's poor inland provinces (Li and Zhao 2003). One reason for this trend is increased employment opportunities in coastal cities, but the declining attractiveness of maritime labor also plays a role. If seafaring has always been a hard job, it has become even harder in recent years under the pressure of the market forces. Increased work loads on board ship, polarization in the workplace, and the decline of support structures that mitigate the stress of work all point to the same conclusion: globalization has taken China down the capitalist road, although this occurs in a context that is still shaped by the legacy of state socialism and Chinese cultural traditions. At the moment, officers and ratings still share mess tables and Chinese vessels still carry commissars during the voyage. It is unclear, however, how long the "floating native land" will retain these features.

What do changes in the Chinese shipping industry teach us about the country's transition from socialism to capitalism? International shipping is atypical in two respects: it is the world's first completely globalized industry (Lane 2001), more deregulated than other industries and subject to extremely rapid technological change. It is atypical also in that Chinese shipping, unlike industries that take advantage of the country's abundance of cheap labor, relies on capital intensification. At the same time, the process of reform in the shipping industry and its effect on seafarers share profound similarities with the reform process in land-based industries. Shipping companies' enthusiasm for modern technology and crew downsizing reminds us, for example, of the strategy taken by the country's textile industry, where the modernization of machinery goes hand in hand with a streamlining of the workforce (Zhao and Nichols 1996). In both industries, profit-sensitive managers have introduced a wide range of institutional and technological changes to reduce costs, especially labor costs which are most vulnerable to market pressures. The remarkable development of high technology in shipping has the potential to improve the working and living conditions of seafarers; however, this potential will not be realized as long as technology is used only to increase labor productivity and company profits. Since China's accession to the WTO, managers in state-owned firms have become even more sensitive to labor costs in order to stay competitive in the market. The implications for Chinese workers are clear: they are likely to lose out in the process of reform, unless they form their own organizations that can stand up to protect their rights and interests, including their right to enjoy decent labor standards.

Acknowledgments

The author would like to thank Feng Tongqing (China Industrial Relations Institute) and Shi Xiuyin (Institute of Sociology, Chinese Social Sciences Academy) for their contribution to the study of the ship political commissar and Shen Guanbao (Department of Sociology, Shanghai University) for his and his team's contribution to the study of the labor market for seafarers in China (Zhao *et al.* 2004). The first project was funded by the International Federation of Transport Workers (ITF) Seafarers Trust and the latter by the Seafarers International Research Centre (SIRC), Cardiff University, UK.

Notes

1 The definition of "PRC ships" or "PRC fleets" here refers to vessels that are beneficially owned by PRC state shipping companies and crewed with PRC seafarers.
2 Data in this section and the section on the political commissar have been reported in Zhao (2002).
3 This section has been substantially informed by Tony Lane's discussion on technological development in world maritime industry, *The Impact on Seafarers' Living and Working Conditions from Changes in the Structure of the Shipping Industry*, The JMC Report, ILO, 2001.
4 TEU stands for "Twenty Equivalent Unit." A 20-foot box is one TEU, a 40-foot box two TEU.
5 It is interesting to compare the trend in the PRC fleet and in OECD fleets. In the

early 1980s, "progressive" ship owners in Britain and Norway tried to flatten hierarchies on board, largely in order to lower investment and operating costs for differentiated living quarters. This reform met strong resistance from officers and was hence aborted. However, efforts are still being made to reduce certain aspects of the ship hierarchy in OECD ships.

6 Lida Junghans (Chapter 4 in this volume) describes Chinese railways as "semi-militarized" and subject to strict political and ideological controls, which, however, have been eroded in the reform period. These observations also apply to maritime shipping.

References

BIMCO/ISF (1995) *The Worldwide Demand for and Supply of Seafarers,* Warwick: The Institute for Employment Research, University of Warwick.

Cai, Ping (2001) "Seafarers on Land," online, available at: http://www.clidrary. com (accessed 15 November).

COSCO (Chinese Ocean Shipping Company) (2000) "Modern Enterprise System," online, available at: http:/www.cosco.com.cn/history3.asp (accessed 10 May 2001).

COSCO (Chinese Ocean Shipping Company) (1997) *The Handbook for Shipboard Political Commissars,* Beijing: The People's Transport Publishing House.

Frazier, Mark W. (2002) *The Making of the Chinese Industrial Workplace: State, Revolution, and Labor Management,* Cambridge: Cambridge University Press.

Grey, Michael "Chinese May End Manning Shortage," *Lloyd's List,* 20 July 1999, 5.

Hassard, John, Sheehand, Jackie, and Morris, Jonathan "State Sector Reform and Societal Transformation in China," paper presented to 15th EGOS Colloquium, University of Warwick, 4–6 July 1999.

ISL (Institute of Shipping Economics and Logistics) (1998) *Shipping Statistics Yearbook 1998,* Bremen, ISL.

ISL (Institute of Shipping Economics and Logistics) (1999) *Shipping Statistics Yearbook 1999,* Bremen, ISL.

ITF (International Transport Workers Federation) (2002) "Shipping Industry Review," *Seafarers Bulletin,* 16: 8–12.

ILO (International Labor Organization) (2001) *The Impact on Seafarers' Living and Working Conditions from Changes in the Structure of the Shipping Industry,* Joint Maritime Committee Report, Geneva: The ILO Office.

Kahveci, Erol (1999) *Fast Turnaround Ships and Their Impact on Crews,* Cardiff: SIRC.

Lane, Anthony D. *et al.* (2002) *Crewing the World Fleet,* Cardiff: Seafarers International Research Centre, Cardiff University.

Lane, Tony (1986) *Grey Dawn Breaking: British Merchant Seafarers in the late Twentieth Century,* Manchester University Press.

Lee, K.X. and Wonham, J. (1999) "Registration of Vessels," *The International Journal of Marine and Coastal Law,* 14(1).

Li, Jianqun and Zhao, Minghua (2003) "New Seafaring Labor Source in China," Cardiff: SIRC Research Report, Cardiff University.

Lu, Feng (1993) "The Origins and Formation of the Unit (*Danwei*) System," *Chinese Sociology and Anthropology,* 25: 3.

Lu, Xueyi (2001) *Social Trends in 2001: An Analysis and Prospects,* Beijing: Social Sciences Literature Publishing House.

Ministry of Communications (China), Shanghai Shipping Exchange, and Shanghai Maritime University (2000) *Chinese Shipping in 1999: A Development Report 2000*, Beijing: Ministry of Communications.

Schrank, Robert (1982) *Industrial Democracy at Sea*, Cambridge, MA: MIT Press.

Sharma, Krishan Kuma (2002) "The Sea-going Labor Market in the People's Republic of China and its Future," in Tae-Woo Lee *et al.* (eds) *Shipping in China*, Burlington, VT: Ashgate, pp. 18–32.

Shen, Mingnan and Lee, Tae-Woo (2002) "COSCO Development Strategy," in Tae-Woo Lee *et al.* (eds) *Shipping in China*, Burlington, VT: Ashgate, pp. 33–47.

Smith, Chris and Pun, Ngai (2003) "Putting the Transnational Labor Process in its Place: The Dormitory Labor Regime in Post-Socialist China," paper presented at 21st International Labor Process Conference, Bristol, UK, 14–16 April.

Sun, Guangqi and Zhang, Shiping (2002) "Chinese Shipping Policy and the Impact of its Development," in Tae-Woo Lee *et al.* (eds) *Shipping in China*, Burlington, VT: Ashgate, pp. 4–18.

Walder, Andrew (1986) *Communist Neo-Traditionalism: Work and Authority in Chinese Industry*, Berkeley, CA: University of California Press.

Wang, Guang (1982) *Zhonghua shuiyunshi* [History of Chinese Shipping], Taiwan: Commercial Publishing House.

Wang, Jixian (2001) "The Present Situation and Future Prospect of Chinese Seamen Overseas Employment," paper presented to LSM International Manning and Training Conference, Manila, 3–4 November.

Zhao, Minghua (2002) "The Consequences of China's Socialist Market Economy for Seafarers," *Work, Employment and Society: A Journal of the British Sociological Association*, 16(1): 171–183.

Zhao, Minghua and Amante, Maragtas (2003) "Chinese Seafarers and Filipino Seafarers: Race to the Top or Race to the Bottom?" *Symposium Proceedings*, SIRC Symposium 2003.

Zhao, Minghua and Nichols, Theo (1996) "Management Control of Labour in State-Owned Enterprises: Cases from the Textile Industry," *The China Journal*, 36: 1–21.

Zhao, Minghua and Shen, Guanbao (2001) "Seafarers' Labor Market in China: an Overall View," paper presented to Global Labor Market Working Meeting, SIRC, Cardiff University, 30 June.

Zhao, Minghua, Shi, Xiuyin and Feng, Tongqing (2004) *The Political Commissar and His Shipmates aboard Chinese Merchant Ships*, Beijing: Chinese Social Sciences Documentation Publishing House.

Zhongguo hanghai xuehui [China Shipping Society] (1989) *Zhongguo Hanghaishi: xiandai hanghaishi* [Chinese Shipping History: Contemporary History], Beijing: People's Transport Publishing House.

Zhu, Rong (2001) "2001–2002: The State and the Prospect of the Reform in China's State Enterprises," in Ru, Xin and Lu, Xueyi *et al.*, *Chinese Society in 2000: An Analysis and a Prediction – Social Blue Book*, Beijing: Social Science Contributions Press.

Index